This book contains information that can mood, mind and physical wellbeing!

It will show you how you can use powerful energies through exercises, rituals and symbols to:

- take back control and transform emotions of anger, fear, distrust, anxiety and guilt that can take away your confidence, happiness and peace of mind

- set your intentions to heal, release and dissolve attachments to people and situations that bring you down

- assist you in your quest for life lessons on your spiritual journey of self-discovery

- help you to heal the scars on your mind, spirit and body caused by past traumas

- invoke universal energies of light and love for lifting your spirits and healing

- heal and reclaim soul fragments and lost aspects such as confidence, trust, self-worth and more

- assist in healing your heart of rejection and lack of love – opening the way to give and receive love

- create powerful intentions of sealing and protecting your energies from negativity in those around you

- clear the atmosphere of your home and workplace

- direct healing energy vibrations where they are needed anywhere in the world

- assist you in your own process of ascension – raising your vibrations for living in peace and harmony with yourself and your world

Anne Jones is an inspirational speaker, healer and author of self-development books translated into 17 languages. She is the author of the best seller *Healing Negative Energies*.

Love is the Key

Wherever you are on your life and soul journey this book brings everything together simply and beautifully; a truly valuable resource of wisdom, guidance and practical advice. By using ancient symbols to invoke high vibrational energies, How to Heal by Anne Jones will greatly assist you in healing, releasing, transformation and your own personal empowerment.

– Sue Stone, transformational leader and TV presenter

I was immediately hooked by Anne Jones' new book, How to Heal. It is really accessibly and interestingly written. Moreover it is the most comprehensive book on healing I have seen. If you want to be a healer, look no further for, with ancient symbols and detailed instructions this book is a powerhouse for any healer.

– Diane Cooper, therapist, healer and international author

Symbols are powerful icons that have influenced people worldwide, for good or ill. In *How To Heal: Release your past, reclaim your energy, revive your joy*, healer Anne Jones reveals how this power can be used consciously in positive ways; ways that heal. In our pandemic era, this message is urgently needed.

– Larry Dossey (USA), physician and author of *One Mind: How Our Individual Mind Is Part of a Greater Consciousness and Why It Matters*

Thank you, Anne, for your guiding, coaching and healing. It has given me inner peace and understanding on how to influence and manifest a good life.

– AS (Norway)

Thank you for the healing session; I found it incredibly liberating. I was 'stuck' and was questioning my ability to create and move forward in life, and after your guiding hand, I feel very much lighter and now believe in myself and that everything is possible. Interesting to experience the physical rush as the blocks are cleared. I look forward to reading your books and using the symbols... very powerful! Thank you again.

– CH (UK)

I use your symbol healing all the time and feeling the effect of them. Thank you very much! I feel I am empowered by them; I can quickly work for the problems, I or other people, experience, and they are effective!

– YH (Japan)

I feel extremely positive, refreshed, and energetic after our session today. Thank you so much!

– NN (India)

When you talked about low self-esteem, that was me but after you gave me some advice last year I started to feel more positive and found my healing energies became stronger

– BF (UK)

For many years I did not know I was 'programmed'. I managed it so well until I was so good at it and got amazing results for others and not myself. I suffered emotionally and then it manifested into a physical problem. I was hospitalised, I had accidents and still, no one came to help. Secretly I saw a psychologist and he said I had Superwoman syndrome. Nothing worked until I met you and after two sessions, I met a wonderful man and fell in love. From that point I knew I was worthy, and I found the courage to go deeper and cleared the problems that I had.

– AN (Malaysia)

I completed the first module of the symbol healing course; I saw myself hugging my spirit guide. I have a tingling sensation in my hands after drawing the healing symbol.

– NA (Malaysia)

I just wanted to thank you for your beautiful healing session for my mum in December. That afternoon her pain really diminished noticeably.

– MH (UK)

The session yesterday was so powerful and amazing. I am getting more excited about myself.

– YM (Japan)

First of all, thank you so much for the fantastic session. You really do wonders with my struggles and worries, and reinforce strength, energy, and belief in myself. It was as if you managed to redeem so much anxiety and old skeletons of all sorts from my brain, heart and soul. A lot of hooks, blockings and deep-down worries were removed/cleared and processed by your healing. It is fantastic to experience this transformation.

    – AWS (Norway)

Thank you so much for the wonderful energy healing session I had with you. It was truly what I needed, and I feel so much more 'together' than I have in a very long time. You've really helped me get back on track and reclaim my own life path.

    – AF (UK)

I feel so much lighter and happier, and I seem to have so much energy too. Also, people have commented that there was something different about me, as though I am surrounded by white light or something. I feel so blessed.

    – ND (Malaysia)

Since my session, my life feels at peace, and I feel so uplifted. There appears to be more contentment and happiness that at times feels strange, but I welcome that.

    – AR

Thank you for your warm and wonderful healing session today! Your positive and loving energy support has helped in my challenging times. Thank you so much.

    – M

Since you cleared all those past lives imprints of the 'wounded leader', I've felt much happier, relaxed and confident at work. Not just at work, mind you, I'm feeling generally more at ease. I just wanted to thank you again for your immense help and care whilst working with me.

    – VJ

HOW TO HEAL

Love & Blessings

xx Anne j

Anne Jones

HOW TO
Heal

Release your past
Reclaim your energy
Revive your joy

How To Heal

ISBN 978-1-912300-56-3

eISBN 978-1-912300-57-0

Published in 2022 by SRA Books

Printed in the UK

Contents

I dedicate this book to Sally Addington,
who has encouraged me at every step of my journey
of discovery into the world of Spirit and Healing.
Thank you Sal, for being with me through highs and lows,
and giving me zaps and encouragement when needed.

Introduction

In 1995, my life radically changed direction when I heard a voice introducing me to healing. Since then, I have had spiritual experiences in the most bizarre situations and discovered the magic that is available in a blink of an eye for everyone who is open to the impossible. In this book, I want to share with you the powerful knowledge, rituals and symbols I have learnt from those spiritual encounters. Discover ways of invoking and using high-frequency energies to give you back control of your emotions and wellbeing by transforming and healing all aspects of yourself; physically, mentally and spiritually.

Let me start by telling you a little more about the voice that started my journey into healing and its fantastical wake-up call for me in Malaysia. My husband, Tony, had been posted to Kuala Lumpur in his role of company director of a large corporation and I had been reluctantly introduced to the world of the ex-pat wife. I left behind my family, friends, a new business venture and a job, so I arrived with a bit of an attitude! How silly was I for I walked into a company house with a cook – ah, I loved cooking; a gardener – what to do now at the weekends; a driver – it wasn't considered safe for me to drive myself – oh no! At first, I was devastated at the loss of the many things in my life I treasured but very soon I found new friends and had fun with oil painting, editing the ex-pat magazine and teaching the ladies how to use computers (home computers had just been introduced at that time).

Then, just when I had settled down to my privileged new life, wham!

I had been teaching the wonders of cut and paste and printing letters in my computer class all morning and decided to take a rest in the cool of our air-conditioned bedroom. I didn't sleep but I was relaxed on the bed and for once did not pick up a book to read but simply lay down doing nothing. Without any warning I heard a voice speaking to me.

'When are you going to start healing?'

It was a disembodied voice with quite a bossy tone. To say I was startled would be an understatement; shock surged through my body and I immediately sat up straight. The question was repeated and without thinking, I responded.

'How?'

'Speak to Sal,' the voice replied.

The phantom phone went down; the line was dead.

A most extraordinary sensation of excitement and happiness burst through me from head to toe; I felt I had been plugged into a high vibration energy stream, which, of course, in a way, I had, for I had been connected to the full force and power of spiritual energy. I tingled and shimmered for over ten minutes before I got myself back to Earth and considered the message. It felt real and natural despite the weirdness of the situation; I sensed its truth. Yes, I must start healing. I had an interest in the occult and the world of spirit although I had never gone further than visiting a psychic from time to time for a card reading. My own experiences had been limited to sensing the spiritual presence of departed souls still hanging around the earth plane. But I had never taken any serious interest in being a healer nor did I consider I 'had the gift.'

I needed to talk to Sally. I only knew one Sal and she was the 'Miss Piggy' who wrote the restaurant reviews for our magazine. Coincidentally, I was going to a function that day where she would be; this was the first of the many cases of synchronicity I would experience from then on. With trepidation and a thumping heart, I approached her with simple words.

'I believe we have to talk about healing.'

Fortunately, she gave me a huge smile and sighed. 'Good, yes, I will send you some books to read, you know how to heal, but you need to remember.'

And that was about it. The next day the promised books arrived. They were three volumes written by Betty Shine, an amazing medium and healer. I left that day for a holiday back home in the UK and I read the books one after the other on the journey. Everything she explained seemed absolutely right and felt familiar. Her main message was HEALING IS LOVE; just be the conductor of the energy and absorb it for yourself or pass it to a person in need of help. I tried this out on everyone I could pin down during my holiday and had surprisingly good feedback. So, I was off and away on the most amazing adventure of my life.

On my return to Malaysia, Sally solved a mystery that had been puzzling me for some time and explained her cool response when I approached her. Her own spirit guides had requested her to help me get going on my new journey. She suggested she might call me, but they insisted she wait for me to approach her. She had been waiting for a sign from me for a couple of months, which just goes to show how slow I am on the uptake. I learnt then that there are times when it's better to slow down, take time out and sit still rather than fill every moment of the day with action or distraction. It was only when I stopped and did nothing at all that Spirit was able to get my attention. From then on, every day I sat and closed my mind and set my intention to receive whatever Spirit had to offer me. I was visited by a series of amazing spiritual masters and guides who taught me ancient symbols that invoke high vibrational energies to assist in healing, transformation, releasing and empowering. The symbols are simple but very powerful and can only be used with good intent, which meant I could share them with anyone, so I set about doing just that immediately through workshops and writing books.

The symbols can be used to bring in energies for yourself or you can use them to channel the energies for your family, friends and clients. You don't need activation or permission to use the symbols and they invoke the very highest vibrations of healing and light. They act as a language speaking to Spirit directly requesting a variety of healing intentions; the energies then flow through you without being blocked or inhibited by your own self-doubt or lack of confidence in your own skills as a healer. Therefore, if you use the symbols you will definitely channel healing energies.

The symbols are very old, ancient even. I have seen myself in a past life regression as a High Priest in Egypt placing the symbols in a casket and hiding the box in a cavern under the Sphinx where I was instructed to leave them, away from public sight until a time in the future when the consciousness of mankind needed them. It seems the time is right now! Before I used them in Egypt priests were using them in Atlantis. When the priest realised that island was about to be destroyed, the priests escaped and took them off to the mainland and carried them to North America, where they were used by the American Indians, to South America, where they were used by shamans, to the Himalayas and to Egypt.

As well as the symbols, angels and spirit masters have given me insights and knowledge about our spiritual energy and how to strengthen, uplift and heal our heart, soul and through holistic connection, our mind and physical body. I am sharing in this book the techniques they showed me as simple rituals that you can easily master. Through these you set your motivation and intentions of what you wish to achieve; by speaking aloud you send the vibrations of your voice out to connect to Spirit, allowing matching energy to draw in the result you need. The energies and situations you attract with these 'requests' are to counterbalance, dissolve and transform negative energy that is creating a problem for you. You can also use hand and arm movements to emphasise your requests and direct the energy flow. These rituals are not secret and can be shared with anyone who wishes to heal themselves or others.

Since that amazing afternoon in Kuala Lumpur, I have travelled the world sharing the guidance I have received and teaching my own take on healing and the symbols and rituals. I have fought demons; cleared people and houses of the darkest energies; seen miraculous transformations; written books; appeared on television and radio and enjoyed the most fulfilling period of my life.

So, now let me share what I know so that you can heal and transform yourself and if you wish you can help others too.

Journal: Start your healing journey by taking a journal and writing down your intention to heal the symptoms and the root causes of all that makes you emotionally upset, gives you physical pain or mental anguish. Good, now let's get started.

CHAPTER One

Your Spiritual Energy and Why You are Here

Before you can start to heal you need to know what it is you are healing. Every part of you; physical body, mind, emotions and spirit are connected, so you heal holistically. As your body heals your mind and spirit will be affected. As you clear negative beliefs about yourself, so your spirit and body respond. The underlying cause of most of your problems will start as an imbalance, imprint or disturbance in your spiritual energy; as you uplift your spirit, your body and mind heal.

I will start by explaining what I mean by spiritual energy, comprised of higher self, soul, heart, connecting cord, wheel of wisdom and life purpose. We will explore the role of your higher self and the impact it has on the way your life will unfold; your life purpose with its list of life lessons and the challenges they attract; the way life on Earth and its challenges can affect your soul and heart energy and the importance of the connection between these different aspects of your spiritual being.

We will see how your soul becomes wedded to your physical body at your birth and the damage it can experience from your life choices and challenges. In this chapter and through the rest of the book I will be showing you how you can use the symbols and rituals to heal these scars and imprints of your soul and, through their holistic connection, heal your mind and physical body.

Spiritual healing: healing your spirit to heal your mind and body; all is one and all are connected

Here is a schematic that shows the form of spiritual energy in a simplistic way. Of course, energy is a moving and ever-changing force, but this diagram should give you a feel for the various aspects and designation of your spirit.

As you will see I have drawn a line halfway down this plan. This represents the division between the Earthly Realm, which we live in and the Heavenly Realm of Spirit. When you are born only one part of your spirit energy, your soul, comes down to join with your physical body for your life on Earth as a human being. The remaining aspect, your higher self, stays in the higher frequencies of the Heavenly Realm. Your higher self holds the wisdom you have acquired from all your many lifetimes, your soul purpose and your life purpose. Let's look at these components of your spirit in more detail.

Earthly Realm

This is the dense, physical world in which we live. We see and can be seen with normal eyesight and we do not need our inner-sight or psychic abilities to live a good and satisfying life, although we co-exist with spiritual beings that we do not see. The world we experience has generally low vibrations and a heavy atmosphere, which encourages materialistic attitudes and our focus and attention is more on the reality we see and feel than our less obvious spiritual aspects. You chose to come to Earth because it presents challenges that you don't face in Heaven. You can develop your character and learn the truth about love. You have one important goal and that is to find love for others and yourself, to discover the true nature of love, and this quest is only possible on Earth. Here you seek gold amongst the dross, you learn to discern the good from the bad; you will be tempted by the material world and realise which side you want to be on – the light or the dark, the positive or the negative, love or hate. Your journey of spiritual development is ongoing and takes many lifetimes to complete and, as you have probably already discovered, as soon as you overcome one challenge and think you have got over your isms, issues and inner dilemmas then you will be faced with another challenge! One thing you can say about living here – it's never boring.

Heavenly Realm

There are many dimensions above and below the dense realm of Earth. In these, there are many different vibrations of energy: there is light and dark, and good and bad. In these realms, the spirit does not need to connect to a physical form as it does on Earth. There are a variety of beings and entities that inhabit these other realms and they are the source of myths and stories that come through our imagination and our psychic connections. At some stage of your soul's development and journey of evolvement, you will visit some of these dimensions. One that many religious texts describe is purgatory, which offers a particularly difficult and torturous existence for a soul. Here you float with your thoughts, your memories and troubling emotions such as guilt and anger. Only when a soul is ready to release those heavy emotions can it then progress to the Nirvana and Heaven that every soul seeks. In the very highest of these realms, love is the only energy that matters, and this is our goal, to finish our cycles of Earth then we can focus on helping other souls to raise their own consciousness.

Higher Self

This aspect of your spirit is known by different names in different cultures and beliefs, e.g. I AM Presence, Monad, Higher Consciousness. It is defined in the dictionary this way: 'higher consciousness is the consciousness of a higher self, transcendental reality, or God. It is the part of the human being that is capable of transcending animal instincts.' It is your purist and most powerful aspect and is untouched by the challenges and negative experiences that can cause distress and scarring to your soul Energy. It holds the vibration of love from which you were originally created and is the true you, the divine you.

Your initial essence was formed and created deliberately for a specific intention and was formed from the energy and spirit of God, Source, higher Intelligence, whatever description resonates with you. Because you are an offshoot of divine energy you therefore have the same powerful essence as your source. This essence is the highest vibration and we refer to this energy form as unconditional love – a form of love that has no judgement and is fully and one hundred per cent accepting. Unconditional Love is not an emotion it is a state of being.

Your spirit was created from a divine source. You have the same energy and powers as your divine source: The essence of the TRUE YOU is LOVE with the power to CREATE.

We are all created of the same basic essence, from the same vibration of energy, which we call love. Your higher self never changes from this source vibration of energy, and neither does anyone else's. It acts as the common denominator, the same energy for every living thing and ensures that through our spiritual aspect, our higher self, we are continuously connected to every other living being. Through this link of love, you are connected to all other living souls. It is through this connection that psychics can connect to your higher self and can see your life purpose and give you clues to what is likely to occur in your life. You are also able to use your higher consciousness to connect and communicate with the highest forces of light and love – angels, spirit guides and God. You can do this by simply speaking out and asking for guidance or love, even if you don't know who you wish to speak to! Just say, 'I call upon the forces of light and love to help me with... ' We will explore the use of this guidance in Chapter Three.

Higher forces of good are always there to help you; you only need to ask.

Your Soul Purpose

You will be pleased to know you were not made on a random whim but were created for a specific purpose and role and each lifetime you visit Earth, you will expand your understanding and consciousness of that role by experiencing it in a variety of ways. This role is your reason for being and is called your soul purpose. Each time you come on a cycle of life to Earth and you gain knowledge through playing out this role, you not only raise your own knowledge but you raise the consciousness of everybody, of every soul. For example, if your soul purpose is teaching you will have lives as a teacher living in different time zones and in different cultures; you may teach a variety of subjects; you will face life challenges as a teacher; you will be a poor teacher and a wealthy one, you will face temptations of corruption and deceit; you will be searching love through your teaching and you may also be a pupil to experience the other side of your work. If your purpose is to be a healer you will experience this role in many time frames with many different challenges, often facing judgement and even persecution. In this lifetime, hopefully, you WILL NOT end up on a bonfire, but you might be mocked and criticised and your beliefs and skills may be dismissed as hocus-pocus. However, every challenge and difficulty you overcome helps your consciousness to expand not only for your own benefit but for the greater good. So keep at it and don't be discouraged, as the end goal will be well worth the challenging journey!

The overriding purpose of every lifecycle and the goal of every spiritual quest on Earth is to find and experience giving and receiving love.

Connection

Through your higher self, you connect to all that is and at that level thought and intention are instant connectors and creators. So, the clearer and better your personal connection to your higher self, the more powerful you become and the more you will resonate with love. The high and pure vibration of love will then positively affect your mental, emotional and physical wellbeing. I see this connection as a cord or a telephone line, sometimes the connection seems lost, sometimes it is fuzzy and you find it difficult to make decisions and you feel troubled or confused; other times it will be crystal clear and you understand exactly what is your best route forward.

Not only is it practical to be connected but it allows you to live a rich and harmonious life; it helps you be true to your real self rather than to a disguising mask that you use to hide your fears and who you are; it encourages you to be true to yourself rather than project what you think people want you to be.

To be authentic and true to yourself you need to be constantly in touch with your higher self.

Without doubt it is the most magnificent part of you and keeping a strong connection is essential for a spiritually powerful life where you are guided by your higher intelligence rather than driven by emotions and your mind. Later in this chapter I will show you ways that you can keep this connection strong and clear.

Journal:
Can you recall times when you have been driven by a higher force or have been able to know something without being told?

Have you just 'felt' you should do something without a logical reason?

Wheel of Wisdom

You collect the knowledge and understanding you acquire through each lifetime in a database that is forever accessible. This wisdom is your intuition and if the connection between your soul and your higher self is open and clear then you always have access to this amazing depositary of knowledge; it is an instinctive wisdom that is about sense and feel as much as knowing.

I see this database as a wheel with segments like the widget holder on a Trivial Pursuit board. As you gain insight, awareness, or learn a lesson, then a little widget goes into the wheel. Once you have accumulated all the knowledge and insights that your higher self needs to fulfil its soul purpose and your wheel is full, then you no longer need to visit Earth again! Your job is done.

When you intuit the answer to a question raised, you access your higher self-intelligence and wisdom; as this occurs you may get a physical reaction, this is the vibration of truth. You can get a sensation that confirms the truth of your answer. You can get this when you speak the truth or when someone else does. My truth confirmation is a whoosh that runs down my body and the hairs on my arms and the back of my neck rise too. You may feel it another way such as feeling heat, a warm comforting feeling around your heart centre in your chest. A shiver down your back or even Consider inserting 'even' or 'maybe' here to distinguish from the shiver. A sensation that runs around your neck, around your clavicles, your collar bones that circle your neck, which is the source of the saying 'the ring of truth'.

Journal:
Do you rely on your intuition? Do you sometimes know what to
do without understanding why? Do you experience a sensation or
feeling when you get an insight or hear something that 'rings' true
to you? It's worth spending time testing this out for yourself as the
more you practise using your intuition, the more your confidence
grows and your connection to your higher self develops.

Life Purpose

Before you are born your spirit will have a plan in place for your upcoming lifetime. You are not alone in making this plan and are given help and guidance. With my inner sight I have seen large rooms where deep consultations with masters take place before we come back to Earth for the next life cycle. There are many options to choose from and decisions to make before you arrive.

- **Lessons:** What lessons do you want to learn and what challenges are you going to attract in order to get the experiences you need to gain wisdom and perception; to grow spiritually and emotionally?

- **Parents:** Much thought will go into choosing the parents who can give you the genes you need for your life purpose. Sometimes they will be soul partners – souls that you have travelled to Earth with before. Sometimes they are not. You may feel that your family is on the same wavelength to you; you may feel the opposite – that they are aliens! Either way, you will have chosen them for the experiences their personality, behaviour and attitudes will offer and the genes you will inherit from them.

- **Service:** Who are you going to help in this next lifetime – this includes your service to humanity and the world?

- **Soul Mates:** Who will assist you in achieving your goals; challenging or supporting and loving you?

- **Astrological:** What time of birth and star signs support your plan?

- **Goals and Passions:** What major achievements do you want to program into your plan?

You have a complicated plan to put together – I can only believe they have super computers in Heaven to help! Let's look in more detail at this 'to do' list that you compile before your conception.

Lessons

One of the ways your consciousness can grow is through gaining wisdom; to expand your wisdom, you will need the stimulation of experiences. Life would be so simple if we listened and acted on the directions and advice our parents and teachers gave us, learnt from observing what happens to those around us and opened our spiritual ears to the guidance flowing to us from our spiritual advisors. Unfortunately, in our human state, we learn more quickly from experience rather than tutoring or from listening to the advice and guidance of others. You mainly learn your lessons through the situations you are drawn into, the choice of direction you choose and the challenges you face; as you may have discovered humans rarely choose the easy road!

The traumas and bad experiences you have had in your life are not random situations; they will be there to either give you a chance to grow or to impact other people so that they can also grow and understand themselves and our world. As you begin to see your life experiences as opportunities then you change from being a victim and become more powerful, more at peace with yourself and wiser.

Learn the lesson and move from victim to victor.

Learning a lesson or gaining insight isn't something that usually comes overnight. After a bad experience, a wrong choice, a difficult time with people or work, you need time to turn your challenge into wisdom. You will find it difficult and sometimes impossible to discover the benefits when you are emotional or in the depths of a trauma, loss or are suffering; wait till you reach calmer waters then look back and try to see what you may have gained from the experience.

At the end of this chapter I take you through some of the life lessons and associated challenges that you may have chosen for this lifetime with guidance on what you can do to speed up the process of turning your challenges into insights.

Throughout this book I will be sharing ways that you can heal the symptoms and the collateral damage from the challenges you have experienced so far.

No matter what your personal life purpose and plan may hold there are some 'must-dos' in your life purpose list, which apply to all of us who wish to live consciously.

- Positively give out love – radiate love – through whatever you do.

- Live without judgement of yourself or other people.

- Help others whenever and wherever you can.

- Live by your own truth, be honest, and be authentic.

- Live harmlessly – never consciously hurt any person, animal – or the environment.

- Take responsibility for yourself; direction, health, choices.

Parents

If you have difficult parents who have given you a troubled and upsetting childhood, it may seem strange to consider that you chose them. However, you will have picked them for several reasons.

- **A challenge you cannot escape:** parents who cannot give or express love or have deep-seated issues and pain of their own will present you with situations and challenges that can be great teachers of life lessons. As a child you are unable to run away from difficult people and your personality and character will not have developed to the point where you can fight back or out manipulate their harmful ways. These experiences will leave strong, long-lasting impressions on you. If you have been presented with the dark side of life in your early years, it can take many years of your adult life to heal the pain and scars of your childhood, but there will come a day when you realise that many of your problems, fears and inner pain do not come from being a bad person as your parents may have implied, but from the way you see your experiences as defining you. Eventually, you will come to terms with who you are, you will stop blaming your parents for their bad treatment of you and realise that they just couldn't do things any differently; you will start to heal yourself of the anger, fear and emotional turmoil that has sat like a heavy weight inside you. Then, you become strong and can find happiness; you can start to love yourself and your purpose is fulfilled.

A difficult childhood can give you the impetus to move out and make a life for yourself, to become independent and strong in your own right – ideal for successful sportsmen, businessmen and high achievers. It also can pave the way for you to be a compassionate and empathetic carer or therapist as you relate to others struggling with similar home lives.

Parents hurt their children when they are hurting; this is not an excuse but a reason.

Journal:
Did you have a difficult childhood? How did your parents treat you? Did your early life experiences harm you and did you carry the scars for long? Have you begun to see that it wasn't because you were 'bad' but because they were struggling with their own emotional problems? Do you know why your parents were difficult? What did they teach you either by hard knocks, or by helping you to see what you did not want for your own children?

- **A loving and stable start:** The easier start in life comes with parents who are generous, understand you, offer guidance, love you and offer you the stable platform for you to fly from. Your lesson here will be to value their love, to accept their support but to also step out on your own and take responsibility for yourself and not to be dependent on them. The danger is that you can rely too much on their kindness and not find your own feet. A loving and stable start with or without financial security can be the example you needed to enable you to give without expectation of gain and to be generous with your love.

Journal:
Were your parents loving and if so, how did this affect you and what benefits did they bring? Were you a rebel in your teens?

- **The genes you need for your length of life and physical needs:** Your natural parents give you the genes and physical attributes or weaknesses that will be part of your plan. If your intention is to be a world-class athlete and push through limits of endurance, you will need a body that can be developed for this purpose. If your purpose is to show the world that spirit can overcome physical disabilities or challenge society to accept a person who is different, your choice of parents will be involved with this too. I was brought up by my mother and stepfather, but my natural father's genes have given me robust health, which has been particularly useful for the extensive travelling I have needed for my work. Your genes can also give talents that you can utilise in your life plan such as courage to speak out, a good singing voice, artistic skills or the grit to keep going when things get tough.

Journal:
What genes and mental and physical attributes have you inherited that have helped or hindered you?

Service

Another aspect of your life purpose is the service you will give to humanity and the world while you are down on Earth. This can range from helping a friend when they are in trouble to dedicating yourself to saving whales. Each of your lives will have an aspect of service in it. The proportion of your time given over to helping others will grow the closer you get to the end of your cycle of lives and will also depend on your soul purpose. If you are a doctor, charity worker, carer or healer, you will naturally be giving more in service to individuals than a scientist or engineer who will be giving to society and the world as a whole.

Journal:
Ponder on the things you have done for the world, from charity donations, helping neighbours to rescuing a dog or cat. Do you feel there is more you want to do?

Soul Mates

You come for a life on Earth along with other souls who have been your travelling companions in previous lives; we refer to these as soul mates. They are people who will impact your life, support you through your difficult times, take the role of parent or sibling, be your child, be a best friend or act as a love companion. Despite popular myth they are not always coming along as romantic partners! They could come as the partner who came into your life for a brief time then moved on leaving you broken-hearted. Or as the teacher who pushed you hard at school that you hated, or the boss who slapped you down constantly to test your ability to keep going, or the bully at school who was teaching you to stand up for yourself. You will usually have a sense of knowing a soul mate and often they will know you well in an instinctive way, even if you don't particularly like them. They are the people who know you better than yourself! They would know which buttons to press and will know how far to push you. When you meet them for the first time you may feel a sense of déjà vu, a feeling of knowing them without having met them before. They can love you, but beware, they can also challenge you. Soul mates will have appeared in your previous lives but in different roles; mother, sister, lover, etc. You may even feel strains of those old roles being played out in this lifetime, so your mother may feel more like a sister to you, or your daughter may act like a mother.

Journal:

Who do you think are your soul mates? What impact have they had on you? What have you done for them? Does your sister act like your mother or your mother act as your child? What have been the most significant people in your life, either for good or bad, who you have liked or disliked intensely?

Astrological Impacts

Once I would have dismissed the impact on my life of my astrological chart. However, having had several readings from two different methods in the West and in India, I cannot dismiss the impact that the locations of the stars and planets have on our character and life. Each reading has shown me the same tendencies of my nature, the same major turning points in my life and the same choices I will make. The energy of the universe and your own planetary system, without doubt, will have an impact on you and the way your life unfolds. You might find it helpful to check out your sign, not in the daily paper but from a qualified astrologer and see how the planets affect your character and the events in your life. It can be quite revealing to see and understand that some of your characteristics are influenced by the date and time of your birth. You will find that some of the projections for you are possible, some are probabilities and some seem to be dead certs! Your plan of destiny will have allowed for crossroads and options where your free will comes into action and where you can change course from your original route. There are times in your life when strong emotions may disconnect you from your higher self and you may make decisions that take you down blind alleys and diversions. However, whatever route you choose your higher self will bring you back on course despite some dead ends or sideshows. You will always get to your destination eventually!

Journal:
What is your star sign and how do you think this influences your character? Do you recall decisions you have made that have taken you off track?

Goals and Passions

Throughout your life you will experience the drive and push of ideas, inspirations and passions. All these are directions and the force of your higher self guiding you. Some of your guidance you may misread or misunderstand and there will be projects and plans that wither on the vine and goals that you do not reach. Sometimes you will start a project but find too many obstacles in the way and despite your enthusiasm and drive, the project just doesn't fly. Then years later you may find you are drawn to the idea again; this time it may bring success.

One of the factors that contribute to whether a goal is reached or not is divine timing; this is the term we use for the influence of not only your higher self but the greater source of light; you may call this benign and influential creator by different names; God, the Universe, Spirit, Light, the Creator, the Source, angels or Fate – whatever feels right for you. This higher intelligence will know the bigger picture of your destiny, your plan and all the factors that need to come into place for it to be a success and to work for you. We will explore your connection with these forces of light in Chapter Three. We will also look at how you can strengthen your intentions by using the full force of your will and your ability to create and manifest, I will share rituals that help you to clear obstacles that appear to be in the way, blocking off your goals.

> ### *Higher forces for good can guide you as they see your life from the mountain tops as you walk in the valleys.*

Journal:
What are your passions? How do you feel when you are allowing them full reign? Do you have goals yet to be fulfilled?

What is your role in this life?

Relating back to your soul purpose and life purpose there will be a main driver, a purpose that will come as a passion for this lifetime. Here are a few possible roles where you can shine your light and gain fulfilment.

- Healer.
- Carer or therapist.
- Doctor or nurse.
- Leader.
- Working for Justice.
- Active for change in the way we care for animals/the environment/children/the disadvantaged.
- Scientist/researcher.
- Writer or poet.
- Artist.
- Builder.
- Designer.
- Bringing light to the corporations.

- Fighting corruption.
- Protector and defender – The armed forces and police.
- Explorer – physically or through medicine or science
- Vet or carer of animals.
- Agriculture, gardener.
- Motherhood, fatherhood.
- To be a thinker, philosopher.
- Entertainer, actor, singer, dancer.
- Spiritual leader and speaker.
- Business and finance.
- To live a simple and quiet life.
- Politician, leading our society.
- Charity and aid worker.

Journal:

There are many more that are not on this list and you may have several roles while you are here. What do you believe is your life purpose?

Use the following symbol and ritual to help you to connect with and activate your life purpose. You may be a little scared to accept your role either from a lack of confidence or from old fears associated with the role. The symbol accesses the powerful Chamber of Light, which is where you go when you arrive in the higher planes to heal fears and anxieties and reconnect you to your true self after a lifetime of challenges. The energy of the Chamber will help you clear the obstacles of your mind that may be preventing you from fully acknowledging what you are here to accomplish.

Ritual: Activate your life purpose

- Breathe deeply four times.

- Hold your intention to connect to and complete your life purpose.

- Draw the symbol. Draw the vertical line then the horizontal then the first dot in the left-hand corner, then the others clockwise over the head.

- Use your hands to sweep the energies down the entire length of the body.

- Say, 'I connect to and fully accept my life purpose as the plan I agreed to follow in this lifetime. I see all obstacles dissolved and my way clear; now, right now, right now.'

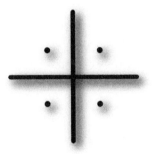

Your Soul

If you go back now to the spiritual energy map at the beginning of this chapter you will see that I have drawn a line halfway down. This represents the divide between the Heavenly Realm, the higher dimensions of existence, from the Earthly Realm, our material world where the energy is denser. In the higher dimensions your life is in spirit form and on Earth is a combination of spirit and physical.

Your soul is that portion of your spirit that comes to Earth for its purpose of gaining experience and growing consciously as we saw earlier in this chapter. Imagine it as an Xbox game. The soul is the volunteer that goes down on an adventure, clasping an action list to its spiritual bosom, acting out a role and often getting battered and bruised in the process. Your higher self is like the father figure that sits above in heavenly peace watching while the child visits this alien and scary world to overcome fears, push out the boundaries, fight of the demons then return with a bundle of precious jewels – the treasure of experience, understanding and knowledge that goes into the repository for the spirit and also raises the consciousness of the entire universe. The collateral damage comes as the isms, fears and scary memories that become embedded in the soul until the next trip to Earth where the action list will include the purpose of healing the scars of previous trips as well as collecting more treasure.

Through the time while you are in your mother's womb you are linked strongly to her spiritually and as you grow towards your birth your own spiritual energies become stronger until the time when you arrive. I have seen a baby's soul flying in and out of a pregnant woman, so I believe it comes and goes through the nine months of gestation and joins permanently at the time the baby takes its own breath and becomes independent from mother. While you are in the womb you will be conscious of the mood and experiences of your mother while she is carrying you. You will hold those memories embedded in your cells and they can affect you through your life and in adulthood, you may recall the feelings of your mother through her pregnancy.

So, when the time is right for your birth, your soul arrives full-on and joins your baby body ready for the joint venture between your spirit and your body for your current trip through our world.

I am often asked what happens if a baby comes earlier than expected, how does that affect them and their planned destiny based on their natal astrological chart. I sense that even early arrival is part of the plan; a joint arrangement between the higher selves of mother and child.

Soul Imprints and Scars

From the moment of your birth you will be facing the experiences that will develop your character and affect you for many years of your adult life; some of these challenges will be quite traumatic. The difficulties that you face in life are mostly drawn to you to spur you on to learn and grow. When you are rejected by someone you love, lose a job or experience a similar trauma, the shock will leave an imprint in your soul. This imprint will hold the memory of the event and the negative emotions that it caused. These negative emotions of anger, fear, guilt, blame, etc. will stay locked in until you are able to heal them. Healing is transforming heavy and painful energy and raising and releasing it as you understand why you attracted the challenging situation or person and what message it may bring. Healing allows your negative experiences and feelings to be absorbed and integrated into your consciousness in a positive way. So, everything that happens to you becomes part of who you are and who you are to become.

No experience of any kind is wasted.

If the imprint is not healed, the low and dense energy it holds will continue to attract similar energy – like attracts like. Until you heal an imprint it will act as a magnet and draw similar challenges towards you. These continuous cycles and repeats become patterns in your life so when you keep having the same situations arriving in your life over and over or you keep attracting the same negative relationships or work situations, you know that there is healing to be done! You need to look hard and long at yourself and see what you are holding onto that is acting as a magnet and most important of all, what lesson are you not learning!

In Chapter Seven, I will be helping you to target and heal these imprints.

Journal:
What patterns can you see in your life? What situations come up repeatedly? Do you think there is something you are not 'getting'?

Ask yourself why you are creating the same circumstances then set your intention to heal the root cause, learn the lesson and move forward.

Protection

Your spiritual energy and your physical energy are precious and unfortunately, the world is full of predators who would like to feed on your vitality. I will be giving you more advice on protecting yourself and your energy in the next chapter but here is a short ritual you can use to call in a shield and I suggest you use it if you want to meditate, pray or even when going about your daily business. Unfortunately, as on Earth, spiritual beings are not all good and some definitely have negative intentions and do not have your welfare at heart!

Ritual: Calling in a protective shield.

A simple and effective way to seal your energy field is to ask for a shield to be placed around your aura.

'I call upon the Forces of Light to surround me with a protective shield; now, right now, right now.'

Spiritual Heart

Your heart centre is the energy centre that sits in the middle of your chest and governs the flow of love – both giving and receiving. If your heart is hurt, damaged or blocked then you may be struggling to create a fully reciprocal, loving relationship. The state of your heart centre is key to your relationships of all kinds including money, work, God, friends, family, etc. so I have devoted Chapter Four to advice, symbols and rituals to heal and open your heart and to attract love into your life.

The core of your heart is the connection point to your higher self and holds the same essence and energy; it is pure love and is the essential you; the true you that is not affected by the scars and imprints that affect your soul. There is a continuous energy link between your heart and your higher self, which is rather like a telephone line. If the line is blocked, you cannot receive your own guidance or be in touch with your intuition. Overload of negative emotions such as anger, fear or guilt will block this link, as will negative self-beliefs such as low self-value and self-esteem. This book is dedicated to healing and clearing these blocks so that you can experience a happy and harmonious life with a clear and open heart and a strong connection to your intuition, life purpose and wisdom. This connection is always present, no matter how blocked it may become when life is tough and you are in the depths of despair. The good news is you can reconnect at any time with your will and intention.

Here is a simple morning ritual that will give the start of your day a spiritual lift; it sets your intention to seal and protect your energy and spirit, to open your heart to give and receive love, to keep your mind open to new ideas and perceptions and to re-establish your connection to your higher self.

Ritual: Morning Ritual – to start the day – protect, open and connect

- Breathe deeply four times.

- Drop your shoulders and relax.

- Call in protection: 'I call upon the Forces of Light to surround me with a protective shield; now, right now, right now.'

- Put your hands together in front of your chest as though you are praying.

- Open your hands and say, 'My heart is open to give and receive love.' Repeat two more times.

- Put your hands together in front of your forehead.

- Open your hands and say, 'I open my mind to the truth and new ideas.'

- Clasp your hands together and lift them above your head saying, 'I am connected to my higher self; now, right now, right now.' Repeat two more times.

When your physical body dies, your soul flows back up your connective tube to reunite with your higher consciousness and returns to the realm of Heaven where you will be welcomed by family members who have gone before and your own spirit guides and angels. You will assess the work you have done on Earth and heal any emotions that you may have taken with you at the time of your death. You will then start to work on your next visit, and so the cycle will continue until you have completed all the tasks your spirit needs, and learned all the lessons required for you to reach the state of peace known as Nirvana, joy, bliss or enlightenment. Through taking on the challenges of life on Earth and learning your lessons, often the hard way you will have raised your own consciousness and also raised the consciousness of all humanity.

In our present time, consciousness is growing and expanding faster and faster. We are now able to connect to people throughout the world with the Internet; we can learn through other people's experiences in a way never seen on Earth before. With empathy we can feel the pain of people's suffering through natural disasters and wars far from home, but we can also be lifted by the joyful experiences of strangers in far off places.

If you are interested in raising your consciousness through the pleasure and stimulation of mixing with other people who have the same mindset and intentions, then you may like to join a Conscious Café group. We gather together normally once a month in groups all over the world to bring together like-minded people who want to explore and expand their own personal growth, to increase self-awareness and to engage in conscious conversations. Details are in Appendix II.

Challenges and Lessons for this Lifetime

Here are some of the lessons you may have chosen to learn in this lifetime.

The Lesson to Overcome Fear

You will have been born with fears and you will pick up other fears on the way. Some will be second hand; you will have taken some of the anxieties that troubled your parents. Some will be created by the media, who thrive on creating sensationalism and fear. Some will be survival fears that help you to avoid danger but the majority and the most impactful will be fears caused by previous bad and traumatic experiences; some of which may have come from a previous lifetime. Whatever the origin of your fear, it limits your life experience; it prevents you from being the best and greatest you can be; it degrades your quality of life; it can even impact your physical health. Digestive disorders, heart problems, headaches and muscle pain are just a few of the conditions caused by fear and anxiety. Without doubt, fear will affect your behaviour and your relationships. If untreated or healed fear can grow unchecked and overcome your mind, destroying the balance and normal thinking and causing paranoia, obsessions, insomnia, panic attacks and suspicions. Many of today's mental illnesses and conditions come from the fears we hold locked inside. If managing or overcoming fear is a lesson you have given yourself for this lifetime, you will be challenged repeatedly with the situation you fear the most.

Fear stifles your ability to live a joyful and fulfilling life.

What can you do?
Unfortunately, there is no quick fix for fear. It will not leave you by simply wishing it away, so firstly it's essential that you acknowledge your feelings; they are valid and there is no shame in anxiety. Through this book I will be helping you to clear and release the root causes behind most of the unwanted and negative emotions that you may be experiencing. As you heal these deeply entrenched scars and imprints created by traumas, you will find the associated fears and anxieties will fade.

If you feel brave you can take steps to face your fear and challenge it. Once you show it who is the master, you will become empowered and strong and never be bothered by it again.

I had a fear of horses since childhood and my worst nightmare was to be close to one. For our retirement my husband and I found a house in the New Forest National Park in Hampshire, England. It's a beautiful area of heath and forests that were hunting grounds for the kings of England and it teems with animal life. From ancient times those living in the forest area, called commoners, can graze their animals on the land for free, so ponies, donkeys, cattle and pigs wander freely everywhere. When I met the vendors of the house we had chosen, a family whose livelihoods were wrapped up in the equestrian world, I told her I was a healer. She immediately asked me to come to the stable in the garden to heal her horse. My heart leapt and I started to shake inside. Oh, no, anything but a horse! I couldn't bring myself to admit my fear; after all she was a champion show jumper and I didn't want to appear a complete ninny. So I followed her to the stable and she introduced me to her beautiful mare. The horse looked me directly in the eye and I gave way to a natural reaction to place my hand on her crown and let the energies of healing flow into her. I focused on her eyes and I felt the healing energies surging through to her, completing our connection. It felt wonderful, my heart opened and my fear disappeared. For the last twenty years, I have taken my dogs for walks in the Forest and we meet up with horses all the time. My absolute dread of them has gone, although I continue to have a healthy respect for their hooves and teeth!

Journal:
What fears do you have? Do you know the cause of those fears? What fears have you already overcome in your life? How did you feel when you resolved them?

The Lesson of Managing Loss

This lesson is one of the hardest to understand. What possible good could come out of the pain of loss, especially of a loved one? There are many forms of loss and all will bring a sense of grief. Everyone will at some stage of their life suffer the grief of losing something or someone. How attached or connected you are will affect the intensity of the pain you will experience. The lesson isn't to be careless and carefree about losing someone you love but rather to allow yourself to come to terms with your loss, to value what you had and to learn and accept that nothing stays the same. The person who has left will be leaving memories and their love will be in your heart and even some of their spirit will stay with you for your entire life and beyond.

When someone dies we don't know why but they will have a reason and another role to perform, either in another incarnation on Earth or in spirit. When my daughter-in-law tragically died from a pulmonary embolism at the age of twenty-five, like the rest of the family, I was heartbroken. In the final stages of her life, while she was on life support, I prayed for her and connected to her higher self to give comfort as she was unable to hear me physically. When she passed over and her soul left her body, it was natural for me to continue my dialogue with her spiritually. I saw her in the heavenly realm and she was surrounded by angels and spiritual beings who were comforting and healing her. She was surrounded by flowers. After a few weeks of our time, I was leading a meditation in a workshop when she appeared in my inner vision. She showed me that she had an important role in heaven; she was greeting other young people and young mothers and fathers who had died leaving young children and loved ones. She guided them in and was their comforter and healer. Knowing the loving woman she was, that didn't surprise me at all.

When my favourite and most loved dog Prince died, a street mutt from Malaysia, again I was able to connect with him in spirit. I was amazed that he was in fact quite an evolved soul, something like a unicorn and he helps me when I am healing an animal. He calls in a group of other animal spirits and they circle the spirit of the animal and send healing.

Not only can a loved one move on to another role but they can also become a spirit guide for the ones left behind. A family of three girls that I know, lost their mother when they were very young, and their heartache was intense and painful for years, but as they have grown older they have felt the presence of their mother with them. I have seen her every time I help the girls; she is a constant and caring guardian for them and there have been many times she has influenced and helped them from Spirit.

Similarly, I keep a close connection to my mother and get an instant response when I throw tricky questions at her and ask her for advice, which is always given with wisdom, love and humour of her earthly personality. This ability to stay connected to her has been a huge solace to me and helped me through the sad days and tearing grief. Here is a ritual you can use to make that connection for yourself. I can promise you that the person you love will be linked to your heart with the cords of love that connected you to them in life; you can use this cord like a telephone line to communicate with them now.

Ritual: Connecting to a loved one in spirit

This ritual will allow you to make a spiritual connection to a loved one or a beloved pet who has passed on. It will help to have something to remind you of the physical presence of your loved one such as a piece of jewellery, a photograph. Also, have a box of tissues nearby! Don't stress or try too hard with the visualisations in this ritual; simply follow the steps. The connection is always there and if you can't make it because you are emotional or anxious then try again another time. When you go through this you are setting the intention of connecting and they may appear to you later in a dream or when you are relaxing quietly.

- In a quiet place, without phones or interruption, in a garden or wherever you feel at peace, sit and relax.

- Bring in your protection; 'Archangel Michael please send your Blue Flame to protect and seal my energy now; right now, right now.' Feel the warmth and love surrounding you.

- Call in your guardian angel and angelic arms will wrap around you – feel the comfort of love from Spirit. 'Guardian Angel be with me now.'

- Breathe in deeply four times and hold the intention that you will be connecting to your loved one.

- Put your hands together in front of your heart centre and part them as you open your heart. Say, 'I open my heart to – the name of your loved one.'

- Put your hands together in front of your forehead and part them as you open your mind to see beyond the physical.

- Clasp your hands together and raise them above your head as you indicate your intention of connecting to your higher self and to Spirit. 'I connect to my higher self; now right now, right now.' Do this four times.

- Draw this symbol and say the name of the person you wish to connect with.

Over the photograph or object that connects you draw, first the spiral from top to bottom, then the upturned pyramid. Do not worry about the precision of the drawing.

- Let your mind and imagination take you on a visit to a favourite garden, beach or place that reminds you of your loved one.

- Speak to them. Don't worry if you cannot visualise them; it's not necessary to see them to communicate with them.

- Tell them of your love, your sadness, how you miss them. Then ask them what they are doing now. Be open-minded – you may be surprised at what they tell you.

I am sending you love and a huge hug to comfort you now; right now, right now, bless you.

This lesson brings other lessons along with it: gratitude, appreciation of love, the lasting power of love, the value of great memories of time shared, the impermanence of life and the need to live it fully minute by minute and day by day.

Of course, we all must leave some time as the famous quotation goes: 'None of us are getting out of here alive,' so live every moment to its fullest, follow the love, follow the smiles, follow the fun. Celebrate every day with your friends and family, put small thoughts, old insults and arguments behind you. Don't let anything ruin your love. Nurture and give your all to every relationship so when they end you have no regrets or wishes for things not said or not done. When the time is right for the soul to leave it will move on, however we would wish it otherwise. Once your loved one leaves you must allow yourself time to grieve and to absorb all that person has given you in memories; allow yourself to move on without resentment, anger or yearning for what is past. You cannot get over grief; you cannot fix or heal grief, but you can allow it to flow through you naturally.

Allow the natural steps of grief to unfold.

- **Denial:** when my father died suddenly, my mother and I felt nothing for several days. We were stunned, numb and emotionless. We couldn't absorb or accept what had happened and we both shared shame that we were acting too normally. Shouldn't we be distraught, shouldn't we be crying all the time? Of course, the shock wore off and we very quickly were hit by floods of tears and great heartache. It is quite normal to feel stunned and unemotional when someone dies suddenly, your spirit is protecting you at the time of your greatest vulnerability.

- **Anger and blame:** it is perfectly natural to feel anger at some point. Even with the person who has passed away. This will fade as you assimilate your loss. You may also feel guilty and blame yourself that you didn't prevent or anticipate their death. You may feel guilty if you were not with them when they passed over, but they had to go when you were not there because it is just too hard for them to pull themselves away from your love when you are present.

- **Pain and Depression:** the impact on your heart and spirit will be immense and you will feel pain in your heart centre which will be broken or scarred by your loss. You will certainly feel low for some time. If you lose a partner that has been with you for some time your spiritual energy bodies will have intermingled, so it will be particularly hard to live without their presence and it will cause a lowering of your spirits. It can help to talk about your feelings to someone outside of your family such as Samaritans or a charity that offers grief counselling. Don't be reluctant to ask for help – it is not a sign of weakness but a sign of wisdom.

- **Acceptance:** acknowledge what you feel and allow your emotions to flow. Know that everyone experiences loss differently and there is no proper way to feel or behave.

- **Absorbing memories and the experience:** as time goes by the richness of your experiences with the person you have lost will become part of who you are.

Create a place of memories in your home or garden where you can go to have your special conversations and recall loving moments.

If you are grieving for a way of life that you have lost or for someone who has chosen to walk away, you will still need time to grieve, but after some time you will feel better if you let go and move forward with your new life.

There are many losses, great and small, that can affect you.

- Divorce or relationship breakup.

- Loss of health.

- Loss of a job or a role – moving from single to married, married to single, etc.

- Loss of financial stability.

- A miscarriage.

- Retirement.

- Death of a pet.

- Loss of a cherished dream.

- A loved one's serious illness taking away your normal and stable life.

- Loss of a friendship.

- Loss of security after a trauma.

- Loss of a home.

What lessons can you learn from loss?

- To value the love you have in your life right now.

- To accept the feelings you have without trying to suppress them.

- To know that your memories are valuable and become part of you.

- To feel compassion and empathy for others who are also suffering.

- To move forward without negative feelings towards yourself or anyone else.

- To move on with your life, accept your loss and treasure the memories.

- To look for the best in every moment of your life and enjoy it to its fullest.

- To value and enjoy every relationship without allowing negative emotions to spoil the love.

- To heal all arguments as quickly as possible – we never know which will be our last encounter with a loved one.

Journal:

Consider the losses you have experienced in your life so far. How do you see them looking back? Can you recall the memories without negative emotions? Do you still yearn for something you have lost, or can you accept it has gone and move forward? What value have you gained from the people who have left your life?

The Lesson of Forgiveness

Forgiveness is a vital part of the lesson of karma, which I will be covering in detail in Chapter Five. Karma is the lesson of cause and effect. What you give out, you give back and is a spiritual law, which means that there is no ducking the issue; there will be a consequence to all your actions both positive and negative; it will happen and is inevitable. Once you have learnt to take responsibility and own these consequences you then need to move to the lesson of forgiveness.

There are two aspects of this lesson. The easiest one is the forgiving of others. With this lesson we learn that the feelings of resentment, anger, blame and hatred are toxic and poisonous – in fact, holding a grudge is like drinking poison and hoping the other person will die. You are the one who suffers when you churn over how someone has hurt you. Of course, you will feel anger and resentment for some time, but if you are wise you will let go of those feelings and accept what has happened. When someone has upset me by bad behaviour or acted with anger towards me, for example, road rage because I am slow to go into a roundabout; I think to myself, how horrible it must be to be in that person's mind. What must they be going through with all that frustration and anger burning away inside them that they get upset over such a small issue? This turns my anger into sympathy! It's a lot easier to forgive someone when you see where they are coming from.

What this lesson gives you:

- Forgiving brings back a sense of peace
- Forgiving allows you to move forward in your life without bringing the anger along with you
- Forgiving dissolves the cords that hold you to the person who has harmed you – it sets you free
- Forgiving releases the tensions in your solar plexus and the stomach caused by the tension of anger and blame
- Forgiving is empowering
- Forgiving makes you stronger
- Forgiving allows you to show compassion.

Blame and anger are chains that hold you back from peace.

How to Forgive

This ritual will lead you through a process of forgiving. Do this when you are ready to move on and when you want to set yourself free from the chains of anger and blame.

Ritual: Forgiving

- Write a letter to the person who has hurt you. Explain how you feel. Release and express any anger you feel. At the end of the letter write your intention of forgiving them.
- Burn the letter and watch the letter and all the emotions that it holds turn into the light of the flame. Your emotions are being transformed from anger back to peace.
- Visualise chains that have been wrapped around you, holding you back from living your life with peace and harmony.
- Say out loud, 'With grace, I forgive you and release myself from your clutches, the chains are broken.' Visualise the chains around you falling to the ground.

- Draw the Release Symbol above three times from bottom left to right, in the air in front of you.
- Take one step forward and say, 'I step forward in my life; I am free of anger and resentment and I am no longer the victim of the name of the person who has harmed you, I release you from affecting my life.'
- Sweep your body as you let go of all attachments and emotions.

Journal:

Is there anyone you need to forgive that holds you back? Does the thought of anyone or organisation still get you angry? Do you think you could release them now and set yourself free?

Unless you learn the lesson of forgiveness you will be challenged repeatedly. Similar circumstances will occur, more people will harm you, and you will keep bringing them into your life till you learn the lesson. Challenges can come from individuals, groups, corporations or government. Once you have let go and moved on without constant reliving the past you will find your life flows more smoothly with less antagonism from others.

Forgive Yourself

The more sensitive you are, the more you are likely to carry guilt. A hardened killer will have no feelings of guilt, whereas some people feel guilty even when they have done nothing wrong! They will worry endlessly about things they feel they should have done.

Forgiving is a great gift to yourself whether you forgive someone else or yourself.

Karma is the state that we create for ourselves when we hurt someone; the spiritual law of karma dictates that whatever you give out you get back. So, if you hurt someone you will be hurt in return, though not necessarily by the same person in the same way. When you do something that breaks your own moral code or that of civilisation or your culture you create an imprint of guilt that sits within your soul. This imprint attracts the challenge of this lesson back repeatedly, until you:

- accept what you have done
- feel compassion and empathy for the person or people you have wronged
- have set an intention not to do it again
- have worked through your atonement (making up for what you have done) and suffered the burden of guilt
- have fully forgiven yourself
- become non-judgemental of yourself and others

Guilt is a heavy burden to carry for the sensitive soul.

Your lesson will not be turned to wisdom if you simply forgive yourself every time you cause an upset! Atone for the harm you have done by bringing balance back into your relationship by giving love in any form; consideration, gifts, time, kind acts; you can then follow this simple ritual.

Ritual: forgive yourself
- Put your hand on your heart centre.
- Breathe in deeply four times.
- 'I send love to the person I have hurt and ask for forgiveness.'
- 'With love, I forgive myself'. Repeat three more times.

Journal:
Do you carry any guilt? Do you often use the words 'I should have' or 'I ought to'? Is it time to forgive yourself and set yourself free? Are you a perfectionist who blames yourself for anything and everything that goes wrong? What can you do to alleviate the burden? What does it feel like to forgive? Is there someone who you are locked into through anger or blame?

The Lesson of Letting Go of Control

Most of us are guilty of trying to control someone at some time in our lives. If you are a parent, you exerted your will over a child to keep it safe; as your children grow you will have given advice and guidance based on your own experiences and that is fine, the duty of care of a parent. However, the issue of this lesson arises from: trying to exert your will over another; attempting to change someone's thinking, manipulating or influencing with your own ideas or attempting to fix someone against their will and personal choice. We usually enforce our views when we think we have more experience, we know best, it's for their best interests and often with the sense that it is a form of love. Even if you are exerting controls with the best intentions it goes against spiritual law and is an important lesson to learn. You cannot be responsible for or dictate the actions of another adult unless you are in law enforcement. Offer guidance and then step back.

Healers should be particularly careful with this spiritual law as we have a tendency to feel the need to put right whatever we see not working and it is tempting to send good vibes to someone with an intention attached. When my mother was struggling with osteoarthritis in her hip and I was away on an overseas trip, I rang her to tell her I would be sending distance healing to her that evening; which I did. The next day, I called back to see how she had felt after the session.

'Wonderful, thank you treasure,' she said. 'I had the energy to clean the kitchen from top to bottom.'

I tried to explain that I had sent the healing for her hip not to clean her kitchen but of course, too late and a lesson learnt. I cannot dictate what someone does with the energy I send! I still send out love to the people or circumstances I know that need light and love, but I now do it with an open hand and let it go where it's needed and used where it's wanted.

Avoid controlling or manipulating – wait until you are asked before giving guidance or assistance.

Journal:
Is there anyone in your life who you feel responsible for even though they are adults, fully functioning and able to look after themselves and make their own decisions? Do you tend to try and fix other people's lives? Are you tempted to carry your adult children, solve their problems, pay off their debts?

Ritual: Letting Go

There are many occasions when this little ritual is helpful. You can use it whenever you feel you are getting too involved or enmeshed in other people's lives, getting too concerned and worrying at night about other people or feeling drawn to fix relationships other than your own.

- Imagine a cord flowing from you to the person or situation involved.

- Visualise yourself cutting it by chopping the side of one hand on the other palm; chop chop, chop, chop. Say, 'I release all involvement and let go of control; now right now, right now.'

- Take one large step backwards.

Continue to send love and help when asked but don't get entangled in another person's journey when you are not invited. They must learn their own lessons and if you interfere by doing what you think is a good turn, you can slow down their progress; they will be drawn back to take that challenge again till they understand and gain their own wisdom. If you are the person being controlled I have help for you in Chapter Two for protection and for releasing attachments and hooks.

The Lesson of Divine Timing and Patience

There is also the matter of letting go of control in your own life; to stop forcing the direction in which your life is going. We often move inappropriately to force situations because we do not have patience. We are in too much of a hurry. We want things to move at our pace, to our timetable. However, you may find that some of your goals, aspirations or ambitions may not match your life purpose. This may be because of:

- **Outside influence:** Your choice of direction and goal may be influenced by pressure from other people who are imposing their views and ideas. These may be very different from what you would choose if you have a clear mind and a strong conviction

- **Decisions based on fear:** You may have made decisions based on feelings and emotions including fear or passion. It is good to make decisions based on your heart feelings and desires, but you will also need to take practicality and reality into account too. Have you the skills? Does the plan suit your lifestyle? Will it fit into any family responsibilities? Do you have the right business skills needed?

- **Driven by duty:** You may feel you ought or should be doing something in a certain way because of your beliefs or sense of duty. If you are here primarily to bring light and raise consciousness, you may feel driven to do work or run a business that is about giving without receiving. If you are driven through duty you may be missing the essential skills and practical knowledge and being carried away with your own enthusiasm to serve.

If you are involved with a project or idea that is not part of your overall plan, then you will find obstacles in your way. You will go down blind alleys and you will feel frustrated and depressed that your great idea is not working. Here are some clues that show you are not on track:

- You don't have the finances to back your project and you can't raise them
- Doors repeatedly shut in your face
- Your project is constantly delayed
- People let you down time and time again
- You feel you are pushing water uphill
- You do not get the support you need.

Eventually, after setbacks and disappointments, you may realise that maybe this project is not meant to be. At this stage, I suggest you put it into cold storage; it may be failing simply because the timing is not right; the reason for its failure may simply be a matter of timing. You may well find that the seed of your idea needed planting, but the full growth and completion may be set for a later date. If you are a 'make things happen' type of person, an achiever or goal setter, then you may well have this lesson to learn.

Some years ago, I visited John of God, an amazing healer in Brazil. My intention was to learn any lessons I needed and to acquire any knowledge that would help me further my work as a healer. As part of the routine of visiting him, I had to stay for twenty-four hours in my hostel room and do nothing, absolutely nothing, no reading, no speaking – nothing. Oh, that was so hard for me! No mobile phone, no computer, no television and no talking. I meditated and slept and meditated and slept and at some stage drifted into a vision.

I rode through the sky in a chariot drawn by eight powerful black stallions. My hands were clasped so tight on the reins my fingers hurt. We flew through the clouds looking down on Earth and I felt the wind blowing my hair; it felt amazing. Then two etheric light hands, old and powerful came around me and took over the reins from me. I was aware of a strong divine presence; I knew these were the hands of God. With divine hands guiding the horses I sat back and relaxed and we went faster and faster; I had a sense of the speed of light as we flew through the sky – it was the most exhilarating ride of my life and with no effort from me at all. When the vision faded I was left with the certain knowledge that I needed to ease up and stop trying so hard in my life and my work; not to push the boundaries and to allow for divine intervention and divine timing.

Let your life's direction and progress flow like the river around obstacles and at a natural pace.

Gradually over the years since then I have allowed myself to relax and allow my progress to flow around obstacles without me forcing the direction. This has been a hard lesson for me to learn because my nature is to push hard and overcome obstacles with the result that my shoulders and upper back have turned into concrete! They are softer now and life is more comfortable; things come more easily. I have also discovered that when I have patience and allow things to take a more natural course, help is always there and I don't have to carry the load on my own.

Faith is surrendering to the inevitable and gracefully allowing for divine intervention and timing.

When you become too attached to outcomes, you will inevitably set yourself up for disappointment and frustration because you are connected, not only spiritually, but also energetically to many people who can influence the outcome of your dreams and manifestations. I have found manifesting works very well if I allow the outcome, the timing and the manner to divine influence. Here is a simple ritual for manifesting your goals, desires and dreams that allows for positive external influences and the best outcome.

Ritual: Manifesting

- Think carefully about your goal or intention. Is it what you truly want? Does it resonate well with you?

- Don't share with anyone who might mock or disrespect your idea.

- Share your thoughts with a friend who is on your wavelength and see how it comes across when you describe your plan. Does your voice sound strong as you speak?

- Set your intentions by writing a description and plan, drawing what your dream looks like in action.

- Set your intention by saying it out loud. 'It is my intention to...'

- Draw this manifestation symbol three times over your writing.

Manifestation Symbol: Draw the symbol in the air in front of you, from left to right then add the dot.

- Put your hand on your heart centre, in the centre of your chest and say, 'I manifest the success of this plan from my heart if it is for the highest good of myself and others.' Repeat two more times

- Release the outcome and let go of your expectation by saying, 'I release to divine intention and my higher and divine self for the how, when and where.' Then chop your hands one on the other as you cut through any attachment strings you may have created with your desires.

Sometimes even though you go through the steps of the law of attraction, which is the law that draws like to like – your vision being matched by the universe – you may find that even with time your goal is not met. The reason can be that you have a deep fear or aversion in your subconscious that is sabotaging your plans. As you go through this book you will find many opportunities to heal these hidden and subconscious fears and unseen saboteurs. By following the steps above you will have set your intention and once that is set, your higher self will find a way to clear and heal all that stands in your way. Also, remember it's perfectly fine to ask for help along the way.

Journal:

Do you have patience with yourself and with life? Could you stop stressing about outcomes and let go? Are you a perfectionist and have expectations and goals that are out of reach? Can you learn to ease up on your expectations?

The Lesson to Open your Heart to Love

This is such an important lesson, for when your heart is closed the energy of love cannot flow to and fro and your ability to give and receive love is inhibited. You will struggle to enjoy life and meaningful and committed relationships. A closed heart will limit your involvement and fulfilment in all aspects of your life.

I wlll be explaining fully the workings of the spiritual heart in Chapter Four, but here is a simple ritual you can perform whenever you feel the lack of love or passion for life.

Option: use an essential oil blend that includes rose, geranium or ylang ylang, better still all three. Anoint your heart centre with it before you start. Rose holds the vibration of love and will help to activate your heart.

Ritual: Opening Your Heart

- Anoint your heart centre by dabbing the essential oil on the centre of your chest, put a drop on each wrist then breathe in the fragrance from your wrists.

- Sit quietly and continue to breathe in deeply four times to a count of four in and five out.

- Gently tap your heart centre four times.

- Keep your focus on your heart by holding your hand on your heart centre.

- Visualise a pink rose in bud.

- Draw the Heart Opening Symbol in front of your heart centre in the middle of your chest.

Heart Opening Symbol: Draw the symbol with the circle first then the lines from left to right.

- See the rose opening, one petal at a time till it is in full bloom

- Place your hands together palm to palm in front of your chest – these now represent the doors of your heart

- Draw your hands apart as you open the doors of your heart

- Reconfirm you are opening your heart by saying out loud, 'I open my heart to give and receive love; now, right now, right now and my passion flows.'

Journal:
Do you think your heart is as open as it could be? Do you need to spend time and effort to heal and open your heart? Is your passion active and flowing?

If you feel you need to release the blocks around your heart and open to love, set yourself the target to do this ritual and others in Chapter Four every day and, with your intention and will, your heart will open, and love will flow from you and to you.

The Lesson for Living Abundantly

This lesson is not just about attracting money but is a lesson in valuing yourself. If you don't value yourself, you won't believe that you deserve the gift of money. To be successful at attracting or making money, put emphasis on healing your self-value and releasing all the blocks that are sabotaging your efforts so far. These blocks are created with your conscious and subconscious mind. If you are struggling financially and have done so much of your life, put this healing as a priority.

The possible causes of blocks to financial security:

- **Previous life:** Bad experiences with wealth and prestige in a previous life

- **Parental influences:** Your parents have feared or experienced lack of financial security

- **Fear of loss:** You fear losing what you have, causing you to hold on too tightly, preventing the flow of money in and through your life

- **Fear of judgement:** Fear of being judged for having a privileged life

- **Not worthy:** You don't feel you deserve wealth.

All those situations are symptoms of imprints and memories from your past and we will be working to heal them in Chapters Five and Six.

Journal:

Do you struggle to make money? Does money slip through your fingers? Are you constantly overspending? Do you lie awake at night worrying about where it will come from? All these are signs of a problem, which is most likely quite deep-seated. Set your intention to heal these blocks to your financial security. Write in your journal your intentions to clear these blocks and heal any imprints to clear all issues around self-value and the ability to receive.

Ritual: Attracting Abundance

- Breathe in deeply four times, count four on the in-breath and five on the out-breath.

- Draw this symbol in front of you three times. This symbol represents an old-fashioned pouch of gold. It sends out to the universe your need to be financially secure.

The Abundance Symbol: Draw the pouch first from left to right in front of you, then draw the line.

- Put our arms out wide, then scoop in the abundance of whatever you wish for; draw your arms in three times saying, 'I draw in an abundance of (*what you need)*; now, right now, right now.'

- Sit for a few moments and think of all you have that you can be grateful for.

- Say, 'I am abundant; I value all have and all I am.'

The Lesson of Giving without Sacrificing Yourself

This lesson comes after the lesson of compassion, which I am sure you have already learnt, this will come from a lifetime when you were selfish and mean-spirited and experienced the consequences, often by suffering deep and painful guilt. Once the important lesson of having compassion for others has been learnt it is easy to go to extremes and to give and give until you have nothing left for yourself. Sacrifice alongside religious and spiritual fervour was common in the last great Spiritual Age; in the Age of Pisces. We have recently moved on from under that planetary influence and we are now in the Age of Aquarius. The Piscean era was one focused on normal folk being guided and directed by strong leaders with rules and regulations, male authority and the need for personal sacrifice and suffering for spiritual growth and development. Fortunately, we have now moved into the Aquarian Age, which is a time to focus on self-responsibility and motivation, making our own decisions, caring for oneself, giving unconditional love, and living with non-judgement and equality for all.

The governing energy in our current age is the Divine Feminine, which brings the energies of love and compassion. Everyone is now faced with the challenge of integrating love into their relationships both personal and at work. We can already see changes in the consciousness of society as attitudes change towards giving equality and respect for women, minorities and the disadvantaged; countries are bringing in laws to enforce equal pay, punishing abuse against women and hate crimes and removing the blocks that prevent all of society equal opportunities. In the workplace we see leadership styles change from fear-based to nurturing and support. The disabled are helped and respected rather than being pushed away into dark rooms. Those suffering mental illness from the results of violence in their work, such as security forces and police, are treated with compassion and understanding. Children are nurtured and not whipped in schools and at home. Yes, thankfully many changes have occurred in the last few years as consciousness shifts, and there are more changes coming, thanks to the Me Too and Black Lives Matter movements.

However, if you were born in the Piscean era you may continue to be influenced by the old consciousness: feeling you must follow rules whether they are relevant or not; sensing your value is less if you are a woman or minority and inclined to put others first to the detriment of your own health and wellbeing. Leaving aside the need to suffer a little while bringing up small children where their wellbeing must come first; for the rest of your life you need to make sure that you are conscious of, and take responsibility for, your own needs and welfare as well as caring for others.

If you are in any of the caring occupations there is the danger that you can give too much of yourself and suffer from burnout. This lesson requires you to create boundaries; to learn when to say no; to take care of yourself rather than sacrifice yourself for others. If you are a giver, this is a hard lesson and you may find you have developed a pattern already where you crash and burn from time to time; making yourself ill because you have overstretched yourself and spread yourself too thin with too many responsibilities.

Journal:

Do you find it hard to say no when you are asked for help or to go the extra mile even when you are exhausted? Do you take time out to nurture yourself?

To prevent yourself from falling, make sure you handle your stresses and the long hours you work by putting plenty of 'me time' into your schedule, even if it seems impossible; try to squeeze a few minutes in each day.

Time for You

- Watch mindfulness YouTube videos and learn techniques to manage stress.

- Take time to breathe slowly and consciously. Breathe in the car on the way to and from work; four counts in and five counts out.

- Take breaks and get outside the building for fresh air.

- Whenever possible get into a park, the countryside or the sea; nature will help clear your energies and calm you.

- Take exercise of some kind three times a week. Buy a FitBit and make sure you get enough movement in your day.

- Use spa treatments, facials and any therapies that appeal – see them not as a luxury but as a necessity!

When you are strong and happy you can give your best to others so nurture yourself.

Ritual: self-Nurture

This meditation will help you to relax. I have recorded many similar meditations on iTunes and on my YouTube account Annejoneshealer. If you do this at the end of the day, burn a lavender candle or essential oils in a burner. If you are doing this in the morning, burn lemon or peppermint candles or citrus essential oils to lift your energy.

- Find a quiet space.
- Put your feet on the ground, preferably barefoot.
- Drop your shoulders.
- Breathe in deeply four times. As you breathe out let go all the worries and anxieties of your day. Breathe in fresh uplifting energy.
- Sweep your hands across your shoulders and down your arms and visualise all the responsibilities of your role falling away. Do this several times. Say, 'I release all the burdens of my work; now, right now, right now.'
- Think of the Earth beneath your feet. As you breathe feel the strength and nurturing energy from Mother Earth rise up through your legs and into your body. Sit for a moment and allow her supportive energy to fill you. She gives water, food and shelter. She is the spirit that sustains you.
- Let your body relax and the tension leave you as you continue to breathe slowly and deeply and allow yourself to be nurtured by nature.

There are more rituals and exercises in the next chapter, where I will show you how to let go of the attachments of other people's negativity and neediness.

The Lesson of Self-Acceptance

Once you have learnt to live without an ego, with humility and without arrogance, the next and, in my opinion, much harder lesson is to live with self-acceptance. Why do you find it so difficult to value and accept yourself? Possibly, because you have yet to learn that no one is perfect and we all have our faults. Perhaps you have been made aware of your weaknesses rather than your strengths by parents and friends or you have compared yourself unfavourably with your role models and people you admire.

Journal:
Are you critical of yourself? Do you beat yourself up because of the
way you look or act? Are you often thinking you could do better?
Do you compare yourself with others and feel inferior?
If you judge yourself and compare yourself badly against others,
you need to heal your self-esteem and set an intention to accept
yourself just as you are. Write this intention in your journal now.

Low self-esteem is a problem that everyone will face at some time in their life. You cannot be confident and self-assured all the time and, under the skin of most of the people you know, there will be self-doubts. How can you boost your appreciation of who you are and be more at ease with yourself?

Let me help you a little here. We looked at the preparation you went through before you started this lifetime. You went to great lengths to choose lessons, experiences and challenges that would help you grow; you chose parents who would suit the life you were coming to live. Everything you needed either to challenge or support you was carefully thought out. So therefore, how can you be anything but perfect for the life you have come to live and the role you have come to play? Of course, there may be some tweaks you would like to make to your personality and there may be healing to do to help you to get back to the real you – to clear the issues and problems that trouble you, but basically, you are what you need to be. So please will you accept this? Will you respect the person you are?

Wear your scars with pride, for they come from the life battles you have won and the source of your wisdom. Your experiences have made you what you are today – so respect yourself for being a survivor and winner.

You can step fully into your power and live your life to the fullest when you accept who you are. You are always going to be different from everyone else because you are unique. You have a unique plan for this lifetime, so you are kitted out differently from everyone else. If you were here to be a concert pianist, you would be born with nimble fingers and a passion to play. If you were to be an explorer, you would have a strong physique and an insatiable curiosity. You have the skills and the temperament for what you are planning for this lifetime so accept who you are and respect yourself.

In classes I get my clients to do this exercise in pairs but you can do it looking into a mirror.

Ritual: Self-love

- Set your intention to see the best in yourself and to overcome all tendencies to be critical.

- Write down ten aspects or characteristics of yourself you like.

- Write down ten skills and attributes you have that help you in your daily life socially and at work.

- Clear your mind of old programming that says you aren't good enough by using your hands and fingers as combs and sweeping downwards around your head. You are clearing your mind of old and unwanted negative attitudes about yourself.

- Say, 'I am releasing and clearing all negative attitudes I have developed about myself; now, right now, right now.'

- Look in a mirror and say genuinely and clearly, 'I respect myself for all I have gone through in my life and the person it has made me into. I accept and love myself; now, right now, right now.'

Don't be discouraged if it takes time for you to completely appreciate and value yourself; don't give up. Take every possible opportunity to see and acknowledge the positive in yourself.

Loving yourself does not exclude your love for others. If you give your love and care from duty it drops your energy. If you give it from your heart it lifts you.

The Lesson to Speak Your Truth

There are many reasons why you might not always speak the truth, or, more importantly, your own truth about what you believe, what you want and what you feel. Here are a few:

- The most common reason for stifling your views is your reluctance to hurt others. Your caring nature will lead you to avoid saying something that may upset a loved one. If you are sensitive and empathetic you would rather keep your thoughts and feelings to yourself to make the lives of those around you as harmonious as possible.

- You suppress your feelings and thoughts because after sharing them in the past you have been either ridiculed or told to shut up, leaving you with a fear of speaking out.

- You have always had a fear of appearing silly or ignorant if you express your beliefs or feelings.

- You may not understand your own reluctance to step forward and speak out, but you have an overriding fear that steps in when you are expected to share your opinions, especially your spiritual beliefs. Your hesitation might come from a scar and imprint from a past life experience. This is often the case for healers and alternative therapists who have been persecuted for their beliefs and practices in previous lifetimes because of religious intolerance.

- You have a shy disposition and are reluctant to get involved in debate or arguments, and you may be very happy keeping your thoughts to yourself.

Journal:

Do you fear speaking in front of strangers? Are you reluctant to share your feelings and beliefs with other people, even friends? Does your throat restrict when you need to speak in public?

In the past, when I had an important seminar coming up at the weekend, I developed a constriction in my throat and my voice disappeared to a whisper by the Friday. I was terrified that I would lose my voice altogether, but when I stood up in front of my audience, my throat opened up and all would be well. Fortunately, this problem has improved over time, as I have worked on healing old imprints of persecution as a healer and spiritual teacher.

I noticed my throat problem was worse when I was visiting a country where women's thoughts and opinions are not respected. I believe that, like many other women who have to go public with their ideas, I was affected by the mass consciousness and attitudes of society. Until quite recently, even in the United Kingdom, women's thoughts were not given as much respect as men's. This situation is also experienced by minorities and I believe as equality becomes the norm attitudes will change, so this universal problem should disappear and we will be only left with our own personal fears and inhibitions. In Chapters Three and Seven I will be helping you clear these blocks and imprints but here is a ritual you can use whenever you wish to step up and speak out.

Ritual: To clear throat blocks and communicate clearly
This will help you to open and clear the energy centre that sits in your throat and affects your ability to express yourself.

- Place something that is pale blue in front of you.
- Sit comfortably and relax your shoulders.
- Call in the protection of Archangel Michael, 'I request protection from Archangel Michael; please, keep me safe.'
- Put one hand on your heart centre and one on your throat.
- Say out loud; 'It is my intention to speak up about my feelings and beliefs fearlessly.'
- Breathe in the colour blue. See a ball of blue light in front of you, see it grow larger as you breathe out blue light into the ball.
- Keep your hand on your throat as the ball grows larger and larger.
- Now, scoop the blue energy ball into your throat and breathe in deeply.

Those are only a few of the life lessons you may be here to learn, others may include:

- **To be happy and joyful.** Why shouldn't this be the very reason for living? Here is a quote from the Dalai Lama, who has often encouraged us to seek happiness. 'The very purpose of our life is happiness, which is sustained by hope. We have no guarantee about the future, but we exist in the hope of something better. Hope means keeping going, thinking, 'I can do this.' It brings inner strength, self-confidence, the ability to do what you do honestly, truthfully and transparently.'

- **To find the positive.** To be grounded and realistic but to find pleasure in little things, to be grateful and to look for the best in situations and people. If you are pessimistic, anxious about the future and your cup is half empty this could be a lesson for you.

- **To have fun.** Do you take life or yourself too seriously? Could you find ways to have more fun and laughter in your life?

- **To manage your carnal desires and addictions.** If you have come with an addictive personality, maybe inherited from your parents this could be a life lesson for you.

- **To live peacefully.** If you are over-anxious and nervous you could be here to find inner peace for yourself. To learn to manage your anxieties and relax.

- **To live without ego.** Your ego is your relationship with yourself. This lesson includes learning that you are unique yet of equal value. If you have a well-developed skill or position in society or wealth, it doesn't mean you are a better person than the rest. Your worth is from the good you do and the love you share rather than the money you accumulate. Also, to learn that whatever you bring is your offering and your gift to the world and is just as precious as anyone else's. A negative ego is damaging and slows your growth so learn to value yourself.

- **To be discerning.** This could be your lesson if you are unable to see the wood for the trees, are impressed by the look and sound of a person without seeing their true worth, or you choose partners who are abusive or lack compassion.

- **To care for and respect your body.** If you have neglected the needs of your body for the sake of your work or domestic pressure, think about taking some time for your body – it will support you well if you care for it.

- **To balance heart and mind – passion and logic.** If you try to solve your problems by thinking rather than intuiting and feeling, then you may need this lesson.

- **To learn that you are more than your body and mind.** To awaken to your potential as a spiritual being.

There are many more lessons and you will have quite a number to either learn or refresh in your lifetime.

Journal:
What do you believe are your life lessons? Which ones have you completed and which ones are you still struggling with? Do the challenges you have faced in your life now make more sense?

Whatever life lessons are set for this life on Earth you will have several challenges to face in your lifetime. Sometimes it doesn't seem fair that some people seem to sail through life easily while others face endless disasters and traumas. Just remember each one of us is at a different stage of our cycle of lives, a different point in our gathering of knowledge and a different level of consciousness. Because we are all here to learn, grow and give service in a variety of ways we will all face different challenges. Each one of us is unique with our own agenda, which will never be one hundred per cent clear until we pass back over into spirit. Accept that there is a plan, a divine plan and one that your spirit and soul put together before you became conscious in this world in this lifetime. Whatever difficulties you are going through or whatever suffering you may be experiencing it will come to an end and will have a purpose that one day will become clear. No knowledge you gain is wasted; no trauma is without reason and your contribution to raising the consciousness of the combined consciousness of everyone and every living thing is outstanding and immense.

Before we move on to look at your energy field, the aura that surrounds your physical body, it would be a good time for you to sit and contemplate what you want to heal. You will have scars and imprints from past challenges that have left a mark on your mind, spirit or body and left you with suppressed emotions and fears that you want to transform. Any negative emotion you experience will be a pointer to some disturbance at soul level. Take time out now to list all those aspects of you that you would like to heal and transform.

Ritual: Setting your intention to heal

- Be clear what you want to heal. You may only know the symptoms, not the cause but that is okay; write down the feelings you want to transform and any physical problems you are suffering.

- Write your intention in your journal.

- Say out loud, 'It is my intention and my will to heal the cause of my... '

- Repeat two more times and end with; 'now, right now, right now.' Loud and clear!

In the next chapter we will look at your aura, your energy field and how the people you spend time with can affect your energy with knock-on effects on your physical and mental wellbeing.

CHAPTER *Two*

Your Energy Field, Your Emotions and the Importance of Protection

In Chapter One we looked at the spiritual energy of your soul and higher self, now let's look at another unseen but powerful aspect of a human being: the aura, the energy field that surrounds your body reflecting your moods, emotions and the state of your mind and body. We see how vulnerable you can be to not only your own negative thoughts but also to those of others. I will share several ways that you can seal and protect your energy field from the side effects of living with people with problems or who have an issue with you.

Your Aura

Every living creature, small and large, is a form of energy; in fact everything on Earth is energy, in a lighter or denser state. There is an aura around every molecule and cell of all living entities in our world from the simplest of organisms to the most complex. Even the leaves on the trees have an aura and if you squint at one on a sunny day you may see the subtle life force that the leaves emit. Your aura will be shifting and changing from minute to minute reflecting the state of your emotions, your personality, the physical state of your body and any imbalance or disease you are experiencing at any given time.

> *Your aura is a subtle energy body reflecting the state of your wellbeing.*

Your higher self is constantly trying to bring you into the perfect state of being – happy and serene, despite all the challenges of your life. When you are happy and harmonious your aura has strong boundaries reflecting a strong immune system; you won't be affected by other people and are unlikely to be bullied. This is your ideal state and your positive feelings will make your aura shine. Think how a happy person lights up a room when they enter. When you are happy every part of your holistic whole becomes strong and bright. Negative emotions will have the opposite effect. Have you noticed that it's often after an emotional upset that you develop that cold that you have been fighting off for weeks? You will see the strong and clear lines around the aura of the man in this schematic – his energy is contained and calm.

There are people who can see auras and the colours that reflect the feelings of the person and this aura is a sparkling bright yellow – like a ray of sunshine.

Journal:

Think of the people you know. Who shines, who has a positive impact on others even without speaking? Who makes you smile when you meet them? Is your aura like this – do you shine right now? If not, do you know why? Can you make any changes in your life or within yourself to enable you to shine, be at peace and calm? Set your intention to have a shining golden aura that lights up the room.

Boundaries and Protection

Mass Consciousness

Everything in our world is connected through the flow of energy. As well as microwaves, television waves and radio waves you are surrounded and impacted by the thoughts and feelings of everyone in our world. Those who are closest to you affect you the most, especially when they are thinking of you. You will be lifted and helped by their positive and loving thoughts and brought down by their negative thoughts of anger, jealousy and blame. Your energy connects you to not only the people you know, but to everyone in the world. You are therefore affected by mass consciousness – that is the combined thoughts and energies of everyone – and you are affected by their moods, their spiritual experiences, their dramas and their thoughts. You are also affected by situations that are occurring in every part of the globe, both good and bad.

Other people's energies can seriously affect your health and wellbeing.

The moods and feelings from family, friends, work colleagues and strangers can affect you quite intensely, which is great when they lift you up but potentially disastrous for you if they bring you down into depression and fear. When Princess Diana died, there was an outpouring of grief around the world that was contagious and affected us far beyond the expected empathy for the Royal Family. As the emotion of the crowd grew so we were all increasingly affected. The intensity of your feelings is affected by the level of your sensitivity but most people feel moved when there is a massive outpouring of grief as with the Princess' death and when there has been a major disaster anywhere in the world. On the positive side, with uplifting emotions you can go to a concert or sports stadium and be lifted to the sky and beyond by the enthusiasm of the crowd, even before the music or game begins.

Other people's thoughts create thoughtforms that amass above and around you.

Reasons to Protect your Energy

- To feel strong and keep your vitality.

- To avoid being brought down or drained by the neediness or dependency of those close to you.

- You are particularly sensitive and constantly affected by the moods, attitudes, opinions and thoughts of the people around you. People with this high sensitivity to the state of others are referred to as an empath.

- You help others through caring services.

- You are a healer or therapist.

- You work in a hospital, surgery or clinic.

- You are a member of the police, prison service, armed forces or ambulance service.

- You work in the corporate world or a financial institution where competition is rife.

- You work in a stressful environment where you are bullied or pressurised.

- You are a teacher or children's nurse.

- A member of your family is distressed, physically ill or suffering from mental illness.

- You are bullied or picked on because of your sexual disposition, race or cultural background.

- You work or live with angry, resentful, jealous or unhappy people.

- You have a dominating parent, sibling or child.

- You feel over-emotional, fearful, anxious or insecure.

If you identify with any states listed, you will need to protect your energy frequently and I suggest you find one or two practices that you can use every day. Follow them diligently and act with common sense. There is no protection in the world that will help you if you choose to step into the traffic with the mantra, 'The angels will protect me!'

Use whichever of these practises resonate for you then you can get on with your life and work feeling safe and strong rather than insecure and weak. In other words, take charge of the security of your energy and step forward with powerful strong steps.

Reinforcing your boundaries
If you are strong, upbeat and vital you will find that needy and vulnerable people will be drawn to you and they can drain your energy. Anyone who is depressed, insecure, or feels they are a victim will be inclined to draw energy from you. Their thoughts and feelings of dependency can create energy hooks that latch onto you. Through these energetic links they sap your energy. You may have noticed how tired you can be after spending time with someone who is going through difficulties. Counsellors and those who deal with people regularly in this situation need to be extra careful. It's one thing to offer support but you do not want to have your energy drawn from you.

I strongly advise you to reinforce your boundaries daily using the simple ritual below so you can preserve your own energy, prevent yourself from being manipulated or dominated avoid being disadvantaged by the effects of other people's issues. If you are in a situation where you are seriously affected by other people's negative intentions towards you or deliberate interference, then you will need stronger protection and I will be addressing this situation in Chapter Seven. Use this ritual every morning and when you are exposed to disturbing energies, for example when visiting a hospital or people you know will challenge you!

Egg Ritual: Re-enforcing your energy field boundary

This is a simple but effective way to strengthen the boundary of your auric field.

- Visualise a large egg and see yourself stepping into it. Step forward to emphasise your intention of entering the egg.
- Hold the intention of strengthening your natural energy boundary.
- The egg has thick walls that allow only positive energies to come through to you. Negative energies and thoughts drop off the outside – only love can get through the walls.
- Say, 'My energy is sealed and only light and positive energies can enter.'

Saying No

To reinforce your intention of having strong boundaries, you need to place limits on how much of yourself you are prepared to give. If you find it difficult to say 'no', take note! If you have a caring and giving nature you may find it difficult to refuse other people's requests for time, attention and help. It is wonderful to help others and certainly giving brings rewards of love and fulfilment, but make sure that you take care of yourself too. Avoid the compulsion to offer yourself and your time when you are very tired and ensure that you don't overstep from kindness into self-sacrifice. Learn to say 'no' when your own needs are compromised; otherwise you will burn out. Then you will be unable to help anyone! Anyone in the caring profession is likely to forget this from time to time as we saw in the Life Lesson of giving without sacrificing yourself in Chapter One. Watch out for the signs of serious fatigue and a sense of being drained by the people you are helping. Respect yourself, care for yourself and create your own boundaries and hold firm to them.

Journal:
Set your intention of working within healthy limits and creating a balanced lifestyle for yourself.

Here are more ways that you can protect yourself and your belongings. You can use them for your family and friends but as with all spiritual practices, it works more efficiently If the one that needs the protection follows the practice personally. I have successfully used all the methods I am sharing here so can recommend all of them. Every day I call in the following protection of Archangel Michael and his Blue Flame when opening to heal or meditate and at least once a day I surround myself with the Golden Pyramids.

Ritual: Invoking the Blue Flame of Archangel Michael

The Blue Flame of Archangel Michael provides protection against negative spiritual activity and helps peaceful sleep. This energy flame has been gifted to us by the Protector, Archangel Michael (you will see him depicted carrying a sword in religious paintings). The flame creates a shield that allows only positive energies and love to come through to you. As spirit activity can interfere with you at night I recommend you re-seal with the flame before you go to sleep to ensure a clear and untroubled night.

Use whenever you need strength and a strong protector with you. It is quick and easy to use and works immediately.

- Wherever you are you can do this with eyes open or closed.

- Call in the Blue Flame and Archangel Michael. Say, 'I call in the Blue Flame of Archangel Michael to protect and seal my energies; now right now, right now. Thank you.'

- Ask for any specific help you need.

Paru's Protection

My friend and wonderful healer, Paru uses this invocation for daily protection.

'I call in the White Light Shield, from above and through my body right down to my feet.'

She suggests you do this every night and every morning before you get out of bed. If you do this for a period of time it will create an automatic protective shield.

Protection Symbol: to keep you and your possessions safe.

This is a powerful symbol and you can draw it over a name, a photo, person or object. It will create a strong protective shield. It also draws attention to your needs from the universe and Spirit. It sets your intention for asking for help and protection and will gain the attention of your spirit guides, your personal protectors and other light beings in Spirit.

Draw in the air in front of you or over whatever you wish to protect. Start by using two hands in the middle of the base line, then up the sides and finish with the 'eye' in the centre. It creates a pyramid, which is a powerful protection. If you want to protect a loved one draw the symbol three times over a photograph or their name.

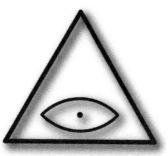

I have created a pendant with this symbol, which you can use to protect yourself, your pets, family and possessions. You can use it as a decorative pendant around your neck or attach to car keys, house keys or hang it in your car. You can put it on your dog's collar.

Elise's Story

Elise, a friend of mine in Malaysia bought a Protection Symbol for her dog and attached it to its collar. The dog was suffering from a skin disease and every day Elise was sending out requests for healing for her dog. The day she put the symbol on its collar, her pet disappeared. She became frantic and spent days unsuccessfully searching the nearby streets. The theft of pets was not unusual in her neighbourhood so eventually she gave up. Four weeks later her dog returned; it walked through the front gate, delighted to see her. The dog was not only fit and healthy but showed no sign of its skin disease. She never did find out where it had gone but she was convinced the Protection Symbol had kept it safe.

Joan's niece

When the niece of one of my clients shared her intention of travelling around the world to Asia and Australia her aunt immediately bought her a Protection Symbol and insisted she wore it all the time on her travels. All went well and the two girls got as far as Sri Lanka without incident. Then the day they were due to catch the Samudra Devi train from Colombo to travel along the beautiful Sri Lankan coast, my client's niece woke with a feeling of foreboding and insisted they skip the train ride and move on immediately to Australia. Despite the protests of her friend they caught a plane that day for Sydney. That day, 26th December, the third-largest tsunami on record with thirty-foot waves swept away the train and took 1700 lives. My client is convinced that the Protection Symbol kept her niece safe and she was guided to leave by the symbol's spirit guardians.

Ritual: Three Golden Pyramids for Protection

The pyramid has always been considered a powerful force of protection and spiritual symbol. Use this for yourself or to protect others, the shape protects and the golden surface will deflect negativity.

- Put your hands together above your head creating an apex.

- Say and visualise, 'I surround myself with Three Golden Pyramids; they protect me from all negativity; now, right now, right now.' Sweep your hands down in a pyramid shape three times.

- To protect others put your fingertips together in front of you as an apex of a pyramid and say, 'I place Three Golden Pyramids over my home; my property, my family and pets are protected; now, right now, right now.' Sweep your hands down as though drawing these pyramids.

Ritual: White Light

This is a popular method of protection used by therapists and healers because it is quick and simple.

- Ask for help from your angels and call in divine white light to surround you.

- Say and visualise 'I call in white light to surround and protect me, sealing my aura; now, right now, right now.'

Protect yourself whenever you are with people who are radiating negative vibes.

Ritual: The Garage Door – an instant guard

If someone becomes aggressive and threatening, put up your hand and imagine you are pulling down a garage door quickly in front of you. I find this particularly helpful when driving and I am hassled by impatient and angry drivers.

Apart from using symbols and rituals, there are other practices you can use to protect yourself and your home.

Essential Oils: Create an atmosphere of strength and protection for you and your home.

Essential plant oils, juniper berry, rosemary, laurel, pine and cedarwood, will uplift and strengthen your energy field. Sandalwood and Sage will clear the atmosphere. Frankincense, Eucalyptus, Cinnamon bark, lemon and clove boost your immune system making you strong and better able to repel negativity. Use them in a spray or an oil burner.

Crystals: Strengthen your aura and create a protective field. Use as jewellery, in your home and on computers and electronic equipment.

Obsidian, black tourmaline, jasper and malachite are a few of the crystals that will create a protective field and strengthen your own aura when you wear them. Malachite and amethyst are good for dispersing the negative energies emitted by your computer. You need to cleanse your crystals regularly as they will absorb negativity from the environment, i.e. wash in sea salt and energise either in the sun or on a large amethyst.

Attitude: appear strong and hide your weakness.

Bullies in physical or spiritual form will always look for weakness. As you heal so you will find you become more resilient and able to withstand criticism, other people's moods and issues and less likely to take negative comments as personal attacks. Take time to heal and work on any issues or problems; as you get stronger and more confident you will become less vulnerable to criticism and judgement. Create the impression that you are strong even when you feel weak and put on a brave face. Finally, laugh; find the humour in even the worst situation; humour is a wonderful way to lift and disperse negativity and it is infectious!

A crime prevention unit did some work on the psychology of mugging attacks and looked into why some people were attacked, often repeatedly, and others were never bothered. They used webcams to watch the way people walk on dark streets in London. They were able to pick out possible victims by the obvious anxiety they displayed as they walked, looking over their shoulders continuously, jumping at the slightest sound and generally looking vulnerable. Those that strode out confidently rather than showing anxiety or peering at mobile phones were rarely selected by muggers.

Journal:
What is your fear – your Achilles heel? What are the buttons that when pressed cause you to become emotional, insecure or vulnerable?

Bullies look for the vulnerable and judge by appearance, so act strong and confident.

How Emotions and Thoughts Affect You

Now we look at the way emotions and thoughts can affect your energy field and what you can do to reverse these effects. The impact of some emotions can be quite extreme.

Angry and antagonistic

Anger can be a great motivator. It is akin to passion and it is the passion in the hearts of activists that create change in our world. There is nothing wrong with feeling angry and if used as a motivator for action, it is a benefit. In fact, it is important to expel and use your anger rather than push it down inside, for there it can fester and will cause damage to your health and eventually make you ill.

When you feel angry your aura will spike, and people near you will sense this. Notice how you are affected by being in the presence of an angry person. Maybe your stomach will churn, your heartbeat will rise, and you will be inclined to move away and avoid them. You can pick up angry thoughts, feelings and attitudes in other people through your sixth sense, your natural intuition, and you can probably see their aura with your inner sight even if you can't see it with your eyes. Anger and fear are associated emotions and are held deep in the solar plexus, so long-term anger can seriously affect your digestive system, particularly your stomach. Anger is also associated with the liver. I can remember scary nights as a child when staying with my grandparents; after drinking, my grandfather would come home shouting and raving – full of anger. He was frustrated with his life; he felt undervalued. He had the resentment of an intelligent man whose education had been cut short by family economics and his anger was constantly simmering under the surface. He eventually died of liver disease for liver is the organ where we hold and store angry feelings.

Journal:

Do you fly off the handle without warning? Do you have triggers, buttons that once pressed send you into a rage? Do you feel resentment towards certain people, society, authority?

We all get angry at times but if you have a constant churning inside, a feeling that you have been mistreated or you're angry at something in your past, flag this up for healing and we will address this in the following chapters.

Causes of your anger and ways to release it
- **Anger that builds into a belief**

Anger is an emotion that can build up slowly from resentment and frustration triggered by your experiences over a period of time. The feeling that you have been treated badly can eventually turn into a full-blown belief that you are a victim; as your negative thoughts become consistent they can turn into thoughtforms that eventually become a permanent aspect of your energy field. Eventually your thoughts may turn into a perpetual state of grievance and cause defensively aggressive attitudes towards everybody and every situation. People holding a grudge will constantly simmer with anger, taking people's comments as personal insults and acting the victim. Hidden and suppressed anger can burn away inside and eventually its toxic nature will cause disease which is exactly what happened with my grandfather.

If long-term anger isn't resolved or healed it can become part of our DNA, which is why we can inherit angry traits from our parents. We will be looking at how you can heal DNA imprints in Chapter Five.

- **Anger caused by a one-off incident**

Anger can come from a one-off bad experience, a trauma that leaves a long-term imprint and sticks in your memory for years constantly troubling your thoughts and disturbing your sleep. The ritual below can help you to release the impact of the experience and dissolve the suppressed anger.

- **Anger from an unknown source**

If your anger has been caused by an incident that occurred when you were very young or if your mind has deliberately blocked it off, relax for there are a number of ways it can be healed and we will be healing the past in Chapter Six. Whether your anger was created in early life or in a previous life, this following ritual will set the way for healing and releasing this most destructive emotion from you and giving you back a sense of inner peace.

Ritual: Anger Release

If possible perform this ritual in a quiet place away from other people; in the countryside, in a secluded garden, in a park or on a deserted beach. You will need paper, pen, matches and a safe place to burn paper.

- Give yourself permission to let your anger come up to the surface to be finally and fully released. Say out loud, 'It is perfectly okay for me to have this anger but now I am ready to let it go once and for all.'

- Write down everything you feel; whatever thoughts churn in your head and any blame you may be holding against yourself or others.

- Write down all your resentments and the way anger impacts your life and wellbeing.

- If you understand the source of your anger, write a letter to the person or people involved; don't hold back; you can use whatever language comes to mind.

- Your anger has now been transferred to the paper so now burn it and watch the way the paper burns; the stronger and more toxic the emotion, the thicker and more yellow the smoke. See how it is being transformed into the light of the flames.

- If your anger is caused by authority or a civil injustice, write in your journal your commitment to influence a change.

- Now shout out to the wind any residual feelings.

- Sweep your hands over your body to get rid of any last toxic energy left behind.

- Give yourself a hug.

- Enjoy a run or walk now and allow nature to lift you and complete your cleansing.

Depression and low spirits

When you are feeling low, miserable or depressed your aura will become dark and shrink close to your body. It will reflect your mood of despondency and the lowering of your spirit. Many of our emotions are driven by the thoughts and beliefs we hold and if you suffer from low confidence and low self-value, these will reflect in your aura. From a healer's perspective we would be looking to find the root cause of the depression and searching for the imprints and old memories locked down in your soul energy that created your low energies. We then send love and healing energies to lift your entire being from negative to positive.

Journal:
Do you suffer from depression from time to time? Do you have a medically recognised depressive state? Do you feel vulnerable?

What to do
Depression, whether registered medically or otherwise is an isolating state, physically, mentally and spiritually; it disconnects you from your higher self and the help you can get from your own spirit. Even when you don't feel like doing anything, try to do the Morning Ritual from Chapter One, as this will ensure that you are protected, give you some strength, connect you to the power and your higher self.

While you are depressed and inward-looking, your defences are down and your boundaries are weak, leaving you vulnerable and easily bullied and dominated. Make use of the boundary strengthening Egg Ritual.

Depression takes you down to a low dark place and isolates you from the love and life you need it takes you far from the light; start to recover by intending to heal the cause.

When you are depressed, you lose motivation and sink into a dark place; your thoughts become negative and you feel disempowered to make the changes in your life that would pull you up and out of the pit. Like most people, I have suffered bouts of depression, and initially I will allow myself to sink and allow my negativity to flow. I feel that when you are forced to come out of the darkness you will put up a resistance. Sometimes it's better to simply let yourself wallow for a while. When you're are ready, try to look towards the light; spend time with uplifting people, watch stimulating movies or listen to your favourite music. It will be light, positive and uplifting energy that will help you to recover. My own solution is to do something creative – once I can bring myself to sit down and start to paint or write, my energy will begin to lift. Find your own personal recovery button – do what works for you.

Some ideas that may help you:

- step outside, look at the sky, focus on something of beauty
- do some form of exercise even if it is walking around your garden or your building block
- play music
- buy flowers or pick some from your garden
- run a bath and add drops of essential oils such as peppermint, frankincense, bergamot, grapefruit or lemon
- if your depression is persistent, check with your doctor – you may have a hormone imbalance and if there is no obvious physical cause don't hesitate to ask for expert help – there is no shame in depression

Journal:
Keep a note of what triggers your depressive moods and write down your intention to heal because nothing changes for us until we set our intention.

Irritability

An irritable and niggly mood will also create spikes in your aura similar to anger but smaller; they are not threatening, but they can be upsetting and off-putting. Irritable people are not great to be with and they send out vibes that can disturb the harmony of those nearby and make them agitated too. Irritation can come from a frustration that you feel about your situation, the behaviour of those around you or a sense of being overwhelmed so that you cannot manage or cope. You may feel irritated by being thwarted in reaching a goal, whether it's meeting a deadline, getting stuck in traffic or someone's reluctance to open the way forward. Whatever the reason the energy you radiate can be far-reaching and upsetting for people with whom you connect.

Journal:

Do you get frustrated and niggly often? Do you know what triggers your mood?

What to do

If you are affected primarily by other people's attitudes, behaviour and lack of respect for your own needs, put yourself into a bubble of protection; use the protective Egg Ritual. If your irritable moods are caused by your own thoughts and desires, write down in your journal what it is you need to do to set this right.

Journal:

What changes do you need to make in your life to prevent these moods? What healing do you need to heal your sensitivity? Is guilt at the root of a frustration with yourself? Are you spending time with people who do not have the same ideals and beliefs as you?

Overloaded, distracted or stressed

There will be days when you take on too much; when your 'to do' list is overflowing, and your attention is pulled in a number of directions. Many thoughts and concerns may be running through your mind fighting for attention: you must pay those bills, there is an urgent deadline to meet, when will you have time to make that dental appointment, what to buy for supper, last night's argument with your partner and your daily workload; all vying for your attention and focus. When you are in this state of mind, with your thoughts going in numerous directions, your energy is also pulled and pushed all over the place. Your aura will look like an octopus! Tentacles everywhere! This has the effect of wearing you out, draining and dissipating your energy and by nine o'clock you are asleep on the sofa.

Journal:
Do you allow your daily to do list to govern your life?
Could you simplify your daily routine at all or take on less? Do you suffer from stress?

What to do

- Never have more than five things on your daily to do list.

- Limit your expectations on what you can achieve in a day.

- Put your list in order of priority and don't feel bad if you don't achieve everything.

- Allow extra time for every journey; there is nothing more stressful than rushing to an appointment.

- Delegate.

Journal:
Are you creating unnecessary tension in your body? Are you living a stressful lifestyle? Is it possible to change and be more relaxed? Do you get driven by 'ought to' and 'should do'?

Ritual: Stress Release

This ritual sets the intention for your body and mind to chill and to release tensions caused by driving yourself too hard and taking on more than your body, mind and spirit can cope with.

- Drop your shoulders. Allow them to come down as far as you can.

- Put your feet firmly on the ground and imagine them to be fully connected to the Earth surface. Imagine grass between your toes and sense your connection to Mother Earth.

- Draw the Release Symbol in front of you three times and hold the intention of letting go of all stress in your mind and body.

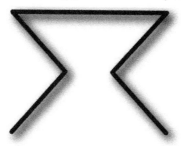

- Using your right hand, press and close your left nostril with your index finger and breathe in through your right nostril slowly then release and close your right nostril with your thumb and breathe out through your left. Repeat nine more times.

- Change over and close your right nostril with your thumb and breathe in slowly through your left, release then close your left nostril with your thumb and breathe out through your right nostril. Do this ten times.

- Use your hands to sweep across your shoulders and down your arms. Flick away all tension and stress.

- Take one last deep breath and blast out all remaining tension.

- Say, 'All is at peace, all is serene within me; now, right now, right now.'

Salt water attracts negative energy.
Keep a bowl of water with sea salt in your office,
workroom or living space; you can flick any
negativity into the bowl.

Shock

Trauma or shock will make you feel you have been smacked in the stomach and your aura will reflect this too. With severe shock, for example a car crash or sudden abuse, your energy may leave your body temporarily – we will look at this situation and how to resolve it in Chapter Six – Healing the soul. All shocks will leave an imprint on your spiritual energy and the emotions that you feel at the time of the experience will be locked into that imprint.

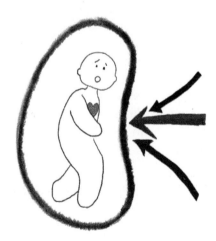

If you allow yourself time and space to release these emotions then you may not have any long-lasting effects; however if you suppress the anger, grief, fear, etc. that came from the trauma you may find that as time goes on, depending on the cause of the imprint, your behaviour can be affected in a variety of ways.

Here are some symptoms from shock imprints embedded in your soul.

- You become anxious or nervous.
- You lose confidence.
- You hold a deep fear that limits your life e.g. you don't want to go out or socialise.
- It can affect your relationships as you become reluctant to commit.
- You have unexplained fears and nightmares.
- You have low self-esteem.

What to do

Straight away after a shocking situation take Rescue Remedy, which is created specifically to release the effects of an emotional trauma or shock to the system.

Ritual: Releasing Shock

Use this simple process straight after a shock, an accident or trauma. I have found it calming and it also releases the impact of the experience before it can settle in.

- Call in protection for yourself or if you are doing this for someone else call protection in for both of you. You can say, 'I call in the Blue Flame of Archangel Michael, thank you.'
- Sweep your hands down over the body from head to toe several times.
- Draw the Trauma and Stress Release Symbol over the injury or over the solar plexus to pull out the imprint of the shock.

Releasing Shock Symbol: Start in the middle then draw in an anti-clockwise direction. Do this three or more times.

- Finish with more sweeping.
- Hug yourself or the person you have helped.

All the healing techniques I will be sharing in this book can help to release any imprints you hold as the aftermath of a shocking experience. In Chapter Six I will be focusing on releasing them, no matter when or how they were created.

Worrying about someone

The energy of every thought and your associated emotion goes to the object of your attention. So whatever or whomever you are thinking about will receive the energy and emotion. If you are sending love to someone or even thinking of them affectionately, then the high vibration of the loving energy will lift their spirits; if you are worrying about someone your negative thoughts will have a low vibration, so they will adversely affect the person – not at all what you are intending!

What to do

Rather than worry about someone, send them good vibes; send them positive thoughts; send them love not anxiety and distress. Visualise them well and happy, not sick and distressed. In the next chapter I will be sharing ways you can channel positive and uplifting energy which you can send to your loved ones, your friends and to places in the world where people are suffering.

Neediness and dependency

In the section on life lessons in Chapter One I shared the problems you incur when you carry people and try to fix them. Now we look at what dependency will do to your aura. When someone is dependent upon your constant attention and support, they will create energy hooks into your energy field and use these hooks to feed off your vitality and boost their own.

Situations when your energy can be zapped by other people

- A person is needy and sees you as a strong and energetic person; they latch onto you, asking you constantly for guidance and support.

- Someone who is sick and inadvertently pulls from your vitality, wanting you to be with them to lift their energy. Just a visit to a hospital can leave you depleted and tired.

- Someone who has no respect for your personal space or time who will text or phone you all the time even when it is inconvenient and intrusive into your private time.

- A family member or friend who is often asking you for financial support, acting as though they can't manage and making you feel guilty if you don't offer help and financial support.

This situation is fine when you are happy to continuously support someone. However, if you don't want someone attached to you and feeding on your energy, you can take any of the following actions to release them.

- Clear the hooks that have become embedded into your aura.

- Step away from the person.

- Encourage them to support themselves.

- Support them in ways that do not deplete your energy.

- Keep yourself protected when you are in their presence.

Journal:
Do you have anyone in your life who leans on you? Do you have anyone with whom you have created a dependency situation? Do you have a friend or colleague who leaves you exhausted?

When someone hooks into you they are charging their battery from your private energy supply.

Ritual: Releasing Hooks and Attachments

Whenever you feel you have been negatively zapped by someone, or you can feel the heavy energies of carrying someone, run through this simple ritual. You can do this for yourself or get a friend to do it for you.

- Sweep all attachments and hooks from your back and shoulders and flick the negativity into a bowl of salt water. Repeat until you feel lighter.

- Say, 'I am free of attachments; now, right now, right now.'

- Make a vow, a promise to yourself to give love and care but to avoid carrying anyone. 'I promise myself that I will give love and healing energies to anyone I choose but I will avoid creating dependency.'

Empower others by guiding, not carrying or fixing.

Thoughtforms: How the emotions of your thoughts can affect you

Every thought that you have whether positive or negative affects the dynamics and state of your aura. So, if you are having a bad day and worrying about money the energy that is attached to those thoughts will be heavy and if your worry is constant your thoughts will hang around your head like black thunder clouds. Because of your holistic nature these thoughtforms will affect the wellbeing of your body, mind, spirit and emotions. So, if you are worrying about money the heavy energy of the thoughtform could eventually make you ill; raising your blood pressure; giving you headaches; creating tension and aching joints. Also, the dark energies of worry are toxic and will tire and depress you.

If you are excited and thinking about a holiday the energy you create with your thoughts will be light and a higher vibration. These light thoughts cut through the dark clouds and help to disperse them. So, when you feel despondent and down, turn your attention and mind to uplifting subjects and pastimes such as music, flowers, a person you love, holiday plans and the thoughtforms of anxiety will soon disperse. Whenever you have a negative thought make it a habit to deliberately focus on something that pleases you. I have a couple of favourite visions that I use, one is a tropical beach with blue skies and golden sand and one is a field of tulips – both make me smile and distract me from the cause of my anxiety.

Ritual: Thoughtform Clearing

Use this simple ritual whenever you feel low, stressed or anxious and your negative thoughts have created heavy thoughtforms around you. It is also an excellent procedure to follow to clear headaches and tension.

- Sit quietly and relax your body.
- Drop your shoulders.
- Use your fingers as combs and sweep through your energy field around your head.
- Flick the negative and heavy energy you release into a bowl of salt water or into an imaginary bowl.
- Do this sweeping until your head feels lighter.

Now we will look at other aspects of your aura and see how the energies move through your body.

Meridian Lines

Spiritual energy flows through your body to all your vital organs along meridian lines. They create a continuous stream of energy through a main central power line and branch lines that supply energy from your crown down to your feet, feeding your organs, hormone glands and nervous system as they flow.

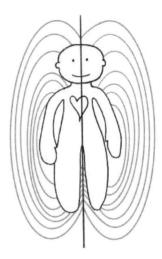

Several alternative healing modalities specifically focus on clearing the meridian lines and all associated organs. With acupuncture, fine needles are inserted at the junction points on the meridians and a reflexologist clears them by massaging the bottom of the feet and toes. In healing, the aim is to ensure that all energy flows smoothly through these lines. The intention of this next ritual is to clear the lines and allow strong positive energy vibrations to flow to all parts of your body.

Ritual: Sweeping

I start every healing session by clearing the meridian lines with this sweeping ritual. This helps to clear any blockages in the natural flow and is particularly helpful for digestive problems, constipation, nasal congestion and difficult periods. It is like a cure-all ritual that can also help with agitation, stress, nightmares, clearing after an argument, releasing negative feelings and so on.

- Put yourself in a protection shield, e.g. call in Archangel Michael to surround you with his Blue Flame. 'I call in Archangel Michael's Blue Flame for protection, thank you.'

- Use your hands as combs and sweep right through the energy field and flick the toxic energies you are shifting into a bowl of salt water.

- Say, 'I am clearing all blockages in the flow of energy through the aura; now, right now, right now.'

- Keep doing this until you feel that your aura is clear.

- Always sweep from top to bottom.

Chakras – Energy centres in your aura

A chakra is a vortex of energy in the energy field where meridians cross. The word chakra is Sanskrit for spinning wheel and if you could see one It would look like this:

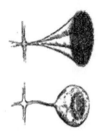

Chakras are a point of reference used in the practice of meditation and healing. There are many interpretations and visualisations of the colour and the way to strengthen, balance and activate them. Yogic traditions have used mantras, oils, crystals and sound to bring power to these energy centres and subsequently strength and healing to mind, body and spirit. Recently the seven-chakra rainbow coloured system has grown with the popularity of yoga.

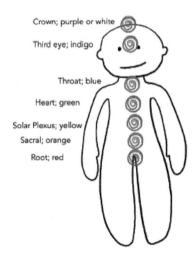

Crown; purple or white
Third eye; indigo
Throat; blue
Heart; green
Solar Plexus; yellow
Sacral; orange
Root; red

To empower a chakra and its associated physical or emotional status, simply draw the healing symbol three times over it and just gently let the energies flow in from your hands. You can check the state of a chakra with the use of a pendulum, a crystal, stone or wooden pendant suspended on thread or chain held above it. You are looking for a perfect spinning circle and the pendulum should reflect this.

Although there are many chakra models that enhance and empower the spirit and body, I would like to focus on a model of twelve fifth-dimensional chakras sourced by Diana Cooper and described in detail in the book she wrote with Tim Whild, *The Archangel Guide to Enlightenment and Mastery*. Diana's system is of great current relevance as humanity and our group consciousness is expanding, shifting and lifting its vibration to the lighter density and more loving state of the fifth dimension. This system reflects the change of your energy body as you expand your consciousness beyond fear and limitations and move from the materially focused world of the third dimension to the love based fifth dimension. As the yogis of old called their deities and their powers into the chakras, so Diana calls in the beautiful and uplifting energy of Archangels.

I have created simple rituals of intention to allow you to bring into action your own power of intention and will. As you connect to each of these chakras let go of resistance, surrender to the energy they hold and allow them to become fully activated and they will assist you.

Earth Star Chakra – Black and White.
Archangel Sandalphon

This chakra is found beneath your feet and stores your potential for your life on Earth. Activate this chakra to feel confident and secure wherever you are.

Ritual: Earth Star Chakra.

This ritual will help you to connect to your potential, to feel at ease with yourself and your situation and to feel secure and safe. This ritual is most powerful when performed outdoors

- Hold the intention of gaining trust that all is well and you are supported.

- Put your feet on the ground, preferably on grass or the earth, without shoes. Sense the immense power of the spirit of the planet beneath you

- Imagine you are a huge tree and your roots grow deep into the earth beneath your feet; know you are connected to the spirit of our planet, Gaia and feel her love and support flowing up through you now, comforting and reassuring you that all is well

- Say "I am secure and at ease and all is well."

Base Chakra – Platinum. Archangel Gabriel
This chakra is at the base of your spine and holds joy and wisdom; when empowered all your material needs are supplied. Know and trust that you and your spirit guides have planned your life.

Ritual: Base chakra
- See a door in front of you. This leads to your path of life.

- Open the door and take with you the wisdom and strengths you have gained from many lifetimes.

- See a golden path leading into the future.

- Slightly ahead of you walks Archangel Gabriel glowing in white light, showing you the way forward.

- Alongside the path are the people and situations who are going to help, guide and assist you on your journey.

- Walk the path knowing all your needs are met and always will be.

Sacral Chakra – Soft Pink. Archangel Gabriel
This chakra sits beneath your belly button and shines with the radiance of love, allowing you to express love through your sexual experience. As this chakra is empowered and balanced so you will attract romantic love that will serve you in every way.

Ritual: Sacral Chakra
- Hold a piece of rose quartz over the energy centre and focus on love.

- Visualise your own conception of love. Feel the love radiating from you to the person or your image of love.

- If you are looking for love, see the door in front of you opening and your vision of the love you desire coming towards you .

- Release any inhibitions or fear around love and sex by cutting through the cord to past pain and disappointment.

Solar Plexus Chakra – Deep gold. Archangel Uriel

Located just under your ribs, this chakra is where you store your anxieties and fears. As your frequency rises so your lower emotions of guilt, shame and fear are absorbed and cleared. This is the seat of your will and personal power; your determination and your ability to manifest through intention. Its golden rays connect you to the Sun, the most powerful star and force of energy in our solar system. Allow Archangel Uriel to fortify your solar plexus to strengthen your confidence and wisdom. To assist in empowering this chakra uses the Solar Logos Symbol.

Draw this in front of your Solar plexus Chakra starting with central line top to bottom, then move around the rays to the right and finish with the circle. Draw three times.

Ritual: Solar Plexus

- Breathe deeply four times as you place your hands on your solar plexus and visualise a bright golden sun right there

- Draw the symbol of the Solar Logos (the spirit of the Sun)

- See a cord of bright sun gold energy flowing from the sun in the sky connecting to your personal sun

- Breath in deeply four more times and consciously draw in the power of the sun's energy.

- Say "I am at one with the spiritual power of the sun and my confidence grows and strengthens now, right now, right now."

- Bathe in the powerful force of shining yellow light and let it flow throughout your body and mind. Relax and enjoy.

Heart Chakra – White. Archangel Chamuel

Archangel Chamuel opens your heart to its deepest levels. Your Heart Centre is located in the middle of your chest and is vitally important in your quest for enlightenment and love. We have seen that opening your heart is high on the list of Life Lessons in Chapter One. When in balance and healed you can give and receive love, allow yourself to see the best in everyone and to fill everything you are and do with love. As your heart shifts into the fifth dimension, it radiates pure white light.

Throat Chakra – Royal Blue. Archangel Michael

The throat chakra is your communication centre and as this transits into the fifth dimension you are able express yourself and share your own personal truth and true feelings; you will be heard and trusted.

Ritual: Throat Chakra

Write down every emotion that has been suppressed. Burn it and see it transform

- Sit quietly now. Slow down your breathing with long deep breaths. Count to seven on the in-breath and five on the out. Take your breath going deep into your solar plexus where you hold your fears.

- Put your right hand on your throat. Intend to release all anxieties about being heard, trusted and respected. Say "I am letting go my fears of being judged, I am able to speak freely and fearlessly."

- Archangel Michael is with you.

- Close your eyes and visualise a rich blue spinning vortex surrounding you; see it getting bigger and bigger.

- Your entire field of vision is filled with swirling rich blue light. Continue to breathe deeply and the frequency of your chakra has risen, you are now heard and trusted.

Third Eye Chakra – Crystal. Archangel Raphael

Your Third Eye is located in the centre of your brow, between and above your eyes. As this chakra rises in frequency it becomes crystalline and you connect to your intuition, you see beyond the physical and the bigger picture of your situation becomes clear. During my Kundalini yoga practice, we focus on this chakra as it allows us to connect to an inner state of calm and takes us away from the distractions of the material world.

Ritual: Third Eye

Optionally, have any of these essential oils in a carrier oil: Frankincense, sandalwood, clarey sage, nutmeg or vetivert.

- Lie down and call in Archangel Raphael.

- Hold the intention of seeing your life, your problems the world through the lens of a greater perspective, see the bigger picture.

- Focus your eyes on your Third Eye, the point between your brows and relax.

- Breathe in deeply four times and drop your shoulders and let your entire body go limp.

- Visualise a crystal ball between your eyes and allow it to spin as it grows in intensity of light.

- Say "My Third Eye rises to the fifth dimension. I see clearly all that is hidden, I see beyond the distortion and prejudice of the material world. I am in touch with my intuition." Lose yourself into the crystal ball. What do you see?

Journal:
After this ritual keep a note of what you see and sense in your journal. What is the bigger picture of your current situation?

Crown Chakra – Crystal clear. Archangel Jophiel
This chakra is located on the top of your head represented by a thousand-petal lotus. When you transit into the fifth dimension it becomes crystal clear. It opens you to your higher self and the wisdom of the universe. Now is the time to clear the clouds of negative and repetitive thought-forms we looked at in Chapter One. When you are fully connected you feel blissful and serene; at one with yourself and the universe. Something to work towards!

The experience of this beautiful connection to spirit comes to me when I see beams of sunlight bursting through clouds representing divine energies and love flowing to Earth. When your crown chakra is open and clear you will feel more in touch with your own sense of spirit and meditating will become easier and more focused.

Journal:
Do you see auras and colours around people or animals? Try relaxing your eyes and slightly squinting and looking through someone – you might be lucky to see their beautiful light force. What colours do you believe are flowing around your crown chakra right now?

Ritual: Crown Chakra
Use to create a divine connection to your own divine self, your higher self. I suggest you follow this ritual whenever you feel low, lonely and confused about which direction to take as you will connect to your own spiritual guidance

- Relax your shoulders.
- Call in the protection of Archangel Michael and his Blue Flame. Call in Archangel Jophiel.
- Sense the force of nature rising from the Earth bringing a nurturing, loving and calming energy stream up through your feet.

- It rises up through your body. As it flows let the tension go from your feet, your legs, your body and arms. Deliberately let go of the tension in the muscles of your face and up to the top of your head.

- Clasp your hands together and slowly raise them above your head. Hold the intention in your mind that you are encouraging your connection to your higher self and guidance.

- Take a deep breath in and breathe out forcing your breath through pursed lips.

- Now place your clasped hand on top of your head and feel the force of your crown chakra waiting to burst up and out. Breathe deeply again and release. You are connected, surrender your problems to your divine self.

Causal Chakra – Shimmering White.
Archangel Christiel

This chakra is above and to the back of your head. When activated it will bring you to the state of peace and calm. This chakra is connected to the moon and the divine feminine energy that has been flowing to Earth so strongly for us all since the beginning of the Age of Aquarius.

Ritual: Causal Chakra

I am entranced by the energy of the moon and I channel the divine feminine energies of love and compassion in my healing sessions. I have recorded a meditation that connects to the energy of the moon; The Moon Goddess on *The Healing Magic of Visualisation* CD 2. Here is another meditation you can perform at the time of the full moon to connect to these beautiful energies.

- Preferably be outdoors where you can see the moon. If not, simply visualise a perfect circle of opalescent white light and hold the intention of raising your energy to the frequency of divine love.

- Surround yourself with the Blue Flame of Archangel Michael. Call in Archangel Christiel.

- Feel yourself drawn closer and closer to the moon and be surrounded and filled with the pearly white light.

- Know that the divine feminine spirit of the moon wraps her arms around you holding you loved and secure. Feel the love that accepts you completely as you are.

- Waves and waves of light flow through you and purify all self-doubt and judgement. You are loved for who you are and all is at peace within.

Soul Star Chakra – Magenta. Archangel Mariel

By activating your Soul Star Chakra you are able to access your wisdom as a master and enhance your spiritual evolvement and enlightenment. It holds every skill, insight and spiritual achievement you have gained through the lifetime of your soul. This gives you access to a huge database of understanding and wisdom.

Ritual: Soul Star Chakra

I discovered this chakra years ago, and every workshop or retreat I held I took the group through this meditation to bring our soul stars together in unity of love and purpose. When people who have the same intention, goal or purpose in life their soul stars connect to become a multi-faceted star, an energy in its own right. The united power of intention is magnified exponentially and the wisdom of every soul in the group is accessible. You can use this ritual for yourself or with a partner, in a business situation, a family group, meditation group, yoga class or with friends. Set an intention as a group and/or get answers to questions.

- If working with others create a circle. Write down and place into the centre the focus and intention of the group.

- Close your eyes, breathe in deeply four times and call in Archangel Mariel.

- Hold the intention of sharing your soul star libraries of knowledge and wisdom.

- Allow your attention to move to the star above your head, know it holds the wisdom of every lifetime.

- Expand your vision to include the soul stars of everyone in your group and see them merge to create a multi-faceted star.

- Say in your head the intention you have set as a group.

- Merge your consciousness with the star and let it lead you to the akashic libraries that hold all knowledge.

- Ask any question you have that needs access to this wisdom. Accept whatever come through to you.

Stellar Gateway Chakra – Golden Orange. Archangel Metratron

This chakra, once activated, is your connection to the universe, source, all that is and all dimensions of time and space.

Ritual: Gateway Chakra

- Surround yourself with the Blue Flame of Archangel Michael.

- Focus on your stellar gateway chakra 18 inches above your head with the intention of expanding your consciousness to be at one with all that is.

- See this chakra blazing into golden orange light.

- See the moon and the stars, see the planets, see how distant universes start to pick up this golden light.

- Your light is now touching all that exists anywhere, anytime.

- Surrender yourself to the full connection of spirit. You are the universe, you are all that is.

CHAPTER *Three*

Channelling Healing Energies

The Power of Love

Healing as described in this book refers to the act of transforming an aspect of yourself or someone else using light energy. As high vibration energy streams enter lower vibrations the energy lifts, releasing and transforming the toxic effects of rejection, loss, imprints and scars from traumatic experiences and emotional pain. The light energy is of the highest vibration and can be described by the word love – unconditional love. Love is a word that is used for many feelings ranging from 'I love pizza' to 'I will love you forever.' We use the word love extensively and there is no harm in this, but I would like to differentiate the love that I refer to throughout this book, especially in this section on healing. The love I use in healing holds no negative associations, no judgement, no conditions, no doubts, no fears. It is a pure and high vibration that, in the spectrum of light and dark, is a dazzling and powerful beam of brilliance. It is not an emotion but a vibration of energy.

Journal:
How does love make you feel? Are you happy with your relationship with love? Do you experience unconditional, non-judgement, all embracing love in your relationships with others and/or yourself? Write down any intentions to raise the vibration of your connections with others and yourself.

Healing; clearing the debris from a dirty pond and filling it with fresh clear water.

Where does the healing love come from?

There are two sources of this very special kind of love. If you recall the diagram of your spiritual energy in Chapter One, it showed that your higher self, your own source of spirit, is made of this divine love, it is your spiritual essence. It flows down from your higher self through your higher chakras to your heart centre. The centre of your heart holds a reservoir of this same pure unconditional love giving you an endless supply that is unaffected by your negative life experiences. So, you have a personal stream of powerful healing love that you can use for yourself or others. To believe in this source of the true energy of your being, it is necessary to accept yourself fully and believe that you really are a divine being – something which most of us struggle with! Believing in oneself as divine is certainly not universally acceptable. It is therefore often easier to consider reaching up to another and higher source of unconditional love. To find this you will need to go beyond the realms of human life to the source of your essence; your creator; God; the Universe; Source or whatever name you prefer to use. Later in this chapter I will share a symbol and ritual that gives you access to this high vibration of energy that you can use for yourself, for individuals, for groups of people and for situations.

Journal:

Do you accept that you are created from and therefore your essence is love? Do you believe you are divine? Do you sense there is a higher force that is a source of love? What would convince you if either of these answers was no?

With your will and ability to connect to the forces of light in our universe, you can become a powerful channel of love energy that you can then direct wherever you wish.

Your Intention to Heal

Spiritual healing, energy healing, pranic Healing and reiki are all methods of using light energy from Source to lift and transform heavy energies. You can use your mind to set the intention of this energy going to where it is most needed whether you are helping yourself or someone else. When I give healing, my intention is set to send it to the root cause of the problem that causes the pain and suffering and I suggest you do this too so that your healing is more than a sticking plaster that fixes the symptoms but goes deeper to the cause.

If you heal the underlying cause of your problem, you pull up the root, so it doesn't grow again.

Here are intentions to use for healing:

- accept that you are divine and a source of healing love
- to connect to the highest vibration of loving energy, from your heart and from the universe
- know that all healing is done by the recipient and not the channel
- set your ego aside and simply allow the love to flow through you to either the pain in yourself or to another
- you are not responsible for any choices and outcomes of healing. You offer the energy; it's up to the recipient to choose how to use it
- the healing energy goes to the root cause

Remember, everything is a form of energy and energy cannot disappear, but the vibration can be changed.

Spirit Guides and Helpers

You can channel healing energies by using the Healing Symbol and I will be sharing a simple procedure that you can follow later in this chapter. However, I find that my healing sessions flow at an even higher vibration when I ask for assistance and guidance of evolved beings in Spirit. Many are focused on guiding and caring from a distance, either groups of people, institutions or motivations or concentrating on you and your affairs. These wonderful souls have the thankless task of trying to keep us on our right path, warn us of danger and, where possible, guide us to make good decisions. I say thankless because we have a habit of ignoring the messages they send and a tendency to go full steam ahead without a thought of spiritual consultation! There are three main types of spiritual being who will assist you with healing: angels, spiritual masters and soul guides. Here is an introduction to each group.

Angels

You will know of angels, for they are pictured everywhere from churches to gift shops and on everything from stained glass windows to tea caddies. Many of the great religions acknowledge the presence of angels; for example, Jesus' birth was announced by the Angel Gabriel; the Angel Jibril (Gabriel) visited Mohammad and shared knowledge and guidance that was later written as the Quran, and the Angel Moroni appeared to John Smith who went on to found the Mormon Church. Angels are neither male nor female, although we tend to refer to them as he and she and are programmed to respond when called. They each have a specific role and job to perform in the spiritual realm. Every now and again one will move into the Earth plane to help a soul in trouble. Doreen Virtue, Sophy Burnham and Lorna Bryne have written great books on the work of angels and true stories of their impact on individuals, particularly at times of great danger. Generally, though, they stay in the spiritual realms and guide and protect us from higher dimensions and they do not come to Earth for life cycles as we do. It is said they were created by God as divine helpers to do God's work and follow his instructions.

There are four great Archangels:

- **Archangel Michael,** whom we see depicted on church frescos and windows carrying a sword. His role is that of protector and is the angel I call to protect me and seal my energies from negative forces when I am healing or opening myself up for meditation. He has an army of warrior angels who will come to your aid when you feel threatened by any negative spirits. There is more on this subject in Chapter Seven.

- **Archangel Gabriel** is God's messenger and is depicted carrying a trumpet. Gabriel is the patron of communications so would be the angel to call if you are not managing to get your message across or you wish to understand the divine guidance that you are struggling to 'hear'; for example, help if you have difficulty working out what is your life purpose.

- **Archangel Raphael's** role is to help with healing and he is the perfect angel to invoke for assistance with your healing sessions for yourself or for others.

- **Archangel Uriel** (Light of God) is the Archangel of wisdom and will bring inspiration and motivation; he oversees channelling of divine wisdom and guidance. He watches over and guides writers and sends insights and knowledge to spiritual teachers.

You also have a guardian angel who is dedicated to guiding and protecting you. You can use the following ritual to connect to either your own guardian angel or any angel who is willing to communicate with the help and guidance you need.

Ritual: Invoking an Angel

This ritual connects through prayer the angel of your choice or non-specific angelic help. An angel may come to you in a dream, when you are meditating or when you are relaxing and thinking of nothing in particular – a difficult state for many of us but one that bears fruit when communicating with Spirit! With this ritual you can send out your desire to communicate with an angel or ask for specific help even for mundane daily tasks; for example many of my friends ask for angelic help when seeking a parking slot! For more involved and serious requests, you may not get an instant response but trust that help will come even though it may take time.

- Have a clear request in your mind.

- Say out loud, 'I call upon angelic help; now, right now, right now. I need help for [say what help you need].' Repeat this twice more.

- 'I release all control and expectation on the outcome and timing; let it be for my highest good.'

- Put your hands up to the sky. 'I let go now, how or when this request is answered.'

- 'Thank you, angels!'

Watch for signs that your request has been heard and look out for the response. Sometimes you will get symbols and signs, for example a white feather is a sign that you are on the right track and that the angels are happy with your progress.

Journal:
Keep a record of any requests you make and then watch for signs that they have been acknowledged and answered. Note when you see a feather or any sign that you are being watched over, protected or guided.

When doors open easily; when good opportunities come your way; when you meet the perfect person to help with a problem; when you feel the synchronicity of life working for you, then you know that the angels are helping and you are on the right path.

Ascended Masters

Every culture has had representations of beings in Spirit that hold the power of wisdom and mystical knowledge; some were depicted as minor gods or deities as in the Greek and Egyptian pantheons, others in animal form, as in pagan belief systems. These are often archetypes of our aspirations of spiritual eminence; role models of how we would like to be or holding the essence of power that we feel above our mortal grasp. Humans have always prayed to these gods to help them with their daily struggles and to guide them on their spiritual path. I have connected to Pan, leader of the spirits of nature and I acknowledge Buddhist and Hindu deities, but most of my help and direction from Spirit has come either directly from Source or from a small number of special beings who are known as Ascended Masters.

This group of powerful beings reside in the higher realms and are focused on helping humans as we trudge through our lives, battling adversity and fulfilling our life purpose. These are spirits who have lived on Earth and fulfilled their full cycle of lives and evolved to the point of enlightenment, so they no longer need to return to Earth. As they have experienced life on Earth they know what we go through, which makes them approachable and empathetic with our problems. Some of them have been known to us for thousands of years, but we learned the most about them through a group of powerful spiritual psychics called the Theosophical Society, founded in the eighteenth century. This society was founded and led by Madam Blavatsky, Annie Bessant and Charles W Leadbeater, and they channelled teaching and guidance from the masters. Alice Bailey wrote books of the channellings of one of the masters, Djwhal Khul, and her books are still in print and available on Amazon.

Here are some of the masters; several may be familiar to you from their role in major religions. See if any of the names resonate with you and if so, you may like to connect to them for guidance on your personal spiritual path.

- **Djwal Khul** – is a Tibetan master, teacher of ancient esoteric knowledge and a channel through Alice Bailey. He guides us to release fear and to see the beauty and positive aspects of our lives.

- **Sanat Kumara** – is an extraordinary, evolved soul who is considered the leading master of spiritual life on Earth.

- **Guatama Buddha** – he came as Prince Siddhartha and evolved and ascended as Buddha and introduced the Buddhist way of seeing life through love and compassion.

- **Maitreya** – although he has served his time on Earth and evolved, he is expected to come to Earth again as the next Buddha, the leader of the Buddhist faith.

- **Kuthumi** – a holder of Ancient Wisdom and World Teacher, he assisted in setting up the Theosophical Society. He had a life as Emperor Shah Jahan, who built the Taj Mahal at Agra, India.

- **Lord Lanto** – he is the master associated with teaching ancient wisdom through Chinese esoteric mystery schools.

- **Mary** – she holds the essence of Divine Mother and visited Earth as Jesus' mother in one of her lives.

- **El Morya** – he is said to have come to Earth as King Arthur and Thomas More.

- **Lady Master Nada** – is a lady master who holds light and love and the value of family. She served in the temple of

Atlantis and incarnated as a lawyer at that time. She defends the law and represents practical service to God through our service to others.

- **Enoch** – is a teacher and sage and is spoken of in the Bible. Enoch has channelled knowledge to me about the heart and soul.

- **Kwan Yin** – she holds the essence of Divine Mother and is a deity in Buddhism. She protects mothers and children and is the protector of sailors. She holds the energies of love and compassion.

- **Saint Germain** – he brings the Violet Flame that transforms negativity for spiritual followers. Said to have had magical powers and was on Earth in Arthurian times.

- **Jesus** – is a Master of Wisdom who brought love back to our world.

The masters guide the use of the symbols I use, a full set of which is in Chapter Eight. Although there is no need to be in touch with these spiritual guides to be a powerful and successful healer, there is no doubt they are a source of great spiritual guidance. Here is a ritual you can use to make a connection through channelled writing where their words come through not only into your mind but guide you to type their responses directly onto your computer or iPad.

Journal:
Which of the Ascended Masters resonate for you? Find pictures that depict the one you are drawn to. Write a list of questions you would like to ask. Keep a record of any sense of communication and messages you receive by using the following ritual.

Ritual: Channelled Writing
You can use this ritual to communicate with a specific Ascended Master or you can put up your question and let any one of the Masters respond.

- Sit comfortably in a peaceful location without phones or interruptions with your computer, iPad or use pen and paper.

- Use incense or essential oils to raise the vibration of the atmosphere, e.g. frankincense.

- Burn a candle to set the intention of bringing in light and understanding.

- Draw the Protection Symbol three times over yourself and your computer.

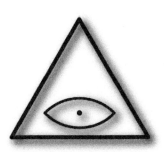

The Protection Symbol: Draw from the middle of the bottom line with both hands, finishing at the apex then draw the eye.

- Draw this symbol three times to set your intention of connection to an Ascended Master.

Connect to Spirit Symbol: First draw the top vortex then the upturned pyramid.

- Say out loud; 'I request guidance from the Ascended Masters now, right now, right now.' Repeat twice more.

- If you have a question in mind say your question out loud.

- 'Thank you.'
- Place your hands lightly on the keyboard and release all controls of your mind and imagination. It can help to stare at your third eye as you surrender to the channelling.

Never be discouraged if nothing happens at first; keep faith that you will get something through and try again another day. I have had absolute nonsense and I have also had the most amazing channellings about the construct of the soul from Enoch, and the Archangels guided me through the workings of the heart centre.

Good luck and happy channelling!

Healing

There are a variety of ways to set off the transformation and raise the energies that cause a healing to take place. First, we look at visualisation and command then we look at the impact that a healing session can have; then move on to build the healing practice using symbols and rituals.

Journal:
Write your healing needs and your intention to open to the vibrations that heal with love and light.

The Power of Visualisation

You are a powerful creator and can utilise your natural powers of creation with your imagination and visualisation. You can create a picture or vision in your mind, forming an energy picture of how you want to be. You can declare a strong intention that sets up a vibration that attracts a matching reality similar to the way we manifest our wishes and goals. Use this natural gift of creating to manifest the health and wellbeing you need. I have recorded healing visualisations available on iTunes or in CD form. There are also a number on YouTube. Here is one you can use for uplifting your energy and a general sense of wellbeing. Read this first then adapt to your own needs.

Create the way you wish to be using your power of visualisation

Ritual: Visualising Wellbeing

- Find a quiet space, turn off your phone and make yourself comfortable.

- Drop your shoulders and relax.

- Breathe in deeply four times, allowing a flow of oxygen to reach all parts of your body.

- Visualise yourself surrounded by blue light and know that only positive energies will come through to you

- Say, 'I allow my imagination to visualise how I wish to be. I see my condition cleared, healed and resolved; now, right now, right now.'

- Close your eyes.

- See yourself in a video walking along a beach, the sun is shining and you are in perfect health. You are carefree and relaxed.

- Allow yourself to walk the beach, pick up shells and do whatever your imagination fancies.

- Hold the faith in your recovery and use this visualisation whenever you feel depressed or overwhelmed by your problems or suffering.

Love and hugs to you. Sending you love and healing right now, xxx.

You have other hidden powers that you can use for healing. We now look at the power of your voice to express positive intentions.

The Power of Command

Every word you say has its own energy, and depending on the emotion and feeling behind the words the energy you express will either lift up or drop your energy levels. Like a mantra that can be used repeatedly to emphasise your intention for yourself, an affirmation can create a positive vibration that holistically helps you to override your own negative beliefs about yourself. For example, if you have difficulty being financially secure you can use an affirmation that you are abundant and financially supported. 'I am financially secure; all my needs are met and I am abundant.' As with the visualisation this sets an energy flow that will attract its matching vibration – like attracting like. Affirmations should always use the present time; use now, not will for will puts your new status into the future and you want it in the present. Always use positive words: 'I am secure' rather than 'I am not insecure'.

Affirmations work well on reprogramming any negative beliefs you have about yourself; use them for self-image, self-confidence, acceptability etc.

Remember: you are created perfectly for your life purpose.

Journal:
Write your own affirmations and use them daily for a month. Repeat them out loud if possible as they have a stronger vibration when spoken. Revisit to see what effects they are having.

Using the Power of Command in a healing session

When I give healing, whether in person or at a distance, I speak out loud. I conduct the energies and send them where I want them to go and what I want them to do. If you saw Gandalf the wizard in Lord of the Rings you may recall him standing on a bridge being chased by the enemy. He put up his staff and hand and demanded in a magnificent and powerful way that they stop. He was using his Power of Command. This is a manifestation of your intention backed by your will and determination through verbal expression. Your words hold a resonance and that flows out as an energy stream attracting the matching response, which is why we use words in our rituals of manifestation. For healing you don't need a staff although some people like to use crystal wands; you also don't need to bellow out your intentions! However, expressing your intention with conviction can be a powerful addition to the energies you channel.

Ritual: The Power of Command for Healing

With this simple ritual you express your positive intention for healing

- In a quiet and secluded place, relax.
- Consider what you wish to heal – keep it simple with one problem at a time.
- Call in your protection to seal your energy.
- Breathe in deeply four times.
- Connect to your higher self by clasping your hands and three times raising them above your head saying, 'I am fully connected to my higher, divine self; now, right now, right now.'
- Say 'Using the rights and authority given to me by Power of Command, I release/heal (*what state you wish to clear or heal*) now, right now, right now.'

The combination of the Power of Visualisation, mind control and the Power of Command can have spectacular results as my friend Marcos found out.

Marcos' Story

My friend Marcos has been working hard on self-healing and the power of meditative practice. Here he recounts an experience he had of healing a long-standing health issue with his digestion using his mind through meditation and the Power of Command through the authority of his voice.

'Sensing there was something wrong going on in my body, I finally got to a personal state of mind where I could meditate very deeply and with no 'mind chatter'. It took a while and, like any exercise for the body, I needed to train to get to this level of meditation.

I use 'My Body' meditation and travel from my toes to my brain and go through every muscle, bone, organ and system. I save the nervous system till the end before I open my energy system using the yogic model of the chakras. I visualise a tetrahedron at the point where each chakra sits. This meditation takes an hour or so. I have music playing in the background. The music enhances my meditation; I use Banco de Gaia's 'Big Men Don't Cry'.

'As I turn into my pineal gland something happens in my mind. Sometimes I am in a remote place, another country, another era. But this time I wanted to do self-healing and at that point my focus was guided to my sigmoid colon and saw polyps sprouting from my colon walls. I felt shock travel through my body, but a strong sense of determination turned that shock into action, and I gathered all my energy and with one thought, just one, I let go of those polyps and healed the colon walls and all the tissue that contracts that part of my body. I told the polyps, 'LEAVE MY BODY NOW; there is no place for you in my body.'

'Twelve hours later during early morning ablutions I happened to look inside the toilet bowl and I saw a lot of blood, dark in colour, with some raspberry-shaped objects. There was no pain involved. I had forgotten my healing meditation of that morning. It was only when I looked inside the bowl that it reminded me of my experience under meditation.

'Since then, I also believe that I cured myself of possible hiatus hernia. This meditation took a lot longer as there were a lot of human emotions to consider and heal. This one was like knitting my diaphragm back to its old shape so that it didn't allow the stomach to roll into its opening and give me that awful reflux I'd been getting for the past two years.'

Journal:
Use the Power of Visualisation and Command and record your experiences.

Experiences during and resulting from healing

Whenever you change the energy of your body, mind or emotions you are likely to have some after-effects over and above the positive results of the healing. Here are some of the sensations and feelings that may come at the time of the healing or afterwards. None are wrong or right and are not indicators that you are doing it 'right' as everyone has different reactions. It can be helpful to share these with anyone you help to avoid unnecessary anxiety.

As the healer you may experience:

- your fingers tingle and pulse, you feel a sensation in the palm of your hands as the energies flow

- ripples running down your back and arms as energies shift and transform

- heat In your hands and arms; your entire body may feel hot or cold as energy shifts.

- a sensation that I call a 'whoosh' when your recipient lets go of a blockage or suppressed emotion

- images or short visuals like video clips that indicate the cause of your recipient's problems from the past, this life or previous lifetimes

- symbolic visions indicating the cause of problems - for example, I see snakes wriggling away when dark and heavy energies such as curses are leaving

- voices guiding you to place your hands on a specific part of your recipient's body

- your heart centre feeling full- this is the love you are feeling for the person you are helping

- the same pain that the person you are helping is feeling - acknowledge it and then intentionally let it go, it is purely a sign and indicator for you to know where the problem is and shows you are fully connected. When I get these feelings I know I can help the person.

As the recipient of the healing you may experience:

- heat either where you are touched or anywhere in the body where energy is transforming

- hot and/or cold shivers as energy moves

- a sense of euphoria while the healing is in progress and for a time afterwards - it's advisable as a recipient not to drive but take time to settle after a session

- sensations of heaviness leaving and a general feeling of lightness that will stay for some time until the body and spirit adjust to the new state

- sleepiness and the need to rest and sleep- it is best to follow these needs as the healing continues after the session

- tearfulness; tears are a sign that suppressed emotions are releasing- always have tissues around when you are healing!

- emotional meltdowns after the healing - it is not unusual to go on an emotional roller coaster from elation to depression for a few weeks after a major shift of energies

- no sensations during the session but you may attract fortuitous and helpful people and situations that offer solutions to your problems

Healing will clear barriers and help you attract what's needed. Healing opens the way to synchronicity and opportunities.

Points to watch when healing

You will be working with the energies of love. They are light and beautiful and quite magical but there are some points to watch. Here is a list of things to avoid, especially when healing other people:

- never share anything that comes up in a healing session; keep the confidence of anyone you help

- always sweep down the body, not towards the head

- always protect yourself and the person you help before you start

- don't direct any healing to the physical heart as pacemakers can be disturbed by a surge of energy

- when working on babies, sweep them gently

- never say you can see a hole in their aura or anything that might shock or frighten someone

Remember, they are the healer and you are a conduit for the energy. Don't make promises of what you can achieve and keep your ego away from the process.

Preparation for a healing session

You do not need any complicated preparations for the techniques and rituals that I teach for healing. Just be centred and emotionally calm. Feel compassion and love for the person you wish to help; the symbols don't work through anger or dislike and the energies will flow with your own intentions of love and care, not through financial gain or ego.

Clear the room

I find it helpful to clear the environment before I start a session; you can follow any of these ways to clear negative energies and raise the vibration of your room. There are more clearing rituals in Chapter Seven.

- Spray the room with clearing and cleansing essential oil spray (see Appendix) or your own mix of peppermint, juniper and sage essential oils in spring water.
- Smudge with sage or frankincense.
- Burn sandalwood, sage or frankincense incense.
- Call Archangel Michael to clear the room for you. 'I call Archangel Michael to clear away and transform any negative energies in this space; now, right now, right now. Thank you.'

Because you are shifting energies and releasing negative and toxic vibrations into the atmosphere it is advisable to have something close by to attract and collect the negativity. Flick any unwanted energies towards one of these options:

- a bowl of sea salt in water

- a large crystal: clear quartz or amethyst are good for this. Cleanse the crystal afterwards by immersing in a bowl of salt water and power it up in the sun or moonlight

- if you have neither of the above to hand you can call in Archangel Michael. He is a very busy angel but is always happy to help! Ask him to transform any negativity you release. 'I call on Archangel Michael to transform any negative energies, thank you.'

Confirmation: If you are helping someone, ask him/her to confirm that they wish to receive the energies you are about to channel.

Ritual: Channelling Energies with the Healing Symbol

You can clear negative attachments and channel healing energies using this simple process; the Healing Symbol sets your intention and connects you to the highest vibrations of universal love. These steps are the basis of all the healing I do; you can add further techniques and symbols depending on your requirements. Follow the same steps whether you are doing this for yourself or someone else; for the sake of simplicity I will be describing how to do this for someone else but you can use the same steps for yourself.

Step One – Protection

- I have given several different options for protection in Chapter Two; choose one that suits you. This is the one I use for healing: 'I call on Archangel Michael to surround me and... (*the name of anyone you may be helping*) with your Blue Flame to seal and protect us, letting only positive energy come through. I call in protection now, right now, right now. Thank you.' Complete the protection by drawing the Protection Symbol three times in front of yourself and the person you are healing.

Protection Symbol: Draw the base line first using both hands, then the sides of the pyramid, then the eye.

Step Two – Assistance

Call in the help and guidance of your own spirit guides and those of the person you are healing. 'I call in my spirit guides and angels and (*recipient's*) guides and angels; now, right now, right now, thank you.'

Step Three – Sweeping

Use your hands as combs to sweep through the energy field, flicking any attachments and heavy energies towards the salt water or crystal. Draw the Release Symbol three times and say out loud; 'I clear and release all negative energies and attachments; now, right now, right now.'

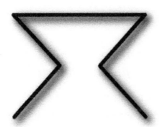

Release Symbol: draw three times from bottom left in front of the recipient.

Sweep the shoulders and neck and say; 'I clear all burdens and responsibilities that are not your own; now, right now, right now.' Do this for a few minutes. Focus extra attention on any sticky energy you may feel; this is congested energy and your sweeping clears the meridian lines that help the natural energies to flow.

Step Four – The Healing Symbol

This symbol connects you to the highest vibration of divine/universal energies and sets your intention to channel through your heart and your hands.

Healing Symbol: Draw the symbol in the air three times from right to left; finish with the dot.

Once you have drawn the symbol, the energies will flow from the chakras in your hands and you can then place them on or near the area that needs healing. Simply hold your hands in place for as long as feels necessary – a few minutes should suffice but it is fine if your intuition guides you to do this for longer. Although the energies flow just as well if your hands are away from the problem area it can feel comforting to place your hands directly on the body, especially on joints or a painful stomach. Check this suits the person you are helping first. Continue channelling the healing to wherever it is needed.

Step Five – Ending the session

Complete the session by drawing in the air over the entire body the Preserving Symbol to seal in the healing energies.

Preserving Symbol: Draw down the front of the body three times. Start with the top half-circle, the bottom, then the centre line.

Give yourself or a client/friend a big loving hug to completely seal in the energy and finish the session!

Step Six – After the session – Release

Walk away from the healing session without any expectations of results and let go of any attachment by chopping the side of your right hand on the palm of your left to symbolise your desire to let go and draw the Release Symbol three times on yourself to disconnect from your client's energy.

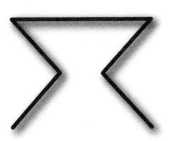

Ritual: Healing to revitalise, balance and re-energise

Follow these steps to uplift and relieve depression, low energy, sadness, lack of motivation, sluggishness and general negative feelings and mindset.

- Complete steps one to three of the Basic Healing Ritual.

- Draw the Healing Symbol three times over the crown chakra at the top of the head and hold your hand there for three minutes letting the energies flow; raising the vibrations of the body, mind and spirit and lifting and revitalising the energy field .

- Continue down the body filling each chakra with healing energies. See the chart below and further details about chakras in Chapter Two.

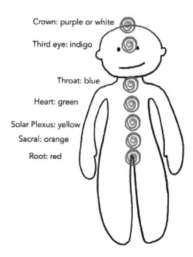

- Once you have activated each chakra with the channelled energies, complete by sweeping healing energies down through the body from top to bottom.

- Seal the new energy in with the Preserving Symbol.

- Complete with a hug.

- Use the Release Symbol on yourself to let go your attachment.

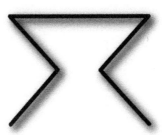

Note: To check the status of the chakras you can use a pendulum, or any weighted drop from a chain or thread. Hold the pendulum over the chakra and you will see it spin around. If the chakra is in balance and strong, the pendulum will trace a perfect circle. See Chapter Two.

Ritual: Healing to bring calm and release stress

- Follow steps one to three of Basic Healing.

- Sweep from head to toe, holding the intention of clearing any disturbance in the aura and calming anxiety. As the aura loses its agitation you will feel stronger and calmer.

- Draw the Healing Symbol three times and place your hand on the crown for a few minutes, then the heart chakra, then the solar plexus.

- Sweep again gently from top to toe.

- Draw the Peace and Harmony Symbol over the heart centre, let the energy flow through your hands.

- Seal with the Preserving Symbol.

- Finish with a hug.
- Detach with the Release Symbol.

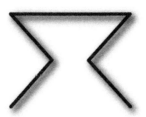

The health of the cells of your body is affected by the level of toxicity in its environment. That environment is composed of your thoughts, attitudes, your emotions and those of the people you work and live with, as well as the air you breathe.

Healing for Physical Problems

Most of the healing methods I have shared so far have been focused on healing and transforming energies that affect your feelings about yourself, your mind and your emotions. In this section I will share ways that you can use healing energies to help relieve physical conditions. Your state of mind, whether your heart is open or closed to love, and your emotional state will affect and cause some of your physical problems. Therefore, when you do any of the previous healing rituals the ripple effects of energy will have a positive effect on your physical state, e.g., clearing the heavy energies of negative thoughtforms around your head can help to clear a pressure headache. Healing the solar plexus chakra can help to clear any blocks in your digestive system and so on.

The spirit of your body

Your body has its own spirit. This is an elemental spirit like spirits of nature that live with trees and plants or inhabit rivers and waterfalls. The spirit of your body needs the same respect and nurturing that we should give nature to enable our environment to stay healthy.

I hope this doesn't shock you but every thought you have about your body affects this spirit! As all negative thoughts and attitudes are toxic and harm you, so your body responds to self-criticism and judgement. Your body and its spirit will respond positively, both spiritually and physically, to nurturing and respect. When I am helping a client to heal their body I always include the body spirit in the healing session. Here is a short ritual you can add to a healing session for a physical problem.

Your body is a living and spiritual gift and will respond to love and care, so treat it with respect and love.

Ritual: Nurturing and healing the body spirit

Use this after step two of the Healing Ritual, after you have requested protection and guidance.

- 'I acknowledge the spirit of my body and I apologise for the pain my anxieties, thoughts and attitudes have caused you. I honour and respect you.' If you are doing this for someone else let them say this, or you say it using their name.

- 'I release all stress and trauma from every cell of my body now, right now, right now.' Sweep your hands down over your body and flick away the negative energies.

- Activate the healing energies with the Healing Symbol then by placing your hands, where appropriate, on the area of the body that is hurting or diseased

- Seal with the Preserving Symbol.

- Finish with a hug.
- Detach with the Release Symbol.

Remember that your body is a living being and needs your love; nurture it with good food and water, respect it by resting when it is tired and treat it kindly. It will be affected by the traumas and challenges of your life and needs your love and respect.

Journal:

What negative thoughts, criticism and judgement do you habitually have towards your own body? What harm do you think your lifestyle has had on your body? Has your body suffered from mental stress and your life challenges? What is your plan to nourish and respect your body in future and show gratitude to the spirit of your body?

Healing specific problems

You can add any of these simple rituals and symbols into the basic healing process or use them as stand-alone procedures. Just remember always to PROTECT yourself and the person you are working with before you start.

Ritual: Healing for fractures and torn ligaments

Healing energies work very well for healing bones. When the surgeon dealing with my mother's broken ankle checked her progress he was amazed how quickly it had healed. She didn't tell him that it was due to the healing I had been giving her. Here is a symbol that you can use either side of the break then place your hands on or over the bones or ligaments.

Fracture Symbol: Use over any break, tear, fracture or displacement

Draw in the air vertically on either side of the break three times each. Draw the long line then the two little lines.

Ritual: Healing for injuries

Use this symbol to remove the shock from a sports injury or accident. It clears the shock and starts the healing process. I have found that there is less bruising when I use this symbol straight away.

Healing Injuries Symbol: Draw the spiral three times in an anti-clockwise direction.

Clockwise motion puts energy in and anti-clockwise pulls it out.

Ritual: Healing for cancer

Cancer of all kinds and autoimmune diseases are complex and the causes are many, but the healing I have shared so far helps by lifting the energy of the spirit, the heart and the body, and balances the effects of invasive and toxic treatments. This symbol helps you direct your healing to the source cells that are damaged.

Draw the first ellipse on the left then the right, then top then bottom. Draw four times.

The symbol directs healing to any cells that are malformed or attacked by viruses or cancer. As you use the symbol say, 'I send love for healing all cells; now, right now, right now.' If the person you are helping is not with you, the symbol can be used with the Distance Healing Symbol – see next section.

Ritual: Healing the digestive tract

Here is a process you can use for any digestive problems, for the oesophagus, stomach and bowels; for indigestion, constipation, irritable bowel etc. Use these three symbols:

1. **Protection.** Call in your protection for you and your client before you start.

2. **Release.** Draw this symbol three times then sweep down over the body from the neck to the toes and flick away the congested energy into a bowl of salt water. Do this for a few minutes.

3. **Healing and balancing the digestive tract** — again flick away any heavy energy into the salt. Do this for a minute. Then draw this symbol with two hands weaving your way up the body and then sweeping down.

4. **Filling with healing energy** – Draw the healing symbol in the air three times and place your hands on or over the problem area for two minutes. Sometimes the pain is not where the actual problem is located so move your hands around the area until you feel heat – this can indicate that you are in the right place.

Ritual: Back Healing

Many back problems are caused by imbalance and misalignment.

These can be caused by an imbalance in your life; working hard and not allowing yourself enough sleep or relaxation; not getting enough exercise because you are busy; taking on responsibilities that are not yours to take and so on. This healing process focuses on bringing your energy field back into alignment to allow your skeletal frame to follow. Shoulder and neck pain can come from the obvious causes of bad posture at computers but can also come from energetic source of burdens from responsibility, as we saw in Chapter Two. You will need to work with a friend to clear and align your own back. Start with protecting both of you.

1. **Protection:** Draw the Protection Symbol over yourself and whom you are working with.

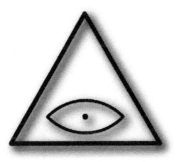

2. **Visualise:** See yourself as a great tree, see your roots growing deep into the ground beneath you and know that you are secure, grounded and supported. Feel strength coming up through your roots like sap rising.

3. Sweep and Release: Use the Release Symbol to clear any heavy energies that you carry on your back:

- people who you carry who rely on you or lean heavily on you

- responsibilities that you have picked up and carry that you are not yours

- worries about finances and concerns for your family that sit on your shoulders

- anxieties about deadlines and work commitments

Draw the release symbol three times then sweep for two minutes.

Say, 'I clear all heavy energies that are weighing me down and pulling me out of balance.' Repeat twice as you sweep.

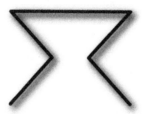

4. Align: Draw a strong line down the spine and down to the floor with both hands saying, 'You are coming back into full alignment; now, right now, right now.' Repeat two more times.

5. Balance: Draw the Balance Symbol three times and sweep this energy down over the body. Say, 'You are balanced in mind, spirit and body. All is well.'

Balance Symbol: draw left oval then right oval then the lines. Draw three times.

6. **Preserve and Set the energy.** Confirm the new energy state by using the Preserve Symbol three times. The top cup then bottom cup and then the central line.

Journal:
Keep a record of all the healing you do for yourself and other people and feedback. You may find you forget what you did for someone as the releasing helps us let of go the memory as well as attachment to their energy. It helps to have a record, so you can check back if they want a healing you have given repeated.

There may be times when you want to help someone or a situation and cannot be there: for those times you can use Distance Healing. This can be as powerful as healing in situ and gives you scope to send healing to lots of people, disasters and world events. All the healing rituals I have shared so far can be included in your Distance Healing process.

Distance Healing

Energy is magical; it is not bound by walls and location! You can send healing to anyone wherever they are in the world. When my husband, Tony, and I lived in Hong Kong I went through some difficult times with my teeth; fortunately, I discovered an outstanding dentist from California. I became a frequent visitor to clear the backlog of work for my molars, plus I wanted to take advantage of his exceptional reputation for fitting crowns. On one of my numerous visits he asked me if I could send healing to someone on the other side of the world. I mumbled yes – it's difficult to talk with a fist in your mouth! He asked me to send healing to his brother-in-law who was in an intensive care unit in Seattle. He had developed leukaemia and was recovering from a bone marrow transplant. Unfortunately, he was struggling with recovery and critically ill; the antibiotics that prevented rejection of the implant had not been working and his condition was deteriorating hour by hour. He gave me his brother-in-law's name and as he continued to work on my teeth I visualised the name in golden lights in the sky. I used my symbols to set the intention and said in my mind, 'If permission is granted from the higher self of his name I send healing; now, right now, right now.' I lay there with this vision of the name in lights for several moments, then disconnected.

The next day I had a phone call from the dentist's wife. At first, I thought she was upset with me! She asked me if I had been sending healing to her brother while in the dentist's chair the previous day and I confirmed that I had. I asked if there was a problem and she laughed and said, 'No, not at all, quite the opposite.' Apparently, at the time I was having my treatment her brother suddenly started to respond to the antibiotics and all his vital organs had gradually returned to life. She asked the doctor in charge what time the apparatus to which he was hooked registered his recovery and it was the precise time I was sending healing to him. I was as grateful as she was. What a wonderful confirmation of the power of distance healing!

Healing from a distance has the added advantage that your emotions are less likely to block the energy flow. When you are face to face with someone you can get immersed in their troubles and if your own emotions kick in they can act as a barrier to the healing. With distant healing, you are less likely to let that happen. It is also very quick – it just takes moments to send the vibrations through. My friend Sally, who helped me start my healing journey, does all her work this way and has done for years since she became ill from an overload of people's negative emotions. Sally maintains that distance healing is much more powerful, and it feels natural to link up with helpful masters, angels and guides. This is easier when working on a higher plane than at a physical level. A couple of years ago I also found that I was heading for burnout and my guides suggested I work at a distance. I now do group healing in my seminars and send out the vibes in online webinars and online healing sessions using Facebook Live.

Since Covid-19, I have been doing all my healing sessions online using Skype or Zoom and the results have never been better.

There are several ways you can set up to do distant healing:

- use a photo.

- write a name.

- visualise a name as I did in the dentist surgery.

- say the name out loud

Ritual: Distance Healing
Either have a photo of the person whom you wish to help or write down their name. I use a printout of a heart and I place the names of the people I wish to help in the heart then I send them healing and love every day.

Protect yourself before embarking on any distance healing because negative energy can bounce back into you if you don't?

- Draw the following two symbols over the picture or name. The first is for distance healing – draw this one once, and the second invokes healing energies.

Distance Healing Symbol: Draw once, start in the middle and draw round clockwise then the line then the dot.

Healing Symbol: Draw three times, from the right top then the dot.

- Say, 'I send love and healing to (*their name*).'
- Place your hands on the photo for one or two minutes, the energy will quickly transfer from you to the person you are trying to help.

Cynthia's Story

I met Cynthia on one of my visits to Moscow. She was attending my healing workshop when I explained the use of the Distance Healing Symbol. She sat bolt upright and stared at me and I felt a frisson of energy flow between us. She continued to stare while the energy flowed from me to her. After the energy calmed she shook herself and asked me if it is possible to send healing to someone in another country? I assured her that a person could be anywhere. As I was explaining the use of the symbol she had been thinking of her sister, who that day was visiting hospital for her cancer treatment back in England. The next day she shared the exciting news that her sister had rung her that night to say that something strange had happened on her journey back from the hospital. She had been feeling very depressed and hopeless about her future when she felt a strange heat coming over her. She stopped the car and after the sensation had faded she was filled with a sense of peace, which was with her still. And yes, the timing matched exactly to the connection we made in the workshop in Moscow. In this case the energies had passed from me to Cynthia, and then to her sister and then to her in UK. Since then I have often used a family member or a close friend as a surrogate to channel and direct energy.

Distance healing from me to you through Facebook

I use Facebook Live to stream healing, but I also record the session so you can still connect to the energies by watching the recording. When I am channelling the healing energies I speak out loud the intentions for the energies to address certain problems. These will include some mental health, some physical and some emotional. I also send a general stream of loving energy for anything that you need.

After one of the earlier sessions, the video and sound failed, although I carried on with the healing session. Afterwards I received this message.

'Thank you so much, Anne, for a powerful healing session!! I could really feel you sending powerful, light pink coloured energy!

Can I ask you a question, please?

During this healing session, I clearly heard you speaking while doing the healing. I wasn't prepared for this, but it was absolutely great!

The question is: Was this you speaking? Or did I receive someone else during this session?

Thank you.'

The lady who sent me this message obviously had strongly developed psychic senses for she could feel the energy (clairsentience), she could see the colour of the loving energy stream (clairvoyance) and she could hear me speaking (clairaudience)! Quite a feat – well done to her!

There are no walls that can keep out your love. Send your love and compassion to someone who needs it right now!

Let's see how we can share these energies and spread them further afield. It can be depressing to see the news with people suffering from wars and natural disasters. You may feel disempowered, ineffective and personally distressed if you believe you cannot help. But you can! By using Distance Healing, you can send love and uplifting energies to lift the vibration of situations, groups and individuals even when you don't know them personally. Use the distance healing ritual to direct energy to places and situations by writing down the specific target and placing your hands on or above your writing. Next is a healing ritual that you can use to clear the negativity caused by mass consciousness which is the combined thought streams (thoughtforms) of people around the world.

Light is stronger and more powerful than Darkness. You see this whenever you enter a room and switch on the light. Switch on your light through positive intention.

The Bigger Picture

You can use your healing skills to affect not only individuals but also situations, groups, countries, war zones, areas of natural disaster and the atmosphere and energy body of the entire world.

Clearing Negativity from Mass Consciousness

You may have noticed that some days you are feeling down even when things are going well in your life. You may be experiencing and being affected by mass consciousness: the accumulation of thoughts loaded with emotions that come from the joy and suffering of everyone; the sadness, pain, despair, hate, anger and guilt that is felt anywhere in the world. When there is more negative energy than light, it will sit like a dark cloud above us, blocking out the light and preventing us from accessing the divine love that pouring down to us every minute of every day. The negativity is a blanket we need to penetrate to make our own connection to this amazing source of light. You may struggle to keep connected through the barriers of your own negative thoughts and emotions, but you are also affected by the barriers put out by mass consciousness. Your intention to penetrate this fog will eventually cause the breakthrough you need. As more of us connect to the light, the better we shall all feel.

Unconsciously, your contribution of light or heavy energy has an effect on mass consciousness as every thought you have is loaded with your emotions. If you have a positive and uplifting mindset, attitude or approach to life, you will be charging up and lightening the overall energy field of everyone. Obviously, you cannot be one hundred per cent positive all day and every day. You will have days when you are low and depressed, unhappy or hurting. But you can deliberately radiate good vibes through a simple meditation that will send out a flow of positive and light energy to ripple through the human energy field and help to clear the dark clouds that hang around us all. Every time you channel in light, every time you consciously radiate this light, every time you send out loving thoughts, you are clearing the darkness and allowing more light into the world.

Use your love as a laser beam to break up the clouds of darkness.

Ritual: Clearing Mass Consciousness

- Relax and close your eyes.
- Set your intention to radiate beams of light from your heart into mass consciousness to affect every sentient being.
- Call in your protection. Draw the Protection Symbol in front of yourself three times.

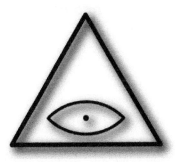

- Call in your guides and angels to assist you. Say, 'All beings of Spirit that have the wellbeing of the world in their hearts, please assist me right now.'
- Draw the Distance Healing and Healing Symbols three times.

- Say, 'I bring love from the Universal Source of Love and Light to my heart; I add my personal love and compassion and send to enlighten mass consciousness; now, right now, right now.'

- Visualise rays of light coming from your heart into dark clouds. See the sun shining through the clouds and filling the world with light.

- Hug yourself! Thank you, every positive vibe helps us all!

Every kind act, every smile, every compassionate thought for friend or stranger will lift the energies of mass consciousness and affect everyone on Earth.

In Chapter Eight there is a meditation using the Silver Ray Symbols to bring peace and harmony to the world. You can use this yourself or better still, get together in a group to send healing to our entire world.

In the next chapter we will take a closer look at the magic of your amazing heart centre and how you can heal the pain of rejection, broken heart, loss of love and lack of love. We will also look at the impact a wounded and closed heart can have on all aspects of your life.

CHAPTER *Four*

Healing your heart centre

Love is the Key to Happiness

Now we come to my favourite subject: the role of the heart centre and the effect it has on your life. Your heart centre monitors the flow of love you give and receive and as love is the key to your happiness it's imperative that you keep it in good working order. Its effects are far-reaching into your life and wellbeing and reflect on every relationship you have, from romantic partnerships to your connection to money. The underlying influence on the wellbeing of your heart is your relationship with yourself, so we will also look at your levels of self-love, self-confidence and self-value. I will be sharing some of the amazing experiences that have shown me the inner workings of the heart centre and share techniques that can help you to open your heart and enjoy a life full of love.

If you seek love, ensure your door is open to allow it in.

Your Goal: An Open Heart

Your heart centre controls the flow of your love and it has filters and shutters that control how much love comes into your life. As love is the nectar of life, this will affect how sweet your life is, how happy you are, how at peace you are with yourself and your world. The very centre of your heart, the core of your heart, is the pure love essence, the divine energy of your higher self and your creator. This is the true essence of who you are.

The Core of
Your Heart
The True Essence
Of You:
LOVE

The Core of Your Heart is Love

The core of your heart is connected to your higher self, through your higher chakras by a cord of the same essence. If the doors of your heart are shut, you cannot connect to that true and very special core of who you are. If the doors are closed you cannot connect to your higher self-wisdom, your intuitive powers, your life purpose and the gateway to the divine. Your ability to be happy, to have inner peace, to know yourself as you really are, to experience fulfilling relationships and to share your love with the world will be limited in some way or another if your heart is closed – even partially.

I am told 'Your heart needs to open'

I went to Hong Kong for a short visit soon after my wake-up message to practise healing. While my husband was working I left our hotel to explore and wandered the back streets of Central where I came across The New Age Book Shop. In years to come I would become a regular visitor of this store, which was the heart of Esoteric Hong Kong for expats and locals alike, and they regularly hosted healers and psychics. On that day they were advertising sessions with a psychic called Jenny Lethbridge, who is active today but now living in Hampshire (see Appendix). Impulsively, I entered and asked if there were any sessions free and, with universal serendipity and synchronicity there was one available in five minutes! She amazed me with her 'knowing' of me and immediately recognised me as a healer, much to my delight. But she brought me down to Earth by telling me that my heart needed to open fully to have unlimited healing powers. She shared much more including The Four Trees Ritual for dealing with difficult negative energies, which I share in Chapter Seven. I left the shop with mixed feelings but set my intention to open my heart, and every day from then on I used the Heart Opening Ritual in Chapter Two.

Journal:
Write your intention of healing, clearing and opening your heart. However you are feeling today, know that you can improve your relationships with yourself, lovers, parents, friends and life in general. Write your own mantra to emphasise your willingness to be open to give and receive love.

When you set your intention and put your will into action, the universe will join in and help you achieve your goal.

How a closed heart can impact your life
If your heart is even partially closed, it will affect aspects of your life. Here are some of the ways the barriers around your heart can prevent life flowing well for you.

- Prevent you from meeting a suitable life partner – your 'Keep Out' sign can be read from a distance!

- Prevent you from receiving the love you need to heal your inner wounds and scars.

- Prevent you from having committed and close relationships with lovers and friends.

- Cause an outer prickliness or armour that deters people at work and play.

- Can create a block to fun, happiness and a fulfilling life.

- Put up a barrier to anything you desire including financial security and all forms of abundance.

- Influence the way you perceive your experiences, casting a pall on the good things in your life and preventing you from seeing your opportunities and blessings.

- Prevent you from seeing the beauty you are and stop you from acknowledging your gifts and skills.

- Put limits on your experience in all aspects of your life.

> ***'Your task is not to seek love, but merely to seek and find all the barriers within yourself that you have built against it.' Rumi***

Compassion is a heart opener

After meeting Jenny, the apparently closed state of my heart sat heavily with me and I resolved to do something about it. I threw myself into my work, pushing myself ever harder by travelling, teaching and giving healing morning day and night. I felt driven and had an insatiable desire to improve my healing skills. Every day I meditated and performed the simple heart-opening ritual I shared in Chapter Two. I was soon to learn that we don't always have instant results from our manifesting, but the subtle shift of energies that are set about by determination and intention will eventually bear fruit as I was to find out in Tibet. After giving a healing session on a visit to Singapore, my client came out of the deep trance created by the healing and announced that Kwan Yin, the Buddhist Goddess of Mercy had a message for me. She took me to the Kwan Yin temple nearby and in a meditation there I came face to face with the deity who would become my spiritual guide for some years to come. Kwan Yin has a very direct approach with messages and she told me in no uncertain terms that I needed to go to Tibet to start the full opening of my heart. Though a forceful being of light, she is also kind and she reassured me that my heart wasn't totally closed. But there was obviously work to be done – under the Himalayan Mountains by a river, so she said! She added that she would give me a further message in a cave. This message shook me as I had been teaching you do NOT have to go and live in a cave in the Himalayas to find spiritual enlightenment and that one could progress as easily in your hometown be it Croydon, Marseilles or New York! So, this guidance took some swallowing. Not for the first time I had to eat my words and readjust my thinking! Anyway, I found some enthusiastic friends who thought it would be fun to trek into the wastelands of Tibet and seek some answers.

Our plan was to meet up in Kathmandu in Nepal and cross the Tibetan border over Friendship Bridge. My travelling companions flew in from Hong Kong and Singapore and I came from London. The day before I flew, the Nepalese Royal Family were massacred by a family member and Kathmandu and its airport were under curfew. The full story of my Tibetan experience is in my book *Opening Your Heart*, but the short version is that I flew into a city under lockdown and rather than spend time acclimatising to the altitude in Nepal we sped off up to the border in a coach piled with provisions and our backpacks. We crossed the bridge and took Jeeps and a truck up into the high mountains of Tibet, navigating narrow mountain passes and sheer drops. We were soon shaken from our city-safe comfort zone and dumped into the land of yaks and prayer flags. I was further successfully 'softened up' by a close encounter with death from severe altitude sickness caused by our guide driving us with maniacal urgency up onto the high plateau of Tibet. Here in a very basic hostel I threw up blood and fell unconscious from lack of oxygen. It seemed our guide had his heart set on taking us to the sacred mountain of Mount Kailash despite my sickness. Fortunately, common sense prevailed, and my friends persuaded the guides that whatever spiritual enlightenment was waiting for us at the sacred Mount Kailash could wait for another time, and they took me down back into the valleys of the Himalayas where a camp was set up and I started to recover.

On the way down from the high ranges, we stopped to pay our respects to the memory of Milarepa, an ancient Tibetan holy man who had redeemed his life as a corrupt businessman by becoming a spiritual recluse. He spent years meditating in a mountainside cave until he eventually cleared his guilt through prayer, became enlightened and in the modern day, has become revered as a saint. The cave had been transformed with Buddhist sacred symbols and icons into a shrine to redemption. We duly gave our thanks and asked for blessings from Milarepa and as I knelt before his shrine I received another message from Kwan Yin. I should slow down, appreciate the gifts I had been given and care for myself more. As we left the cave

I came face to face with a young man whose face was covered in open weeping sores, apparently from burns – a common problem for children left unattended with open fires by parents who work in the fields scratching out a basic living. I was touched by the boy and gave him a handful of money and moved on back to our Jeep.

Later that day in our recovery camp I tried to sleep but my chest was seized by a series of cramps and shooting pains. In horror of a heart attack I ran to my friends who comforted me and sent out urgent prayers into the mountainous wilderness that surrounded our camp. I saw a vision of the young boy from Milarepa's Cave standing before me and I instantly felt his suffering and the suffering of thousands of children around the world who don't have basic care or the love of a mother to wipe away the pus on their faces. I cried and cried and eventually the pain dispersed. I realised that the pain had been my heart opening – in this instance compassion had been the key. Once I had cleaned myself up after the deluge of tears, my friends and I went down to the river that ran by our simple camp and offered gratitude for my recovery and our health and wellbeing. So Kwan Yin was right: cave, mountains, river and heart-opening all in a week – an amazing, scary but unforgettable week! In Hong Kong where my husband was based, I was introduced to a man running a charity that helped villagers in Nepal to build safe fires and set up clinics in the mountain villages. My husband and I have supported him and his work ever since and we went on to set up our own charity, Hearts and Hands for Africa and have introduced safe cooking stoves there as well.

Journal:
Have you experienced pain in your chest that you know comes from being touched by the plight of another? Did you cry?
Tears are the emotions that were locked in from the time your heart closed.

We close our hearts to protect ourselves from more hurt. We close our hearts to manage the emotions that would overwhelm us

I Face the Barriers of Guilt

In Chapter Two, I showed the heart centre as a simple chakra, but a group of powerful angels decided I needed to see another perspective; to learn more of the workings of the heart and see the reason mine had closed. They showed me that, although my heart had begun to open and I may have been good at giving out love, I was unable to fully love myself, a situation many of us experience. Here is what happened to me on a trip to Pondicherry in India some years after my Tibetan trip; a trip that helped me understand the impact of guilt and to begin to see the inner workings of our hearts.

I went to India with two dear friends with the idea of a holiday but also a strong desire to understand myself better. I had been crying off and on and feeling a sense of imminent loss. I felt grief although I had no reason to be sad. Since then, I have come to realise that this feeling is a sign that I am about to go into a new state of consciousness, a shift, and gain a new perception or understanding. It is not uncommon for this to occur on your journey of self-understanding and development. You too may have feelings of loss, confusion and emptiness prior to a shift of consciousness.

On the first day, I had another visitation from Kwan Yin who told me to visit a Church. I had expected to be guided to an ashram or temple not a church! But we were in Pondicherry, an old French colony of India, and there were four large churches still active in the town. My friends kindly came with me to the nearest and I went inside while they went sightseeing. I sat in a pew and tried to relax and meditate. I discovered Indian churches don't share the hush and reverence of our English churches and I struggled with the constant comings and goings of noisy visitors. A statue of Mother Mary looked down at me with a string of fairy lights twinkling around her head and an unsmiling Jesus solemnly stared into the Church, a red light pulsing at his heart centre. I closed my eyes and despite the din eventually slipped into a meditative state.

Beings of light are waiting to help us every step of the way – call them to help

Archangel Gabriel stepped into my inner vision and hit me with the news that my spirit guides would be leaving for a while! This set off a fresh bout of tears! Fortunately, because of the constant crying over the last few weeks I had a large box of tissues by my side. Gabriel explained that I was about to experience an inner journey that didn't require guides other than angels. I was led down a set of steps to stand outside a door, the door to my heart. The angel asked me to enter; the door opened easily and I stepped into a wonderful space filled with light. This, I was told, was the chamber of my personal experiences of love, where I give out and receive love.

In the middle of the chamber a flame glowed brightly. I saw my father who had already passed away, and a beautiful reunion brought on more tears. I realised that, even though a loved one dies, some of their spirit will always be with us in our hearts – how comforting. I saw my pets and friends whom I had loved. I saw everyone whom I had ever allowed into my heart, confirming the expression we use to 'take someone into our heart'. This place felt good and I was quite pleased with myself – it seemed all was well in my heart centre. But there was more to come. Three other angels appeared; I obviously needed a powerful escort for what was to come next! They introduced themselves as Archangels Uriel, Raphael and Michael and led me through an outer chamber to another door. Oh dear, this door was in a bad state. Large rusty locks and bolts held it closed, criss-crossed with long wooden planks nailed to the doors. It appeared to have been shut for aeons. I started crying again – how pathetic, but a sign of more revelations to come! The angels were wonderful. They calmed me down and explained that this door led to my inner heart chamber, which held the essence of unconditional love that was the true me. But I had shut it off due to the guilt and shame I had carried in my heart and soul for many lifetimes. I could either open the door and see what was beyond or step back and continue my life as before. Of course, there was no way I could refuse to go forward. As soon as I decided to progress, they helped me to break down the barricade I had placed there long ago and eventually the door was free to open.

You create the barriers around your heart;
you can bring them down.

As I stepped forward I half expected to enter a room of light but not so, I fell into a pit of darkness! As I tumbled down and down I felt things flying past me as though escaping: old, suppressed emotions and memories being released after being locked down for a long time. Eventually I landed in a dungeon. The angels reassured me that all would be well, but my heart was beating so fast and loud that I imagined the entire church was filled with its fearful hammering. There were three large chests standing in the middle of the dungeon floor. The angels urged me to open them. I was scared but I had to look. I approached the first chest and immediately the lid flew open and I was viewing a video taken from one of my past lives. I was horrified to see myself as a slave driver: a ruthless mean man herding slaves along a dusty road. What a shocking revelation, no wonder I had so much guilt and shame, no wonder my heart was closed! As I watched my old persona act out that cruel life, the angel told me that I could forgive myself; that everyone has a dark life; through crossing into darkness we learn the powerful lesson of karma and understand the devastation to our soul when we make the choice of the dark road of living without love and compassion. It seems that all healers need to step over so that they can be tolerant of others and heal even the hardest hearts. This was little comfort to me at the time but has made sense since. Finally, as the picture was fading, a small boy in the group of slaves turned to me and said sweetly and clearly, 'Forgive yourself, Anne, we have.' Heavens, did I cry then! My heart felt it would burst, which in a way I guess it did; it burst open!

As a healer you can only heal the root cause of wounds that you too have experienced in some lifetime.

I sat for some time in the church that day and contemplated my life. I realised that I had always been looking for redemption; always trying to please others; attempting to be liked; always saying, 'I'll do it' even when I didn't want to and taking the blame for things I didn't do. These are all signs of someone carrying a heavy burden of guilt and the deep toxic imprints of shame. As I considered my experiences with the angels I felt a sense of relief; I began to understand myself better. Over the next few days I visited the other churches in the area.

The subsequent meditations took me into a shining bright inner core of my heart and I saw the connection we have between our heart centre and our higher self. I realised how guilt and shame can be powerful barriers to love. By bringing down the barriers to my heart and by healing the reasons I had put them there, I felt liberated and able to connect to not only my own sense of self-worth but to divine powers everywhere in our universe. The experience helped me to be more adept at opening the hearts of my clients and healing the deepest wounds that we all hold from our past.

Do you carry guilt?

Journal:
Is old guilt and shame blocking the way to the core of your heart? Is guilt affecting your relationship with yourself and others?

Here are some indicators and signs that you may recognise in your own life. Do you:

- step back and put other people first as a habit even when you know you are depriving yourself and affecting your health?

- want to please and look for approval even from people you don't particularly respect?

- work too hard trying to achieve despite negatively affecting your wellbeing?

- say 'yes' to requests for help even when you are exhausted?

- never feel really satisfied with yourself or your achievements?

- judge and criticise yourself and your achievements?

- undervalue yourself, give away your possessions, your skills and your time for free or for a minimal charge?

- think it is far more important to give rather than receive; beyond the natural kindness of a good and loving heart?

- dislike yourself to the point of self-harming?

- tend to sabotage the good things that happen to you and feel you are not worthy of happiness?

Loving and giving are the keys to happiness but not when they destroy your health

Journal:
Does any of this section sound true for you? If so, do you recall anything in this lifetime that you have done that may cause you to feel shame or guilt? Do you think you may have been born with guilt? You may not have done anything particularly wrong but if you personally feel the shame then it can be enough to close your heart.

Shame

Shame is the most destructive of emotions that is reflected in negative feelings about yourself, leaving you judgemental and self-critical. It destroys a positive ego and sense of worth and leads to low feelings of self-esteem, self-value and self-confidence. It is hidden deep and often covered up with bravado, intense activity and layers of protection.

Shame can come from not only your own actions or omissions but can be a result of someone else's actions. You can pick up shame from:

- being bullied (why didn't I stand up to them, I am weak?)
- sexual abuse (why didn't I manage to stop it happening?)
- not getting the job you desired (I must have failed in some way)
- being abandoned as a child (I was ugly or unlovable)
- being programmed by parents and teachers to believe you are unworthy (they say I am not good enough, so that must be true)
- being rejected for another by a partner (I am not good enough, not beautiful enough, too fat, etc.)
- being ashamed of your association with parents, society and culture (I hate being associated with those people, I am ashamed of their behaviour)

Shame will seriously compromise your ability to love yourself and acts as a powerful barrier against love.

It is so much easier to forgive someone else than it is to forgive yourself. It is easier to feel compassion for the suffering of others than it is for yourself. Healing and recovering your self-worth is hard but when you do master it you will experience an amazing transformation. Before you start this next session, use this visualisation to bring up your compassion, which is love triggered by your sense of empathy.

- You are wandering the dark streets of a city at night. You see a young girl cowering in a doorway. She is dressed in tatty clothes and obviously unloved, alone and lost. This child has been rejected by her society for a misdemeanour against society's laws and has been judged and thrown out. You are the only one who is seeing her pain. What will you do? Will you pass by or take the child into your arms and give them the love she needs to survive?

Empathy awakens Compassion

Ritual: Opening your heart centre with compassion
Keep hold of your sense of compassion while you do this next session.

- Call the great Archangels Gabriel, Uriel, Raphael and Michael to be with you to protect and guide you. Feel their presence as they wrap their wings around you; they love and protect you.

- Set your intention to open your heart by putting your hands together in front of your chest as though you are praying. Your hands represent the doors of your heart. Open and drop them down now.

- Set your intention to treat yourself as you would treat an abandoned child. Feel your compassion and wrap your arms around yourself.

- See that child now in your arms and see it morph into the spirit of yourself – your neglected divine aspect.

- Draw this young version of you towards your heart.

- Say whatever comes to you to console this child, forgive it and love it with all your heart and soul.

- When it stops crying take it closer and closer until it enters your heart where it can be loved forever.

- Say, 'I am forgiven, all shame is healed. My heart is free to open completely.'

Journal:
Write down how it feels to be compassionate to yourself. What else can you do to allow forgiveness to heal the guilt and shame? How does this session make you feel?

Ritual: Opening your heart to receive love
Do this whenever you feel that you have closed down and when you feel ready to bring love back into your life.

- Call in protection and your guides.

- Relax and drop your shoulders.

- You are standing in a beautiful hallway with high ceilings supported by marble pillars. The walls are covered in bookcases holding everything you have learnt in this life. You are in the Halls of your Mind.

- Your guide steps up and takes your hand and leads you to large wooden doors that open onto a flight of steps leading downwards.

- Walk down the steps knowing you have the love and kindness of your guide to assist you.

- See the door to your heart centre at the bottom of the steps, open this door and step inside. See who is waiting there for you.

- In your own time advance to the back of the chamber and find the door to the inner chamber, the core of your heart.

- Let the angels help you pull down any barriers. Use the Release Symbol to help you.

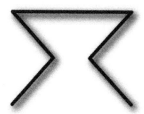

- Step through the door. You are stepping into a beautiful chamber of light and your own higher self is waiting to receive you. Feel the love as you are embraced by this pure aspect of yourself.

Whenever you doubt yourself or feel that you are not worthy in any way, go back into your heart and feel the pure love of your true essence.

To remind yourself, tap your heart centre when you feel the need to reconnect.

My quest to fully understand the workings of the heart centre continued some years later in Norway.

Heart Spheres

On a visit to Oslo, Norway, I was asked by a young healer to help her open her third eye. She felt that her psychic abilities, although greater than most people, could be improved even further and believed that there was something inhibiting her. I did the obvious thing, which was to focus on her third eye chakra to clear and heal it, believing this was the cause of her blockage. I couldn't feel any heavy energy in her chakra and started to wonder if maybe there was no block, when I was intuitively guided to change my focus and direct the healing to her heart centre. I didn't know why I felt this would help but trusted my guidance. As I worked on her heart I had a vision of her in a previous life being persecuted as a witch. As the vision unfolded I felt the fear and the pain she went through in that lifetime, and although I hadn't shared what I was seeing my client began to sob. Obviously, the healing was working. I sat meditating on this as my client allowed the energies to heal her old imprints and release her fear of opening to her inherent psychic skills. I was shown that there are several chambers or spheres around the core of hearts, and these relate to the many different types of relationships and love connections that we have. Her issue was with her work, her psychic skills and healing abilities. She had been ridiculed and killed for her work, so that aspect of her heart had been broken as society turned against her: even those who she had helped with her skills and care had walked away from her. This had left her with imprints of rejection and that sphere of her heart had closed; it was this closure that inhibited and limited her work in this lifetime.

You close your heart to protect it from the pain of past experiences. To open it you need to heal the imprints of pain and release old emotions locked inside.

There is a heart sphere or chamber for every type of relationship. Some of your heart spheres may be fully open, some completely shut and many somewhere in between, depending on whether you have been hurt by your experiences in that sphere. E.g. your heart may be open to giving and receiving love with your children but your relationship with your mother and father may have been painful in which case that sphere could be closed. Many people struggle with personal relationships and have barriers and difficulty showing empathy or commitment, but have a full open heart with compassion for animals.

The sphere or chamber that I was taken through by the angels in Pondicherry was the one relating to close personal relationships, the sphere where people we love very much leave some of their spirit for the rest of our lives. Not only people, but animals too; I was thrilled to see my first dog, Prince.

This chart contains examples of the relationships you could have with different people and aspects of your life. You may be able to think of more and some may not be relevant to you. For example, I know my Labradors would have a huge sphere for their relationship with food!

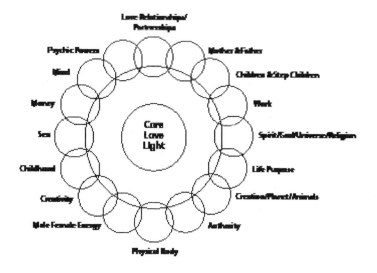

Journal:

Looking at the spheres in the diagram, which of yours do you think are open or closed or partway? Do you know why?
Write down your experiences that have affected the state of your heart.

The impact of spheres on your ego; your sense of self

Your sense of self is damaged when any of your spheres are scarred, broken or closed. For example, when you are rejected by someone you love, you can start to doubt yourself and your self-esteem will take a knock. If through all other aspects of your life you have a good flow of love, this lowering of your self-esteem will soon be healed. If you are suffering from lack of love in many areas of your life, then your self-confidence and self-esteem will stay low for longer. A young man brought up neglected by his parents and surrounded by gangland culture may have his sense of self badly affected; he will either suffer the pain or push it down, close his heart and put on a cloak of bravado.

There are too many possible scenarios and spheres to cover in this book but to give you a taster, I am going to take you through three that might affect you. The spheres or your relationships with parents, finance and partners.

The Sphere of Parents

Many of my clients in their middle age are still carrying resentment and blame for the way their parents treated them or for not showing them love. Unfortunately parents are not angels – how wonderful our world would be if they were! They are humans with issues, frailties and scars. We are not always wanted or expected! My own mother most certainly wasn't looking to have a baby (me) with her husband, a man who she had come to despise. Fortunately for me, although I wasn't planned, she fell in love with me when I was born so I wasn't affected, but many children are. Early experiences of lack of love can leave scars long into your life and these scars and imprints can cause you to put up barriers towards your parents, blocking the flow of love between you. There are situations where parents are blamed even when they have done nothing abusive, cruel or unkind and have loved their children. In teenage years it seems a trend to blame parents for all feelings of inadequacy or inner turmoil, but when we get older we can usually see that they did what they could and were a reflection of their own difficult childhoods, culture and background. Once we wake up we can see that many of our issues come from way before we were born.

Expectations of our parents have changed a lot in our current era. We now expect closer parenting from fathers, we expect parents to put children first, to be emotionally empathetic and so on. In my grandparents' day the father was purely expected to be a source of economic support, and with larger families children were far more independent than now. As times change so do expectations, and expectations are the root of most suffering – disappointment, hurt, resentment etc.

When you blame another you turn yourself into a victim.

If you are the victim of abuse from either of your parents, focus on healing the impact and scars on your heart. Your goal will be to reach neutral feelings about them and not let yourself be defined by the way they treated you.

If your relationship is very painful, consider stepping away but be aware that rejection can cause them pain. Send them healing and visualise your heart sphere open and healed. Keep yourself protected in your egg whenever you have dealings with them.

Journal:
Did your parents give you love and support?
Would you say they have lived up to your expectations as parents?
Are your expectations realistic based on your parents' background and experiences?

The Sphere of Finance

I discuss our relationship with money in several sections of this book; it is an important part of our lives and will often reflect our sense of self-worth. When the sphere that interacts, relates and manages your finances is blocked you may find that you have bad luck in money affairs; you accumulate debt; your money 'goes nowhere' and you are always short; businesses lose their profitability; you don't get pay rises and so on. This aspect of your heart will have closed because of something negative you have experienced around wealth, money or finances. Later we will look at imprints from past lives that affect your relationship with wealth but here we see how your heart doors can also close to protect your inner self, your ego, from being affected. You close your heart to prevent the sense of worthlessness from permeating your heart and destroying your self-esteem completely. You close down, and this will reflect in your attitude to money.

- You may pretend you don't care about acquiring wealth.

- Your business affairs can start to fade as you fail to send love and passion from the core of your heart, your true self.

- You give away all your money because of a sense of being contaminated or judged for being wealthy.

- You attract bad luck in your business affairs and lose money easily.

Sometimes when a sphere closes it can have an impact on another sphere. Here is John's experience; the sphere of his children and the sphere of his partners affected his finance/business sphere.

John's Story

On one of my working visits to Hong Kong I was invited to work at the Mandarin Hotel. This was a very different venue for me and I wasn't sure how it would work because most of the guests were visiting on business. My first client was a businessman and he asked me to help him improve his business. He had been extremely successful for most of his working life, but then some years ago his enterprises began failing and whatever he did, he could not recover his original good fortune. We discussed his family life and he told me he was divorced and his only son lived with his wife. Although I don't normally have requests to improve business I decided to step out of my original judgement and open my heart and let the energies flow. I realised an aspect of his heart was closed. I told him to put his hands together to represent the doors of his heart and to open them if he wanted to let down the barriers he had placed there, whether deliberately or not. He became emotional; as he opened his hands and the barriers fell away he sobbed, and I felt a huge shift of energy.

He shared his grief at losing constant contact with his son. We discussed this and how it had affected him; his bitterness towards his wife and his own sense of guilt at causing the marriage to break due to his workaholic tendencies and extensive time spent away. I took him through a ritual of forgiveness for his wife and himself and cleared his karma. He left with a spring in his step and a huge smile on his face; he was already starting to plan a holiday with his son. Afterwards he wrote me a letter; he felt so much kinder towards his wife and they had formed a better visiting plan for him and his son. AND his business was picking too! A good result all round – simply by opening his heart.

Ritual: Open and heal your heart sphere of finances

This ritual takes you through not only a heart-opening but also forgiving the person or organisation that upset you and caused your heart to close. When a heart sphere is damaged it has impact on your self-esteem, in this case your sense of self-value will be affected so we include healing for this too.

- Call in your protection and your guides and angels.

- Say out loud your intention e.g. 'It is my intention to open my heart sphere that governs my relationship with money.

155

and wealth.' If you know who or what was to blame for your situation say, 'I forgive ...; now, right now, right now.' Repeat four times.

- Draw the Release Symbol three times over your heart to show your intention of letting them and your hard feelings go. Hard feelings towards a person or organisation will place a barrier over the entrance to your heart sphere.

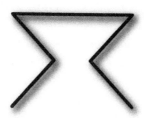

Release symbol: draw from left to right in front of your heart centre.

- Draw the Heart Opening Symbol three times.

Heart Opening Symbol: Draw the symbol with the circle first, then the lines from left to right.

- Put your hands together in front of your heart centre to represent the door of your finance heart sphere. Open them to show your intention of opening the doors of your heart. Do this three times, saying; 'I open my heart to allow money to flow, to bring success to my business affairs and to create financial security; now, right now, right now.'

- Draw the Healing Symbol three times over your heart and channel love and to your sense of self, which sits around your heart of hearts. Say, 'I heal my sense of self-value; now, right now, right now.' Repeat two more times.

Healing Symbol: Draw the symbol in the air three times from right to left; finish with the dot.

- Complete the session with the Preserving Symbol to hold the energies in place.

Preserving Symbol: Draw down the front of the body three times. Start with the top half-circle, the bottom, then the centre line. Repeat two more times.

The Sphere of Loving partnerships

As this sphere is the most problematic one I will be spending the most time with it. We are nearly all affected at some time or other with issues around romantic love! If you have been in love at any time the effects will be profound, and if you have lost that love the experience can affect you deeply for a long, long time. In this session I will explain how you create powerful connections through your loving thoughts and feelings and how these can, in turn, cause you great distress when the love ends. We look at why you can feel so much pain in your heart centre at a break-up and why you can be so seriously affected by love that has long gone.

Broken Heart and Heart Strings

When two people fall in love, their constant thoughts of love for each other create powerful connectors between them, so strong that they become etheric cords that tie them together.

When you are in love, the cords will give you a sense of oneness; you may find you finish each other's sentences; get a sense of what the other one is thinking and feeling and calling each other at the same time. Initially the cords between you are light, bright and flowing with unconditional love. When the love is balanced and equal both feel strong and supported, your spirits are uplifted with the constant flow of light energy and you see all in your world as wonderful! These powerful connectors can continue to support you and feed you with positive vibes as long as the two of you are both feeling the love. Unfortunately, not every love story continues harmoniously as the lovers walk off into the sunset, and very often other emotions begin to creep in and spoil the vibration of the cords. As soon as one partner loses interest or loves less, then the balance is lost. When one loves more than the other, controlling and manipulating behaviour can creep into the relationship with the cords being used as puppet strings.

Heartbreak

When someone you love leaves, you will almost certainly experience heartbreak, not just the grief and pain of losing someone you love, but as their cord is pulled from your heart, your heart centre will feel the trauma of the withdrawal. This is the pain you feel in your chest – it truly is a heartbreak you experience and the energy of your heart centre will be torn. If the person you love walks away and no longer cares for you but your cord to them remains strong and you think of them frequently, you will continue to feel anything from discomfort and sadness to intense searing pain and grief. Here is a diagram to show what happens when the cord is pulled out. Your heart sphere is torn in two!

Your cord will still be attached to the missing partner and keep you connected. This can make it difficult for you to move on and get over your loss. The following ritual will help you to:

- detach your cord
- refocus your mind away from what you have lost and be present
- clear negative feelings in an existing relationship
- clear your yearnings
- clear cords of anger and bitterness
- release emotions that churn away inside you that are either near the surface or suppressed
- release you from the restrictions of controlling or manipulating behaviour
- clear the barriers that you have put around your heart

Attachments and expectations cause suffering – set yourself free – let them go.

How can cutting the cords help you?

Are you ready to let go and step into a new phase of your life? Then get ready to cut your cords of attachment.

I have seen many outcomes from cutting cords and letting go, every one of them positive. Here are some of the effects of releasing attachments and the stories that highlight powerful results. I have changed these reports slightly for the privacy of those involved but they will show you the potency of this therapy.

Unblocking the way for new love

If you are still attached to an ex-lover you can be blocking new love from coming into your life. Your current connection and cord will act as barriers blocking the way in. Clear your redundant cord, which is attached to the past and holds hope for a resurgence of lost love, to make way for someone who might be close and ready to bring love to you.

Sandra's Story

Sandra, a 28-year-old attractive blonde, was the first person I helped with the Cutting the Cords Ritual. She was finding it difficult to move on from a powerful relationship she had three year earlier. She could not get her ex-lover out of her thoughts and dreams, although she had not heard from him for years. His memory and the time they had been together 'haunted' her.

She had met Oliver when working overseas and had fallen in love immediately. He was fun-loving and attractive – her perfect man. He wined and dined her with style and panache and totally bowled her over. Soon after they met she moved into his apartment and they enjoyed a year of fun, high living and passion. They were ideally suited and both enjoyed the same lifestyle and each other.

For reasons outside her control, Sandra had to return to the United Kingdom. Oliver soon followed for a visit and to her delight he asked her to marry him. He returned overseas while she stayed on in England and began to put the wedding plans into action. Unfortunately things began to fall apart. He called her less and less and there was no further mention of the marriage. Eventually it became clear that their relationship had ended.

She came to see me three years later; she still hankered for him and thought of him constantly and held hopes that he might turn up on her doorstep one day and renew the relationship. She'd had a number of boyfriends since their split-up but her heart wasn't ready for anyone else. Could I help her to move on?

Firstly, I checked that she really and truly wanted to disconnect with this past love. I suggested she try calling him to check that he wasn't planning to return. She had his number and pushed the phone at me when he answered! He admitted that although he still thought of Sandra often, he had a new partner now. I told him we were going to cut cords with him. He asked if this would hurt him and I laughed and said no, but thought it might teach him a lesson if it did! So after a few tears as the realisation finally sank in that he was not going to return we went through the cord-cutting process.

As Sandra cut the cords I felt a great whoosh of energy rush past me, a massive release! Immediately she felt lighter and free of the heavy energy of the cord, which had turned into chains holding her down. As Sandra left the room, I had a vision of a man waiting on the sidelines, waiting for an opportunity to step into her life. Within months she had met a lovely man whom a friend had been trying unsuccessfully to introduce to her for over two years; eighteen months later they were married. One of the reasons that Sandra found it so hard to let go of the relationship with Oliver was that her relationship hadn't had a clear-cut ending and she had been left dangling on the end of the cord.

We need some form of rite or ceremony for major beginnings and endings in our lives, such as marriage and divorce. We need to commit or disconnect from one phase of our life to another. For many, cord-cutting has proved to be a powerful closure to situations and relationships and an opening for a new phase.

The courage to leave an abusive relationship

Cutting the cords and expressing your true emotions can give you the courage and impetus to walk away from a disastrous partnership. This was the case for Sarah.

Sarah's Story

Sarah had been struggling in an abusive relationship for years. Her mother Hayley was worried as she stood on the sidelines watching her daughter get weaker and sicker. Hayley was filled with fear. Sarah was terrified of her husband and couldn't find the courage to step away; this is a common situation for people locked into a relationship with a partner who, with mind games and manipulation, slowly destroys their independence, depletes their free will and scares them into submission. Every time Sarah tried to leave he would plead with her and apologise for his behaviour; he pulled at her compassion and promised to treat her better. Each time she would forgive him and stay. She was locked in by fear and compassion. Eventually, Hayley persuaded her to come to one of my workshops and crossed her fingers that the cord-cutting would do the trick. Sarah wept through the workshop – not an uncommon experience for someone who has been battered by emotional blackmail and stress for a long time. A year later Hayley came to another of my workshops and shared the good news that after the cord cutting Sarah had found the courage to leave her husband, had fallen in love with someone new and was already planning their wedding. Hayley was brimming with happiness at the way her daughter had turned her life around.

Instant Results

Sometimes the results of cutting and letting go of your expectations can have an instant effect. This was the experience of a lady who came to an evening workshop in Malaysia.

Lulu's Story

Lulu was fed up with her boyfriend. She was very attracted to him, but he would blow hot and cold and he hadn't called her for over four weeks. She wanted to know if she had a relationship or not. She felt she was dangling – which she was – on the end of his cord! She went through the first phase of the workshop; she had set her intentions to cut her cord to him; she let go of expectations from him and had released her emotions by writing them and burning them.

At this point I gave the attendees a break to have drinks and cake and relax. Lulu put her phone on to check on her children who were at home. She gave a shriek, 'He's called,' she shouted. 'For the first time for four weeks and he's driving up from Singapore tonight, a four-hour drive, I can't believe it.' We applauded the success of her evening's work so far. She told me afterwards that they sat up all night and discussed their feelings and decided to let go of romantic expectations and stay as good friends. She was pleased with this outcome and as far as I know they are still good mates.

Sue's Story

Short and sweet. Sue came to a workshop on the Thursday and cut her cords to past attachments, and on Friday met the man of her dreams! And she is still with him two years later.

Cords of Anger, Resentment and Hate

We can be attached with cords created from thoughts of love, but negative thoughts and attitudes can create cords too. For example, if you hold anger and resentment for a boss who fired you or a friend who treated you unfairly, then cords or attachment will grow. You will then be tied to the very person who has hurt you and your consistent feeling will continue to feed the heavy energy that connects you to them. This will drain your energy and lower your own spirits. If someone has harmed you in the past and you can't bring yourself to forgive them, the least you can do is cut the cords to them and move on in your life without the chains of anger holding you back.

My story of corporate betrayal

This is an experience I had with a company that treated me unfairly. I worked in the international division of a computer company and despite achieving all my goals and targets, my boss replaced me with an old friend of his. I was devastated and went into an instant meltdown that lasted a couple of days. Later, I received an apology from the CEO who was nervous I would sue the company for wrongful dismissal. I decided not to take the company to arbitration as I had been with them some years and up to that point had enjoyed a great relationship. But I continued to seethe. I was not only furious with my boss but also his second in command who had been a friend of mine; he hadn't raised a finger to help me and that had been a great disappointment. They offered me another placement, but my pride and faith were damaged, so I left and joined another company. I continued to let anger and resentment churn inside me. After several months of sleepless nights where I envisioned myself setting about my old boss with a meat cleaver, I decided I needed to move on! After all, I was simply reliving the worst moment in my career and that wasn't doing me any favours at all. So, I wrote down all my feelings and cut the cords to him and my old friend and threw myself into my new job.

After a year I had achieved good results with my new company but was unhappy with the long commute time, and when I was approached by my old company to take up a fabulous new position in the South African office, I accepted. When I arrived back I was greeted warmly by old colleagues, but the head of the department had gone. He had been sacked and my old friend had been off sick since the decision to re-employ me was announced. He eventually came back to work and I gave him a hug and told him the past was gone and I had no bitterness left. He cried with relief. I know I wouldn't have been asked back, nor would I have been able to return if my heart had continued to be full of anger and bitterness.

Improving other people's relationships
Although you cannot deliberately interfere with other people's energy other than sending love, your own releasing and letting go can change energy dynamics that can have positive outcomes for other people. As you disconnect and release any negative emotions held in the ties and cords, you clear the way for associated and connected cords to become free; the way rescue workers untangle old fishing lines that trap birds – as the lines are untangled the bird flies free. Here is a good example of the impact that releasing embedded emotions and negative attachments can have on others.

MaryAnn's Story
A few years ago, I gave a series of seminars in New York. MaryAnn was enthralled with the symbol workshop I ran in a downtown recording studio used in the past by several famous sixties and seventies rock

bands. The event had become a truly magical experience with the power of symbols plus the exotic location. The next day MaryAnn sat through the Cutting the Cords workshop and told me in true New Yorker style that she felt it wasn't working for her.

'Nothing like as powerful as last night,' she declared.

I pressed on and persuaded her to get involved which she did reluctantly.

'Can I cut the cords for someone else?' she asked.

'No, but you can release your own connection with the person or people involved' I replied.

She huffed and puffed, obviously cynical and unimpressed. Two weeks later I received a letter from her.

Some forty years ago she had broken up with her husband and since then had little or no connection with him neither had he been in touch with their daughter Suzanne. Maryann had long got over any residual feelings about her husband and this was why she had been cynical about cutting the cord to him. However, she had gone ahead and cut the cords, holding the intention that it would free any negative energies between them. She willed him to get in touch with Suzanne because her daughter was suffering from severe depression and MaryAnn felt that a visit from her father would help her. Amazingly, the day after the workshop she had a phone call from her ex-husband! He had felt a powerful urge to be in touch with the family and was upset to learn of Suzanne's ill health. He immediately got touch with his daughter and already she was showing signs of improvement.

MaryAnn admitted she had never let go of the anger she felt towards him and she was especially bitter over his lack of attention to their daughter. By expressing her feelings and letting go her negative attitude she had cleared the energies and opened the way for him to connect again.

Cutting cords can release emotions and attitudes

As well as setting yourself free from the past, cutting the cords can also help you to improve current relationships where the first flush of love has faded and negativity is creeping in. This process can revitalise and cleanse any relationship: lover, friend, work, child and parent. Here are some of the emotions and attitudes that can be souring your relationship and can be cleared as you cut through the toxic cords that may be developing.

- Anger.
- Bitterness and resentment.
- Guilt about something you did.
- Blame – blaming them for a situation you are in.
- Jealousy – you are suffering unwanted feelings of envy about someone or something.
- Frustration and irritation – someone or a company not acting fast enough for you.
- Revulsion – if you keep deriding a prominent character or politician, you are feeding them with your attention and bringing down your own energy.
- Fear – if you constantly think of a situation or person that fills you with fear you are constantly re-establishing your connection to them.
- Expectation – if you expect more from a person than they can give.

Journal:
Do you have a relationship that could benefit from a refresh? Write down all those that you could improve and plan to perform the ritual below for them all, not necessarily in one go but over time cleanse and clear all toxic relationships.

Situations that can benefit from cutting the cords
- Improving a current relationship of any kind where negative attitudes or emotions are spoiling your connection.

- Letting go of your desire to live in the past e.g. a home or country you have left behind, a work situation that has changed etc.

- Releasing yourself from the toxic feelings of anger and hate for someone who has harmed you.

- To express love that you may regret not sharing with

someone who has died. Your attachment through guilt can prevent them from moving on spiritually.

- Letting go of any attachment that is causing you distress and stopping you from enjoying the moment.

- You are restless and expecting more, you have expectations that are not fulfilled. Let go of the need for more

Happiness as contentment comes when you don't want more
Now are you ready to cut your own cords? This is a powerful healing process so give yourself time and space. I am sending you love as you go through this. Good luck!

Ritual: Cutting the Cord
The ritual comes in three parts. You can modify this to suit your own situation and make it appropriate for the releasing you need.

- **1. Releasing old negative emotions.** Express all emotions and feelings that you have around an attachment that you now wish to release.

- **2. Transforming these emotions.** Burn your writing so that all emotions transform into light energy in the flames.

- **3. Setting yourself free.** Place a thread around your wrist to represent the cord of attachment and break it.

Journal:
Write down the names of the people or situations that you wish to release. Write down why you want to let go.

Before you let them go, write the benefits you have taken from your experiences with them. What lessons did learn from your time and association with this person? What strengths have you gained? Have you grown stronger as a character?

Part One – Releasing Emotions
The most effective way of releasing any dark and heavy feelings that you may have bottled up for a long time is to write them down. As you write, the energy of your emotion moves into the ink and paper and is released; negative feelings are toxic; you need to clear them

from your spirit, your mind and your body. You can write what you feel in letter form, although it will never be posted, so you can speak directly to the person concerned without harm. If this doesn't suit you just let your feelings flow onto the paper. We often hold onto our feelings for the sake of our family, for fear of losing someone or from cultural pressures. This is now your chance to say everything that you haven't said or that you have poured out to friends but still churn in your mind day after day. You can be as explicit as you wish and let any anger and venom held within you go into the paper once and for all. This way of releasing causes no harm to you or the person involved but is a great form of healing. Don't share the contents of your letter with anyone but focus on the sense of letting go and setting yourself free.

A love letter: You can write a love letter to someone who has passed away. This will enable you to share all the love you have for them and anything you wish you had shared while they were alive. You can also share some of your latest experiences and family news. When you burn this letter, know that they will receive it in Spirit and will know what you are feeling and sharing. This will help you let go of regrets, guilt and bring them closer to your heart.

Part Two – Transform by Burning
Once you have written your letters and expressed your feelings in your writing, your emotions will now be in the paper. Burning the paper will transform the emotions and feelings that you have written. Watch the flames turn the negativity into light. The smoke disperses the energy, sometimes as thin white wisps, sometimes yellow and thick when heavy energies are being released. Congratulate yourself for this powerful healing.

If your circumstances prevent you from burning the paper, then tear it into the smallest pieces and flush it into a drain or waste bin where it cannot harm anyone. As you do this visualise flames consuming the paper. Hold the intention that these toxic feelings are released forever. Goodbye!

Part Three – Cord Cutting Meditation

- Either tie a cotton thread around your wrist or get someone to help you to do this. The thread represents the cord of attachment that you wish to release. You may have more than one cord to break and this is fine, but to help you focus don't do more than three in one session and preferable put all your focus and intention on one.

- Find a quiet spot where you can meditate without interruption. Turn off your phone. Make yourself comfortable. Drop your shoulders and relax by breathing deeply four times.

- Call in your protection: The Blue Flame of Archangel Michael, the Protection Symbol or Three Golden Pyramids. Say; 'I am protected, my energy is sealed and only positive vibrations can come through to me.'

- To ground yourself: imagine your feet develop roots that grow deep down into the ground, down through the many layers of the Earth's surface, through underground streams and rock beds, deep to the heart of Mother Earth. You are now grounded and secure.

- Visualise yourself walking through woods on a sunny day. The sun shines through the trees creating pools of light on your path. There is a cooling breeze and you are the perfect temperature.

- In the distance you see an old red brick wall. This wall surrounds your personal healing garden. The garden of your heart. As you get closer you notice a wooden door set in the wall and you walk up to it now.

- Open the door and step inside, close the door behind you. You are now in the most beautiful garden. It is filled with your favourite flowers, shrubs and trees. Take time to enjoy the peace and serenity.

- Follow the path that leads you through the garden and you will pass pools filled with lotus flowers and water lilies. Fountains and tumbling streams sparkle in the sunlight.

- Keep following this path and it will take you deeper and deeper into your heart garden. Feel the love.

- Eventually you come to an inner garden. This also has a wall around it. Enter through the gate.

- This garden is filled with pink roses. See a bench seat where you can rest. Sit there and enjoy the sight of hundreds of roses in full bloom surrounding you.

- Mist flows into the garden. At the far end, the person that you wish to release appears. Sense and see the cord that still links you to that person. Say whatever you wish as a farewell.

- Break the cord around your wrist as you let them go and set yourself free.

- The person you are releasing will leave the garden now. Spend a few moments focusing on the positives that you have gained from knowing them and the experiences that you have shared.

- In your own time, leave the rose garden that represents the Core of your heart but know it is always there for you to find love and peace. Walk back down the path out of the outer garden, down the path, through the woods and back into the room.

- Well done! Congratulate yourself with a big hug. Bless you.

To help your heart centre recover, you can apply a healing balm, such as heart balm (see Appendix) or rose essential oil. Wear gemstones such as pink rose quartz or green tourmaline or place under your pillow.

Breaking Patterns

So many of my clients have problems in either starting a relationship or finding that none develop into loving and committed partnerships. When I discuss their choice of partners I often find a pattern; that their partners have similar characteristics and they treat them in similar abusive or negative ways. Patterns develop when you fail to learn the lesson of being discerning in your choices and continue to follow a set mindset or belief. A girlfriend of mine had an abusive father, then married a man who regularly beat and terrified her; her next partner didn't beat her but didn't respect her, putting his adult children before her constantly. Finally, she learned her lesson which was to value herself enough to have a loving relationship and she broke the pattern; she chose a man who respected and loved her. Many of my clients have gone through any number of failures before they wake up to realising that they are worth better choices.

Jill's Story

Jill came to see me after she had terminated a disastrous relationship. She had been left by her lover and, from what she said, this was just one of her many disastrous relationships during her adult life. She was drawn to overbearing, dominant men and ended up being abused by them. As a reaction she began to make connections with men who were either under-sexed or homosexual. Her move towards homosexual men was her way of protecting herself by drawing her towards 'safe' relationships. She wasn't happy in any of these relationships and looked to break the pattern of her choice of sexual partners.

I sensed this was a pattern she had contracted to change in this lifetime, so any intent and focus on this problem would be beneficial and work well for her. I led her through a healing meditation; to visualise the word 'abuse' carved in wood and to see herself breaking this up with an axe. She told me afterwards that she was into the visualisation immediately and found it incredibly easy to break up the wooden block.

As she threw the chippings onto the fire, I saw many women from around the world burning wooden effigies and plaques inscribed with the words of their pattern of choosing dominant and abusive men. These women were laughing and crying and throwing their offerings with abandonment and joy, such a wonderful release for them all. When we release a negative ingrained pattern of thinking or behaviour we can affect many others; linked by our spiritual and energetic connections to those with similar vibration, experiencing similar situations and holding similar beliefs and attitudes. As we shift they feel the change in energy dynamics and it lifts them and helps them to also change. If enough of us consciously move away from being mistreated in any way, then eventually all humans will choose to be treated equally and fairly. We have seen this recently with the MeToo movement.

Everyone is connected; you impact the world with your positive choices and love.

If you were brought up in an environment where you were abused, then there is a very high possibility that you will find yourself in the same situation again. It is imperative that you take responsibility for breaking the pattern to rescue your own self-esteem and also to save the next generation from repeating the process.

Jill felt totally empowered and lightened by the experience of her release. The last I heard she was in a loving relationship.

The impact on your heart and soul will last forever when you:

- make a positive choice about your life direction or a partner

- raise your vibration by choosing love and respect for yourself, not fear

- release negative attitudes and expectations of yourself, others and life

- decide you are worthy of a loving partner, not a bully or abusive one. Walk away at the first signs of obsessive or abusive behaviour

Journal:
Are there any patterns in your own relationships? Do you find yourself drawn towards inappropriate or unsuitable partners? If so, I suggest you follow this next ritual with the intention of breaking the pattern and believing that you can have a successful and equal, balanced relationship without abuse where you are respected and loved.

Ritual: to Break a Pattern
- Write down the pattern that you wish to break.

- Acknowledge and write your intention of breaking your pattern. Trust your intuition to guide you to a safe and supportive relationship. Say, 'I choose a partner who loves and respects me.' Repeat twice.

- Either follow these next steps in an open safe place or visualise yourself doing them.

- Take a piece of wood and either engrave the words that represent your pattern or write the pattern you have followed repeatedly on a piece of paper.

- Break the wood into pieces or tear up the paper and throw it on the fire. Say, 'I am breaking the pattern forever; now, right now, right now.' Repeat twice.

- See the fire consume the old pattern and transform it into light.

- Well done. Keep yourself connected by using the Morning Ritual in Chapter One and listen to your intuition when entering into any new relationship.

Being Open to New Love

After you have spent time clearing and healing your heart, you may feel you are ready for a new loving relationship.

Keep your heart open and:

- do the Morning Ritual regularly; it will keep you protected, connected and open your heart ready to receive.

- send distance healing to the people you know need help; this will exercise your heart and like any muscle, it will grow bigger and stronger.

- help others; giving brings more than good karma; it expands your heart.

Make yourself happy.

- Don't look for someone else to make you happy. See a partner as someone to share life's experiences and to help each other grow, but don't expect them to make you happy – this is your job!

- In your journal write down a list of things that make you smile and lift your spirits, and focus on them as much as you can.

- Do you enjoy your work? If not, what work could you do that would make you happy?

- Spend some time in nature – animals, birds, the countryside and the sea will all help to lift you up. Get out of the city for a while.

- If you are struggling, spend more time on activities and being with people rather than analysing and pondering why you are not happy. Not many people will take too deep an investigation into whether they are truly happy. Most of us make the best of what we have and enjoy what we can. Seeking perfection can be a depressing task.

- If life is hard and you are suffering, lift yourself up and refocus on something that can lift your spirits. When my husband Tony had cancer and I felt overwhelmed with worry, I simply went up into the clouds and sat there. Everything seemed less challenging from up there!

Dating

Although Internet dating can be frustrating, it sets your intention that you are open to meeting someone and sends out that message to the world. It also keeps you focused on mixing and connecting. Don't sit at home waiting for love to knock on the door! Unless you plan to fall in love with the Amazon delivery man!

- Keep your sense of humour!

- Don't waste time with a prospective partner once you know that you are far from compatible.

- Let your relationship build slowly, texting, then phone calls, then coffee dates, then and only then meet for an evening.

- Forget about perfection! There is no such thing as the perfect partner. See the overall package of a person and overlook a few weak spots unless they are ones that really matter to you.

- Don't give up! There will be someone who you can share time with – even if your hunt is not leading you to a perfect partnership; sharing, spending time with someone and having fun can get you back into the zone of commitment and deeper relationships.

Use discretion and discernment in choosing your relationships

- When you are meeting someone for the first time, use your discernment and don't be bowled over by looks and image.

- Check out how a person makes you feel and respond accordingly. If you feel a bit nervous or your stomach has negative flutters, step away. If your heart feels as though it is expanding and warm, then step forward.

Look for happiness within yourself before you look for someone to make you happy

Good luck and enjoy the journey of finding romantic love – keep that Sphere of Loving Partnerships filled with fun, laughter and sharing!

Before we leave this chapter on your heart and relationships, there is one more relationship we need to address and that is your relationship with yourself.

Your Ego – Your Relationship with Yourself

Let's have another look at the diagram that shows the heart spheres.

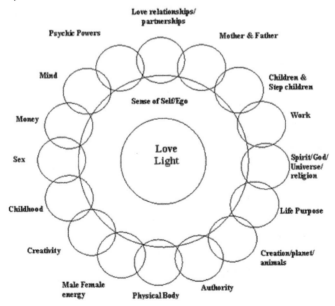

175

Around the core of your heart, your true self, you will see a ring that represents your ego. Your ego is your sense of self, this can be inflated – you think you are pretty amazing and better than most, or it can be deflated – you are self-critical and consider yourself inferior to other people. Often, we refer to these two states as having a positive or negative ego. Your goal is to improve your relationship with yourself and to have a balanced ego which neither creates arrogance nor is so self-effacing and critical that you more or less disappear. So here are some steps you can take to improve your relationship with yourself.

For a balanced ego make it your aim to:

- be aware of who you are, acknowledge your traits, skills, strengths and weaknesses

- accept yourself without criticism but know what character aspects you would like to strengthen, develop or dissolve

- value yourself and acknowledge what you can achieve

- understand that depression can be caused by self-criticism, aiming above your abilities, seeking perfection and unrealistic aspirations

- be as kind and loving to yourself as you are to others; giving yourself breaks and treats and not driving yourself too hard

- be aware when the hardships and challenges of your life are affecting the balance of your sense of self; when your self-esteem, self-confidence, self-control, self-worth are being compromised. Then take a course of action to rebalance your life

- make sure you heal yourself and rebalance the giving and receiving aspects of your relationship with yourself

Ritual: Rebalancing your Ego
You can follow this to help you restore a healthy and positive Sense of self.

- The key is to have all the spheres of your heart pulsing with love and with a full connection between the sphere and your ring of confidence – your ego, your sense of self.

Set your intention to come to that state now by saying 'My goal is an open and healed heart filled with love.' Repeat twice more.

- Say, 'My ego is in total balance; now, right now, right now. Draw the Balance Symbol three times in front of you.

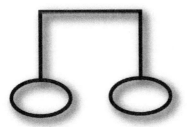

Balance Symbol: Draw left sphere then the lines then the right sphere three times

- Draw the Healing Symbol three times over your heart and place your hands on your heart centre. Feel the love filling all the spheres of your heart and flowing into the centre filling and healing your ego as it flows.

Healing Symbol: Draw the symbol in the air three times from right to left; finish with the dot.

Your heart is a beautiful place where you can love and accept yourself and where your happiness lies. I suggest you spend most of your time there.

In the next chapter, I will share the consequences of guilt, as well as the law of karma, the impact of broken promises and the long-term effects of spiritual vows.

Journal:
Keep a note on the changes, if any occur in your relationship as you work on your heart.

CHAPTER *Five*

Karma, Past Lives, Guilt and Vows

We have seen how guilt can close the door to your heart of hearts and your true self; how it can limit your life, change your perception of yourself and damage your sense of self-worth. Now, we will look a little closer at the spiritual implications of guilt and shame. I will lead you through a healing to clear some of the repercussions of your actions that have left you with remorse and regret. We will see how the consequences of broken promises or spiritually-made vows can have a very long reach and seriously affect your life and your sense of ease with yourself.

What you give out, will return.

The Law of Karma

The Spiritual law of karma declares that whatever you do to others will have an impact on yourself – what you give out will come back to you. Energetically whatever vibrations you send out will be matched in return, although not necessarily from the same source. Karma is the law of cause and effect. Every time you think or do something, you create a cause, which in time will bear its corresponding effects. Therefore, if you give love then you get love back; if you cause pain to others you will suffer at some stage in the future – either in this or a future lifetime.

Your positive vibes will come back to you and your negative vibes will also – this is often called good karma and bad karma. From an onlooker's perspective, karma can seem like retribution for someone who has acted harmfully; from an insider position it can seem like personal bad luck. One of our lessons is to accept responsibility for our actions and to understand the Law of karma.

Karma acts as spiritual justice.

Guilt

Guilt can bring you pain and suffering: stabbing sensations in your solar plexus, pain and discomfort in your heart chakra, weakness and dread that saps your energy or a sense of worthlessness that affects your self-esteem and confidence. Guilt affects you in many ways; through your mind – creating negative beliefs and perceptions of yourself; your body – gnawing away at your solar plexus and bowels creating acidity and digestive problems; your spirit-blocking your heart with your sense of worthlessness and disconnecting you from your higher self and God. Emotionally it can trigger anger and frustration that spills out to the way you treat people and so continues to feed the karmic flow and attracts more negativity into your life.

The level of guilt you feel will be determined by your awareness and empathy for those you have hurt. Someone with a low level of compassion and understanding of other people's feelings will not be too concerned about the fallout of their actions. They will therefore not be so aware of or suffer from guilt. This doesn't mean that their karma is less! They are likely to blame the negative situations that their karma attracts as bad luck or someone else's fault. It can take this person some time to wake up to their responsibility and claim the cause of their bad luck.

If, on the other hand, you are sensitive and conscious of the feelings of others, you can be racked with guilt and its side effects for even the smallest misdemeanour.

Relief from Karma

How can you relieve the feelings of guilt? How can you clear your karma? What if your 'bad' action was in another lifetime – like my life as a slave driver?

Your higher self is forever directing your soul to clear imprints, heal the pain and to work through and clear your karma. It is constantly trying to guide you to finding love and inner peace. So as soon as you start to suffer from guilt it will be leading you through atonement, retribution and forgiveness, in other words, clearing your karma.

Your higher self will guide you to atone and clear your karma.

Atonement
The antidote to the flow of karma – its boomerang response – is ever, love. The forces of karma can be calmed and cleared through loving actions: caring for others, giving unselfishly, making time for other people; by showing compassion and kindness through thoughts and actions. The outward flow of love will also ease the pain that comes with guilt and will help your 'clean your karmic slate'. The Buddhists believe you rack up points for every good deed your do.

David's Story
This is a story of a loving and sensitive soul, a man with a kind heart who suffered from his own demons. From the age of fifteen David became troubled. His emotions took him high and low and he developed a negative attitude towards his schooling and family. The belief that his father was the cause of his inner turmoil continued into his early twenties. They affected his state of mind – or maybe his state of mind affected his emotions, but he suffered depression and suicidal feelings. He didn't believe in love. He developed unexplained and untreatable physical ailments, severe headaches, sinus problems and fatigue. He found solace in a relationship with a beautiful young woman and they had a child. But the negative feelings persisted and he sat at home while his wife took on three jobs to support him and their child. He couldn't explain why he felt so bad, why he couldn't show his wife the love she needed. When their child was very young his wife died tragically, and he blamed himself for not recognising her problem and not saving her. Whether he could have saved her we will never know, but the result was that he was even more affected by the demons of his mind and emotions.

He continued to blame others for his situation but took on the responsibility of his child and looked after her well, although the barrier around his heart caused by the guilt prevented him from responding to her emotional needs. He cut himself off from his friends, avoided his family and blocked off the windows of his house – a reflection of the barriers he had placed around his heart. His negative thoughts about his situation created stronger and darker thoughtforms that took on their own energy and appeared as demons to torment him and he fell into a state of psychosis. He believed his child was being stalked and they would both be killed by unseen protagonists. He lived in a constant state of fear.

One day he had a dream/vision and heard God telling him that his bad luck and troubles were not caused by his family, but were created by his own attitudes. He then turned full 180 degrees and started to consciously blame himself. His psychosis reached desperate levels and he entered hospital for treatment. Years later he is still taking medication to control the anxiety and unprovoked negative thoughts of his condition. But when he left hospital he took responsibility for his own situation and set off on his road of redemption. He dropped the role of victim. He began to put his daughter and her feelings, needs, desires and expectations first in his life. He opened his heart to his family and the beautiful soul that he is shone out to the world. After twenty years of unselfish devotion to his daughter he has found peace of heart if not of mind. He is still sick, but his physical problems have cleared, he sleeps well at night now, he has reunited with his friends who all adore him, he is a positive and loving member of his family again. He has cleared his karma.

Much of David's karma came from a previous lifetime but as with all past life 'unfinished business' it was reflected into this lifetime, giving him the opportunity to heal and complete the challenge, to resolve incomplete steps of his evolving journey to the goal of his soul. This goal is the same for all souls: to find total peace with oneself, to become fully conscious, cleared of all imprints and negative beliefs and reach the state referred to as enlightenment; to be filled with light.

What you can do consciously to clear your karma:

- drop the role of victim
- take responsibility for your own happiness and inner peace.
- help others with kindness and unselfish acts
- put love as your highest priority; for others and yourself

Journal:
Do you think you are suffering the results of the law of karma
in a positive or negative way? If you feel you need to atone for
something, some thoughtless action or hurt – what do you plan to
do about it? Make it a priority to clear the air, seek forgiveness and
move on with love.

My Karmic Gift

Twenty or so years ago I was sitting in the kitchen of a dear friend in Kuala Lumpur, Malaysia (I will call her Karen). It was late and we were having a deep discussion about our parents and our childhoods. Whereas my story was a happy one, not so for Karen. She was born and brought up in Singapore, where her paternal grandfather had built up a wealthy and thriving business empire including a shipping line between his homeland of China and Malaya; he also had factories in mainland China and Singapore. Karen's father, Desmond, was one of thirteen children; he was a gentle and kindly man with a big compassionate heart. One day he was walking through the main street of Singapore when he saw a young woman being beaten and thrown into the gutter. Life was tough and rough in the days of post-war Asia and this was not an unusual sight, but the plight of the girl touched his heart and he picked her up, took her home and cared for her. Quite quickly he fell in love with the woman, whom we will call Daisy.

Desmond's family would never have approved a marriage with a woman who had been on the streets and described as 'a used shoe'! So he set her up in an apartment as his mistress and they had two children. For the men of rich Chinese families this was no big deal and very common. In time his family set up an arranged marriage for him and despite his love for Daisy, he accepted these plans as a dutiful son should. On the night before the wedding his mother discovered an old woman outside the gates of the family home, burning paper and incense, blowing the smoke into the house and garden and chanting. She turned the woman away and kicked the pile of burning paper with bound feet until they were extinguished, but by the time she had returned to the house, she lost the power of her legs and for over two weeks she was unable to walk. At the time there was talk of a curse, but nobody thought more of it. But it appears that a curse had been cast with the intention of more mischief than just to take the strength from the old lady's legs. Despite sleeping with his beautiful and desirable new wife Desmond could not consummate the marriage. After a year of trying the marriage was dissolved, by which time Daisy was pregnant with their third child. Hoping this one would be a male and a legitimate heir, he and family friends pressed his parents to allow him to marry Daisy despite her background. Reluctantly they agreed. Daisy was delighted and couldn't wait to give birth to the boy she so desired, for a son would make her an accepted member of this rich and influential family.

Unfortunately, and with great anguish she gave birth to a girl, my friend Karen. Daisy was furious and throughout her childhood despised and rejected Karen; she treated her cruelly and never once showed her any affection. She took her own inner pain and scars from her troubled past out on Karen; she certainly had a reason for her closed heart and cold-hearted ways.

Pain turns to cruelty.

That night in her kitchen, Karen shared her mother Daisy's dreadful background. Daisy's mother, Dorothy had been wife number four of a rich Chinese man in Singapore and had given him five children. When he died, wives one, two and three took all his money and threw Dorothy, Daisy and her siblings into the street. They lived in desperate poverty until the two oldest girls reached thirteen and fourteen; she then sent them to work in the equivalent of an escort agency and the family lived off the money they made. Once the girls reached the marriageable age of sixteen, Dorothy sold them into marriage to old men. Daisy's husband died when she was in her early twenties, leaving her quite well off. However, soon after his death she fell in love with a playboy. He quickly went through her money and when it had all gone he forced her into prostitution. One day she turned against him and refused to work so he beat her nearly to death and threw her into the gutter, which is where Karen's father found her. There is no doubt that the awful experiences of her young life had left her scarred and bitter.

Despite her rescue from the street and the kindness of Karen's father, the past had left its mark and as she grew up my friend became the focus of her mother's hardened heart. She attacked Karen's dog, she killed birds that ate her seeds when she planted out a vegetable garden and she punished her for the smallest misdemeanour. Karen's father tried to protect her but he shied from confrontation and found it difficult to stand up to his wife's aggression, and although his wife turned against him too, he continued to love her. Daisy became more and more discontented and the final straw came when the mass of fortune left by Desmond's father disappeared into the hands of the newly formed Chinese and Singaporean governments, leaving the family comfortable but not mega-rich. She took all the property that had been given to her by Desmond and placed in her name – something she had demanded to counteract her paranoia of being left destitute again and left him poor and heartbroken. Karen looked up at me at this point in the story and she said:

'My father then lost the use of his legs; he couldn't walk and has been bed-bound ever since.'

Shocked, I looked at Karen and felt a strange frisson passing through my body.

I said, 'That is such a karmic story.'

As soon as the words were out, I felt a massive surge of energy and the electrical appliances in the kitchen revved up and went into overdrive; the fridge, the water cooler and the ceiling fans all came on in full force. Then I saw a vision like a moving video showing me a number of past lives Desmond and Daisy had shared; each one showing powerful emotions and either one of them getting hurt in their love affairs. As the vision faded, I felt a mega surge of light energy filling me and a powerful voice told me I had been given the gift to clear karma. As the sensations faded I opened my eyes to see Karen staring at me open-mouthed.

'There was a bright light shining from you and filling the room,' she said. 'Oh, my God that was amazing; I need a cup of tea and a cake!'

I laughed and said, 'And I need a large whisky.'

I realised afterwards that clearing their karma also cleared the powerful curse that Daisy had paid the old woman to put on the family. The curse not only paralysed Desmond's mother's legs and made him impotent in his arranged marriage, I also made Desmond paralysed once she no longer wanted him and who knows, could also have lost the family their fortune!

After their karma was cleared, Karen was able to have a reconciliation with her mother and her father passed away peacefully. From that day, I have been able to help people shift their karmic burdens when their higher self and their soul feels that lessons have been learnt and when divine grace is given. I am simply the channel to allow this grace to flow through to enable the releasing of the heavy energies of guilt and shame and raise the vibration so that guilt can also be released. The results can be beautiful and life changing.

Clearing karma is an act of forgiveness and divine grace.

With karmic clearing and healing, you can change your life around. Here is a typical outcome from Peter whom I worked with on the phone. I cleared his karma and channelled healing to him during the session. This is an excerpt of a letter I received from his wife afterwards.

Anne, life for both Peter and I has improved dramatically, financially things have taken a turn and we were able to buy a new house. My daughter Barbara is expecting her first baby in July and we both feel generally that an enormous weight has lifted from our shoulders. We can't thank you enough for the intervention with the Archangel Michael to release the karma that was making this life miserable.

Journal:
Do you feel you are affected by karma created by your past actions?

Ritual: Clearing Karma
It is hard to clear your own karma other than through atonement and forgiveness, but this ritual can help you connect to divine grace. We hand over the ability to release the guilt and clear the karmic slate and, as in all healing, let the higher self decide if it is for the highest good. If you have a valuable lesson to learn and have not yet learnt it, you may choose to continue to carry your karmic debt.

- Stand in front of the person you are helping; they should be sitting, relaxed and calm.

- Call in their guides and angels to assist in the healing.

- Call in protection. For example, say; 'I call in the Blue Flame of Archangel Michael to seal and protect your energy, only positive energy can come through to you.'

- Draw the Power Symbol over their head three times.

Power Symbol: draw the two loops, left then right. Then draw the two short lines, the curve and lastly, the dot.

- Say, 'If it is for your highest good and with Divine Grace, your karma is cleared; now, right now, right now.' Sweep down the entire body to the floor.

- 'Your karma is cleared, all guilt released and all transformed into wisdom; now, right now, right now.'

- Complete the session by drawing the Healing Symbol and filling the person with loving light energies.

- Finish with the Preserving Symbol.

Karmic Cords and Vows in Relationships

Karmic cords are those that are created by promises and vows and can pass from lifetime to lifetime; they lock your soul into a connection and commitment. Vows made in churches, temples and sacred places can have very strong and long-lasting effects and, without you knowing, can affect your life and relationships in this lifetime. If you break a vow, you immediately set off a karmic reaction and this too can affect how you feel towards someone and can attract negative reactions. In Karen's parents' situation they were locked into an ongoing path and pattern, chained by their past actions and promises that had been made long ago in past incarnations. Here is the story of one of my clients who knew that her relationship was affected by some powerful negative forces from her past.

Pamela's Story

Pamela had an unusual problem. Her current relationship with Frank was one based on an overwhelming sexual drive that drew her and her partner together with an amazing and insatiable force. This might have been wonderful, but they were not compatible in so many other areas. He was a very religious man and would rather abstain from earthly affairs and material matters. He wanted to live a simple and quiet life. She on the other hand, was vivacious and fun and desired a fuller and more uplifting lifestyle. She was extremely spiritual but believed that we are here to live our lives in this reality to the fullest and to enjoy ourselves on our route through! She smoked, he didn't, she drank, he didn't, she socialised, he preferred his books, she loved sex and felt great afterwards, he felt full of shame! Despite their differences, there was a strong pull towards each other and this had turned into love, so their incompatibility was upsetting her and she felt the need to release the push and pull energies between them. She felt locked in by the sexual drive that was bonding them together. She was convinced this was a karmic connection and that they had probably lived together in the past. She also said she was prepared to sacrifice the relationship rather than let it continue in this unsatisfactory way.

Before we cleared the cords, I did a scan of her past and saw a couple of interesting lives flicker before me. I saw Frank as a priest besotted by her. She was a prostitute in that lifetime and teased and taunted him with her sexuality. He could not restrain himself and had a tumultuous affair with her. He died in great torment, filled with guilt and the shame of breaking his spiritual vows of celibacy. In the second lifetime I saw a similar scenario but this time he was a monk and he ended the relationship and his torment by strangling her! No wonder she felt so strongly drawn by this man! However, I must put it on record that she is by no means a harlot in this lifetime!

When we came to the cord-cutting exercise I saw a whole bunch of cords that were completely entwined. She tried pulling them apart, but we needed to resort to cutting. She did the majority of the cutting with our hidden helpers and I assisted. It was hard going, but eventually most of the cords were disconnected with just three left, one being black. The black one was the most difficult and I believe represented the negative emotions of shame and guilt that came from those torrid past lives. When this last cord finally broke we both felt a huge energetic release. It left her feeling quite weak and she needed a great deal of healing afterwards. Later she told me that after that session he lost his sense of shame about sex and they had a perfectly balanced relationship, honouring their differences but with great love between them. They married and lived happily together for many years till he passed away.

Indicators that you are karmically tied to someone

While you are on the higher planes before you arrive, you set up promises and arrangements with other souls to help you to learn lessons. They will create situations and experiences that challenge you. See Chapter Two Life Lessons. You may have made vows in a previous lifetime that are locked in through all subsequent life cycles; for example I have cleared vows where people have promised to love someone forever and ever; which can prove to be very challenging when personality, cultures and genetics change us so much from one life to the next. Modern marriage vows have a get-out clause. They say, 'as long as you both shall live.' Vows made in previous lifetimes can draw us into relationships that simply won't work.

Here are some clues that you may have made a promise or a vow.

- When you meet, you are immediately drawn to each other, even though you cannot understand why.

- You have a relationship that is a 'can't live with' and 'can't live without' situation. No matter what your partner does you get drawn back to them even when the relationship has become toxic.

- You feel yourself being drawn into a relationship that you know isn't right for you, but you feel you cannot escape.

- Some relationships are not love matches but people we meet as our bosses, workmates, friends, neighbours and spiritual advisors. These can also be karmic and you can feel trapped and unable to walk away despite negative feelings.

My first marriage was to a lovely man whom I felt I knew well from the moment we met. The pull was so strong we seemed to fall into each other's arms. However, in our relationship, we were more brother and sister than lovers. We got along well, and we enjoyed each other's company very much, but the intimate side of our marriage was non-existent. It was sad to break up but as I look back I can see that we had past life commitments and promises to be together that didn't work with our current incarnations. However, we helped each other through the formative years of our early twenties.

Journal:
Do you think you are tied to someone who isn't suitable for you or from whom you feel you would like to step away?

Ritual: Clearing Karmic Vows and Ties

Use this ritual for setting yourself free from any commitments you have made in the past; particularly vows made in past lives that lock you heart and soul into connections that aren't appropriate for your life this time around.

- In a quiet place, turn off phones and make yourself comfortable and relaxed. Drop your shoulders and let your body go soft.

- Call in your protection and say, 'Only positive energies can come through to me; my spirit and energy field are sealed and protected.' Ask Archangel Michael and your guides to be with you.

- Release yourself from all commitments to people who are not appropriate for this lifetime. Say out loud four times; 'I release and dissolve all vows, promises and contracts that no longer serve my highest good, I release them now, right now, right now.'

- Visualise cords connecting you to the person you wish to release, see a pair of golden scissors in your hand now.

- Use the scissors to cut through the cords that bind you.

- Use your hands to chop through the cords by cutting them in your palm now. Say, 'Dissolve and release all karmic ties that no longer serve me; now, right now, right now.'

- Well done. Give yourself a hug!

Journal:

Write down all the positives that came from that relationship. By doing this you are transforming the energy and not one moment of the time you have had together is wasted.

Now we look at how karma, past life situations and vows can affect other areas of your life.

Your past will have left impressions on your soul memory and even when karma is not involved, you can find that some of your current difficulties can be traced back to contracts and vows you made in the past. Also, negative experiences can have left you with fears that prevent you from wholesome and expansive experiences in this life.

Following are examples of situations I have come across frequently with my clients and ways that you can clear the imprints.

The Impact of Vows and Imprints from your Past

Vows and imprints creating financial difficulties

Your ability to attract money, hold onto wealth or even be comfortable with having more money than you need to survive can be affected by a vow you made when you were in a religious order in a past life. I have had many clients who have money issues; either feeling guilty to have money; fearing losing money; fearing lack of money, and many who feel that to be spiritual, they should give away all their possessions and wealth.

There is nothing spiritual about lack or poverty.

Possible reasons:

- vows of poverty made when serving time as a monk or nun

- persecuted or reviled for your wealth

- loss of happiness as your wealth increased leading you to swear you would never be rich again

- being killed for your money

Having money gives you the choice to be generous and help others.

Ritual: Clearing vows relating to poverty

- Clear your vows. Say three times, 'I release and dissolve all vows of poverty made in any lifetime. I release them now, right now, right now.'

- Repeat this mantra daily; 'I accept the abundance of life, I am open to the flow of money and accept financial security; now, right now, right now.'

- Use the Abundance Symbol.

Abundance Symbol: draw in front of you from left to right then add the line.

Allow yourself to be in the flow of abundance.

Vows and Imprints affecting conception

A midwife came to me for healing sessions because she had been having difficulty conceiving. Doctors found her husband had a low sperm count and she had a condition that could make her infertile, but she hoped I could help. My immediate thought was that her experiences in her work with difficult births and side effects, had left her with fear and that was blocking her from conceiving. But one day I saw one of her past lives; maybe two hundred years previously, when she had buried five small children. Devastated and heartbroken she leant on the mantelpiece of her living room and swore, 'I will never have children again.'

Ritual: Clearing vows and imprints around childbirth

- Clear any vows you made after difficult births for you or as a husband, also clear vows that you have made in a female lifetime swearing you will never give birth again. I think that there may be quite a few women making this vow! Say, 'I release and dissolve all vows that I have ever made that prevent me from conceiving and having a healthy child, I release them; now, right now, right now.' Repeat two more times.

- Use the Fertility Symbol. Draw it three times over your body

Fertility Symbol: Start drawing from the top and finish with the dot.

- Use this mantra or something similar, 'I am fertile and I conceive with joy and gratitude.'

Most of us have at least 12 redundant vows.

Vows and imprints creating difficulty finding a loving relationship

During a workshop I discussed the vows that we made in past lives living in religious orders as monks, nuns or followers of strict religious laws. I explained how the vows of chastity can make you fearful or reluctant to have sex. One of the women in the group burst into tears as she realised this was exactly the problem in her marriage. We cleared her vows, although it didn't help her current relationship, and soon after, she divorced. But she soon found love and fulfilment with a partner in another country and she seemed to be very happy with her sex life too!

Ritual: Clearing vows of chastity and imprints from abuse

- Clear any vows of chastity you may have made in past lives as a follower of a religious order or cult. Say three times, 'I release and dissolve all vows of chastity I have ever made in any lifetime. I release them; now, right now, right now.'
- Set the intention to clear and heal any imprints you may be holding from negative sexual experiences, such as rape and abuse from this or previous lives. Say three times, 'It is my intention to clear and heal all imprints caused by

sexual abuse.' You can complete this healing when we do more work on imprints in the next chapter.

- Set your intention to open and heal your heart.

Heart Opening Symbol: Draw the symbol with the circle first then the lines from left to right.

- Put your hands together then open them as you say, 'I open my heart to receive love fearlessly and joyfully.'

Vows and imprints causing blocks for light workers

Many healers, whether they act as spiritual and energy healers or work through therapy, find it difficult to step fully into their role. Very often this is because of a legacy of fear from a previous lifetime when they were persecuted. Society hasn't been very kind to healers in the past and even herbalists were branded as witches and burnt or drowned. If you would love to practise healing but have a fear of stepping forward, you may be affected by a negative past life experience and/or a vow not to do that work again due to the persecution. I have cleared hundreds of such hidden trauma imprints for therapists who either self-sabotage their own careers or simply feel that their opportunities are blocked.

Journal:
What, if any, fear or reluctance do you sense when you say out loud that you are interested in being a healer?

Ritual: Releasing vows and imprints for light workers

- Release any vows you may have made to avoid healing or being known as a healer. Say three times, 'I release and dissolve all vows that prevent me from moving forward as a healer, I release them; now, right now, right now.'

- If you feel anxious at the thought of being known or seen as a healer or any reluctance or blocks around your career progress, then you need to set an intention to get to the bottom of it and identify the imprint and heal it. Either see a healer yourself, or a past life therapist. I will lead you through a regression later in this chapter and you can then access the cause of any reluctance or fear you may carry.

- Face the fear and conquer it by stepping up and giving talks about your work. This will heal and dissolve any past life imprint very effectively.

- Create a mantra to help you with any anxiety. For example, 'I am a channel for the light, all is well and I am blessed.'

Past life impacts on your current life

As we have seen so far with vows and imprints, your past can seriously affect your present. Your wisdom and understanding, your level of consciousness and your spiritual attainment all come from the lessons you have learnt through many lifetimes. But many of the challenges you faced to attain your 'karmic points' of enlightenment can have left quite troublesome memories deep down in your subconscious; fed by the imprints at heart and soul level and brought in from one lifetime to another. If you don't clear these imprints they will stay with you into the next life. In the next chapter I will go deeper into techniques for clearing and healing your soul, but here we will look at the impact of past life experiences and resulting fears and phobias. Understanding where your anxieties come from will start the healing process and in many cases be enough to entirely clear the old imprint.

Journal:

Do you have any inexplicable phobias or fears? Have you had any reluctance to follow certain pursuits or lifestyles since childhood without any understanding why you feel that way?

My fear of horses

All my life I have had an unreasonable fear of horses. As a child in London we lived next door to a coal yard, which used horses to pull the drays, so I was close to and exposed to horses from a young age. However, whenever I got close to one, I felt an inexplicable fear churning in my stomach and I felt all the symptoms of a panic attack. When my husband and I moved to the New Forest where ponies roam unattended everywhere, I decided it was time to find the source of my fear and heal it. I had a friend take me back to the lifetime where the fear began; I ran from a house in the centre of London straight into the path of a carriage and horses. My last moments were filled with the sight of flashing hooves falling down onto me. I went through a releasing and healing process and since then I have lost my desperate fear. However, I give them respect and won't go near mares with foals, but at least I don't tremble at the sight of them anymore or have horrendous nightmares about them!

This leads me to one of the more bizarre fears from a past life.

Wenche's fear of pigeons

One of my clients had a fear of pigeons, and as she lived in the centre of a city, this fear caused her a ridiculous level of stress every day. We discovered her fear came from a memory of being surrounded by pigeons while she was lay dying after being attacked in a city in a past life. When she realised that the pigeons played no part in her death she started to lose her anxieties, and on my next visit to her country she told me her fear had almost entirely disappeared and she was now feeding them on her walks through the city.

Many people have a fear of insects, mice and birds but an overwhelming favourite at the top of the list is the fear of spiders. Up there is also a fear of rats – which is understandable as they are dirty and dangerous. Arachnophobia fear may well come from a memory of being shut in a dark place – perhaps a death experience. Bearing in mind that in the past, most of us had less than comfortable homes and many people certainly died in some pretty ghastly conditions.

Déjà vu

Déjà vu means 'already seen'; it is the feeling that you have been somewhere before, a sense of recollection and despite it being your first visit, your surroundings are familiar to you. This strange sensation can come from visiting somewhere you lived in a previous life, or from a set of circumstances that mirror a past experience. Generally we don't recall our previous lives unless we are in meditation or therapy; on the other hand, children will often have memories.

Eamon's earliest recollections

My girlfriend Brenda remembers as her family walked the streets of Hackney near their home, her young brother Eamon pointing to a nearby street and saying, 'That's where I used to live.' His mother, a strict Catholic didn't believe in reincarnation, so she shushed him up and told him he was talking nonsense. But he persisted, saying, 'My other mother was there,' pointing to a bomb site in the street. This happened consistently much to his mother's distress until he went to school at the age of five.

As you heal your past, you heal the present; as you heal the present you heal your past.

Ritual: Past Life Regression and Healing

This regression technique was given to me by Janet Thompson, one of the best regression therapists I know. You will need someone to hold your space and sit beside you when you do this. Find a quiet and peaceful place; make sure you will not be interrupted and turn off your phones. Clear the space with a room clearing spray or juniper or sage in spring water, or smudge the room by burning sage or frankincense. Before you start, write your intention to go back to heal your fear or phobia. You should allow at least an hour for this process.

- Your helper can read out these instructions and have a pen and paper to take notes of the information you share and insights you gain. The helper should keep the regression moving but not put words into your mouth. Keep sharing what you feel and see. If you get unduly stressed (crying is okay), remember you are looking at this as if it was a video and you can come out and back to this lifetime whenever you wish.

- Lie down and make yourself comfortable with a pillow for your head and cover yourself with a blanket.

- To start your session both you and your helper call in protection and your spirit guides.

- Say out loud your intention to find the past life that will help you to find the cause of your problem and heal it.

Your helper should read the following to guide you:

- Close your eyes and relax, let your body go soft and drop your shoulders down.

- You are in a corridor and walking towards a lift. Press the button to call it to your floor.

- As you wait for it to arrive, your spirit guide steps up to join you. Don't worry if you cannot identify or see your guide clearly; just know that he or she is there with you right now.

- The lift arrives and you and your guide step inside. You are on the tenth floor and you press the button to take you down to level one.

- The lift goes down slowly, one, two, three floors. All is well. You are going down to the past.

- You are now at the seventh floor, sixth floor, fifth floor. Down, down. You are getting closer and closer to your past.

- The lift continues its progress down to the fourth, third, second, first and finally the ground floor.

- The door opens and you step out into a light and airy corridor. On either side are doors that can lead you to your different lifetimes. At the far end is a pure white door that leads to a healing chamber.

- Ask to be guided to the door that leads you to the answers and the cause of your problem.

- Open your chosen door.

- As you step in, you will be taken back to a time past. Look for clues to let you know where and when it is and share everything you see and feel.

- Spend time now sharing your feelings and everything you see and experience.

- Are there any people around you?

- Are you a man or woman?

- Describe your clothing and your surroundings.

- What is your state of mind?

- What are you doing there and what is going on in your life?

- Keep focusing on finding the cause of your problem.

- Once you have discovered it, move out of the room and along the corridor to the healing room.

- You are met in the healing room by angels who fill you with light and love and clear the pain of old memories and scars of traumas.

- After some five minutes or so, slowly leave the healing room and walk along the corridor, back into the lift and back up to your current life.

- Give your helper a hug! Well done.

Frequently Asked Questions

Q: What if I can't see anything when I am regressing?

- A: Allow yourself to relax and you may feel some emotion or feelings. Allow your imagination to feed you with whatever it picks up from your subconscious. If you don't feel anything at all, try another lifetime, go back into the corridor and pick another door. If you still don't feel anything, the reason could be that you have not had your previous incarnations on Earth but on some other planet or dimension. You would be advised to go to a Regression Therapist who could take you to other lifetimes in other dimensions. See Appendix II.

Q: What do I do if I don't know if a problem is from a past life or if I can't manage a regression?

- A: Past life situations and the challenge they offered you to grow will nearly always be repeated in this lifetime so there is no need to be concerned if you don't know if a problem is from a past life. There will be a situation in this life that will draw your attention to the underlying spiritual 'lesson' or development that you intend to gain. Hopefully and most likely, there will be a gentle reminder of your past, so although you may have been tortured for going against the religion of the day, in this lifetime you may be finding it difficult to get your therapy business off the ground and have some opposition from your family – not nearly such a frightening or traumatic experience. You can overcome these blocks and resistance by bravely facing and walking towards your fears – one step at a time.

Remember who you are and reconnect to the best you can be.

Using past life recall to empower and uplift
Although past life regression can be an extremely powerful tool for healing, it can also be a great way to empower yourself. You can choose to go back to a lifetime when you were spiritually empowered, a successful business person, a skilled teacher, happy and contented or a powerful and respected leader. You can use regression to help you with whatever aspects of yourself you would like to enhance by going back to a life when these were strong for you.

Harjeet's Story
My friend Harjeet and I travelled to India, the home of her ancestors for a holiday and she found a new perspective of herself. This is her account of her discovery of a valuable, hidden identity.

October 2017, sitting in the café of the Trident Hotel, Mumbai, having breakfast, I became aware of a haughty and arrogant feeling sweeping through me. It was clearly distinguishable and quite different from my normal self. My awareness of this alien energy stayed with me for the next few days and a picture of a highly powerful Indian lady was emerging in my mind; I could feel her energy and personality. I know when something persists in my mind it is more than imagination. It is something trying to gain my attention, so I allowed it to stay. I felt like an observer of this woman.

When we arrived in Kerela, Anne took me through a past life regression to find her in context. I immediately connected with her. She was beautifully dressed in the style of a grand, rich woman living around the 1800s. Her jewellery was stupendous and densely covered her neck, forehead and wrists. Anne asked a series of questions and it emerged that she had inherited a vast amount of land upon which people lived and worked. She was caring but shrewd and knew that looking after her people would make them indebted to her. She was powerful and used every part of herself including her femininity and attire, to entice and impress. Although she knew how to seduce men, she never married because this was a time in India of extreme patriarchy and female disempowerment; she chose to be alone rather than subjugate her power and authority to a man. Anne asked her whether that was the advice she would give me. The woman said no. That it was different today, that a woman could be in her power, be respected for her independence but still be in a loving relationship. I asked her name. I think she said it was Babita.

I felt she emerged at this point in my life to bring in a quality of feminine power. One that was a combination of the feminine energies of beauty and nurturing along with self-empowerment, self-respect and strength.

At the end of our holiday when checking in at Kerela airport, the check-in agent called to her colleague, 'Babita.' It was the confirmation I needed.

I have since selectively chosen the aspects of my past identity that I admire; as I move forward into the next phase of my journey her confidence, self-respect and strength have become fully integrated into my persona. Thank you, Babita!

Harjeet is a business leader in this lifetime. She is also developing a program to show how love and respect for employees is the new consciousness of business and a powerful way for CEOs to bring spirituality into their businesses; creating a cohesive and harmonious working unit and improving company performance. Her details are in the Appendix. If you work with her in the future, see if you can identify Babita!

When regressing to find a lifetime where you excelled or had a powerful and positive character, follow the process as above, but state in your intention at the beginning that you wish to go back to a lifetime when you had an empowered and strong identity and character.

Regression therapy for physical problems

Although regression therapy is extremely efficient for releasing fears it can also be very successful for healing physical problems that have their roots in a past life. Some of our physical weaknesses come from our genes but some come from physical trauma in a past incarnation, as we will see in Marian's story.

Marian's Story – shoulder pain and low self-esteem

Marian had been suffering from a painful shoulder for years before her session with past life regression therapist Janet Thompson. She had found no respite through normal medical treatments or alternative therapies: chiropractors, osteopaths, acupuncture and spiritual healers. Alongside her physical problem she suffered from extremely low self-esteem, despite being highly educated, attractive and articulate.

Janet took her back into her past using a version of the regression process I shared above. She went straight through the door of her choice and into the life to the root cause of her problem. In the present in Janet's therapy room she flung herself forward in her chair moaning and jerking with her arm out straight. After a few minutes she collapsed back into her chair and shared her experience with Janet.

She had been captured by a group of men and tied by her arm to the back of a horse, which then dragged her along the ground, dislocating her shoulder. Eventually, beaten and broken she was left for dead. She was conscious of her spirit leaving her body looking down and seeing her lying in the mud; she was aware that she had been wearing a pale blue monk's robe. Her spirit was traumatised by the experience and she recalls feeling sad and guilty that she had failed God by not completing all she had planned in that lifetime.

Marion went home and meditated and gained further insights. She realised that her guilt and sense of failure as a monk had caused her low self-esteem in this lifetime. She saw the work she had done as an Albigensian, a Cathar, in 12th century France, and realised she had done all she could in that lifetime and had in no way let God down. From that day her self-respect improved amazingly and her shoulder ceased to cause her any discomfort whatsoever. Well done Janet, and well done Marion! A great healing.

When someone has a physical problem that cannot be healed by conventional medicine or alternative methods then it's worth checking for a past-life cause. Many of my clients come to me as a last resort, having gone through normal medical channels first.

When working with physical problems, keep in mind that the body has its own spirit so include that in your healing practice. Here is an example of a healing for someone with feet and ankle pain that I recently did at a distance.

Mary's Story – feet and ankle pain

Mary's problem was extreme pain in her feet and ankles that had become so intense that she couldn't work, and caused her not only to suffer from the pain but also depression. Although I didn't do a full regression for her, I got the feeling that her problem came from a past life and I sat and connected to her and her feet for a few moments. I saw chains wrapped around her ankles and someone torturing her feet. I felt that she had more than one life where her feet were targeted – a real challenge to her for moving forward. I also felt that she had some karma – maybe she needed to forgive her persecutors. When I cleared her karma, I felt a very strong shift of energy and also when I cleared the imprints from the past from the spirit of her body. She confirmed she too felt the energy of her feet shifting.

Imprints from the past are energy and the vibration of energy can be changed.

In Chapter Two, I showed you to use channelled healing energies of love to heal the physical body and the associated spirit. In the next two rituals you can focus your healing deeper – on the root cause.

Use your pendulum to identify whether the cause is in a past life or the present.

- Call in your protection and guides.
- Hold your pendulum (a weighted object on a thread or chain) with your index finger and thumb.
- Ask these questions:
  - is the source of this problem from a past life?
  - is the source of this problem from this lifetime?
  - is it ready to be healed?

Ritual: Clearing physical problems from a past life

You can follow a past life regression, as I shared before, or you can do this next ritual that is specifically focused on healing physical problems you suspect were created from past life experiences. I shall refer to the person you are helping as a client just for simplification. Have a bowl of water with dissolved sea salt nearby.

- Let your client lie down for this session. Although this is not a regression, they may well connect to their past life experience as you are working on them. If they start to feel or see scenes from their past encourage them to share with you, then you can comfort them, telling them that this is just a video of the past. You are helping them to heal not only the memories but the impact they have on their body.
- Call in protection for yourself and your client. Call in their guides and angels and your guides and angels.
- Ask your client to open their heart: lead them through placing their hands together to represent the doors of their heart; ask them to open the doors to their heart.
- Ask your client to open their mind: placing their hands together in front of their forehead to represent the doors of the mind; ask them to open the doors to their mind.
- Ask your client to let the spirit of their body be open to receive the healing; placing their hands together in front of their solar plexus; ask them to open the door to their body.
- Address the spirit of the body, 'Please, dear spirit of (your

client's name) receive the love and healing we send you. Please forgive us for the pain you have been through from actions, thoughts and emotions that may have harmed you.'

- Draw the Release Symbol and sweep through their body from head to toe as you say, 'I release and transform all negative memories or imprints on your body that came from a past life, I release them; now, right now, right now.' Flick the negative energies you are releasing onto the bowl of water.

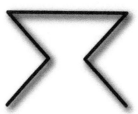

- Draw the Healing Symbol and channel healing to all the chakras with the intention that you are filling their body with healing energies and repairing all damage done.

- Now focus your healing on the areas where they are suffering. Use hands-on if it suits you both.

- Complete with the drawing the Preserving Symbol and giving each other a hug.

Ritual: Heal your own physical imprint

Use this ritual to work on yourself to help heal any long-standing ailments or physical problems. The focus is the spirit of your body that has been affected by the past life trauma. It needs love and nurture, respect and gratitude.

- Call in your protection and spirit guides to help you with this session.

- Set your intention to focus on your body and its spirit by placing your hands in prayer in front of your solar plexus then open them saying, 'I am open to receive love for the spirit of my body; now, right now, right now.'

- Draw the Healing Symbol in front of you three times, then draw it over the part of your body that hurts or is affected.

- Draw the Release Symbol and say, 'I release and transform the energy of imprints; now, right now, right now.'

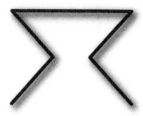

- Say, 'I clear the karma that lies between me and my body; now, right now, right now.'

- Bless your body by bathing the part of your body that is suffering with blessed water. Use the Healing Symbol to channel loving energies into the water.

- Now bless it with words of love, using your own words to show your gratitude and love. Feel your love and kindness pouring into your body and its spirit.

- Complete with Preserving Symbol.

When you respect and love your body – it will respond and support you

We will now continue to look at ways we can heal your soul and go deep into your subconscious and find hidden imprints and scars holding emotions that may have been suppressed since childhood.

CHAPTER *Six*

Healing your soul

In Chapter One we looked at the formation of your spiritual energy. Now I want to show you how the soul is deeply affected and impacted by your life experiences both in this time on Earth and previous incarnations. We will be looking at the imprints, scars and long-lasting memories that sit deep in your soul and how you can heal them.

The more you heal this life cycle, the less to do next time!

How the past impacts the present

Imprints hold negative emotions of past events, locked in time and locked into your spirit. Because they hold heavy, negative and toxic emotional energy they lower the vibration of your spirit, which in turn affects your mind, your general state of health and happiness.

They also act as mini magnets that attract more negativity into your life, ostensibly to create challenges that will wake you up to learning life lessons and allowing your soul to grow stronger spirituality and raise your consciousness – your knowing and understanding of people and spirit. Unfortunately, we often see the bad things that happen to us, not as opportunities to grow, but as bad luck and misfortune and it is easy to feel like the victim. As a victim you will feel disempowered and out of control of your state of mind and physical state, so you can spiral down into depression.

When you realise that, in many cases, you can rise above what has happened, you become the controller and can reclaim your personal power. In the book so far, I have shared many ways that you can rise above your issues and heal your emotions, and now we will look at how you can target the root causes of many of these issues that are suppressed and held down at soul level in the form of imprints.

Soul Imprints

Traumas and harmful experiences, either one-off's or over time, create imprints – scars in your soul. These imprints are like fists that clutch the memory of the event and hold the emotions that arose at the time of the trauma. They are low vibration pockets of energy and they nearly always hold fear and often anger. Not only do they act as magnets repeatedly drawing in similar negative situations to the one that created them but they also lower your energy overall causing depression, sadness, low spirits, and a general lack of vitality and drive. They also affect your mental and physical wellbeing.

Imprints are the buttons that people press that stir you up! They are your sensitive and vulnerable points, and they flare up when you get close to the memory of the past – you will get emotional, either crying, frightened or angry when a situation or a conversation comes close.

Here is a summary of the indicators that you have unhealed imprints.

- You can find no reason for an illness or physical condition that flares up from time to time, e.g. migraine headaches, psoriasis, irritable bowel, painful joints.

- You are running on lower than full energy. You feel exhausted and tired without a medical reason.

- You have a deep feeling of sadness.
- You get emotional and flare up when certain subjects get raised.
- You get defensive when criticised.
- You have fears deep inside; as we saw in the last chapter these can come from memories of past life experiences that are still locked into you.
- You are on the spectrum of a personality disorder such as:
  - Paranoid
  - Schizoid
  - Antisocial
  - Borderline
  - Histrionic
  - Narcissistic
  - Avoidant (or anxious)
  - Dependent
  - Obsessive-compulsive personality disorder (OCDP).

Healing Imprints

Fortunately healing can help you to release imprints and can cut short the cycle of repeatedly going through painful challenges. Healing can also help to heal and release the symptoms and managing techniques you develop to cover your internal pain and discord. You will need to be open-minded and accepting of the higher vibrations that will raise the energy of the imprint, and allow it to transform into understanding and wisdom.

Healing will bring emotions to the surface that you have suppressed for years. Just let the emotions flow as they come up and don't try to hold them back in – they need to be released. Be prepared to let go any attitudes and mindsets that you have developed over the years to manage your inner hurt, for these will be supporting and confirming the idea that you are a victim. Continuing to blame someone else for your condition, no matter how valid, will not help you to feel better. Healing your imprints is key to moving forward.

True healing and transformation come when you heal the root cause, not the symptoms.

Ritual: Healing Imprints

Have a bowl of water containing sea salt nearby to collect the negative energies.

- Call in your protection and guides and angels.

- Envisage the past journey of your soul as flowing into the right side of you as a straight line. This line is a timeline that links you back to the time of your birth then beyond that through to the time your soul was created.

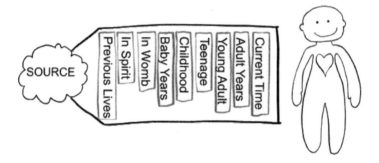

- Starting from your heart centre sweep and clear the timeline that will show in front of you like a video of your life going backwards. You will be healing all the traumas and hurts that you have gone through in your life. Start with your current situation, then back through your adult life. Gently sweep and draw the Healing Symbol to channel energies that will transform the imprints. Say out loud what you are doing. As you know your own life, you can identify each of the times when you have been damaged by negative or traumatic experiences.

- All the time imagine that a video of your life is showing slowly in front of you. Sweep all the time and flick the negative energies into the bowl of salty water.

- Move back through your adult years, young adulthood, through your teenage and baby years, time in your mother's womb, where you can be affected by her experiences.

- Through your conception to the time you were in Spirit integrating your previous life experiences and planning this lifetime.

- Then continue back through past lives to Source and the time you were created. All the time using your hands to sweep.

- Complete the session with the Preserving Symbol.

You can do this for someone else by standing or sitting in front of them. Let them sit and starting from their heart centre heal their timeline to their right.

Soul Fragmentation

To cope with horrific or extremely traumatic experiences, the mind and soul will push away part of your spiritual energy and cellular memory, fragmenting your soul and suppressing your conscious memory of the events. This is not a conscious act but a protective and automatic reaction and one that allows you to continue to function. This situation can occur for people experiencing childhood abuse, bad accidents, sudden loss of a loved one or the scenes of carnage and threat to their lives in conflict or acts of terrorism.

Soul Fragmented

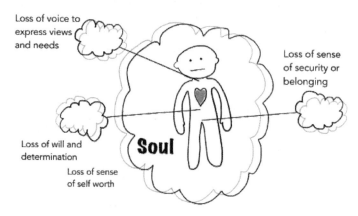

Loss of voice to express views and needs

Loss of sense of security or belonging

Loss of will and determination

Soul

Loss of sense of self worth

Clive's loss of feeling whole, feeling incomplete

I first discovered the phenomenon of fragmentation during a healing for a man I shall call Clive. Clive was a wealthy businessman who had been slightly depressed and struggled with low energy for many years, indeed as long as he could remember. He lay on the couch and I sat channelling healing energies for him; I was shown a vision, like a video, of him as a child hiding under his bed. Something had terrified him. I connected to a dark force that explained that he had taken John's soul at this time. I bartered with him demanding he return it. After a few surreal minutes he accepted the coin I offered then suddenly I felt a strong sense of his soul returning. When we finished the session, John sat up and said, 'Wow, that's amazing, I feel whole again. I haven't felt so together for years.' I didn't tell him exactly what I had done, I thought he might find it a step too far, but

I asked if he had experienced any trauma in childhood. He nodded and looked grim but didn't share what terrible thing had happened that had driven him under his bed. My sense of this is that it wasn't his entire soul that he had lost but a significant part of his spirit and energy had been lost at that time and my intervention allowed him to reclaim it.

Abused children are adept at pushing their darkest memories away and at the same time pushing away aspects of their own spirit. As they do this so they lose not only their memory of the events that caused their pain, but they lose feeling as well. So young people who have been serially and repeatedly abused can lose their gentlest emotions and empathy for others too. They may then turn to a life of crime with little regard for the feelings of others. They can lose their sense of self, of respect for self, lose self-confidence and self-value.

Less extreme cases cause aspects of one's nature to be pushed out and seemingly lost but they are always there, and through healing can be reclaimed and re-integrated. When part of your memory and soul has been pushed away, you will lose or weaken the aspect that was threatened by the abuse or trauma. This is often trust, confidence or self-worth.

Although soul fragmentation can come from a sudden and dramatic experience, it can also come from a flow of negative comments over time. You are, of course, most vulnerable in childhood especially if you have parents who are themselves dysfunctional or struggling with their lives.

Typically, you may lose any of the following aspects or functions.

Your Voice
Your ability and willingness to express and share your feelings. You may also have a problem with your voice; you may suffer throat infections or people may find it difficult to hear you. If you are told your comments are not wanted; you are shouted down or told your views or feelings are wrong, then eventually you will stop expressing your feelings or views and your voice becomes redundant and you stop communicating.

Your sense of security and belonging

If you were put up for adoption, taken into care or lost your parents in a tragedy you may well have lost your security. This can make you feel ungrounded, not able to settle in one place, moving from job to job, finding it difficult to put down roots or commitment. In adulthood having your house repossessed, experiencing a very difficult or traumatic divorce or being left by your partner can also make you feel insecure, isolated and detached.

Your self-confidence

If you have had a bad accident such as a car crash the first thing that goes is your confidence, this can occur for any traumatic experience especially if you are personally responsible.

Trust and Faith

Trust and faith are lost when you are betrayed or deeply hurt by someone you have trusted and depended upon; let down by someone who you have allowed close into your life and heart. If in your childhood, your parents, teacher, or sports coach hurt you there is a strong possibility you will have lost your faith. You will then find it difficult to trust adults for some time. This can seriously affect your ability to commit to loving relationships of all kinds, friendships and partnerships, even in business.

Courage

This is an aspect that can be easily lost by anyone in a military role, in the Armed forces or Police once they have been overexposed to danger and/or been injured in service. If you have had a role protecting society or individuals in the front line in dangerous situations, your courage is bound to be vulnerable. Once you have lost this you may feel scared, insecure and have a strong desire to step back from danger and that is natural. Unfortunately, you may take on a sense of judgement that can also bring shame and loss of self-esteem. You may find you can pull back this element of your soul by finding a new path, a new role that gives you back your self-worth.

It takes courage to face each day when you have post-traumatic stress disorder.

Your Will

When you lose your will, your ability to make decisions and your drive – you lose your power. This vital part of you may be lost after an abusive attack, a loss of family, or you may have been dominated or overwhelmed by a strong character over a period of years. If a parent or partner makes decisions for you, eventually you stop using your own ability to make decisions for yourself and your ability to choose is no longer used. You will feel you cannot make decisions and become indecisive and unsure of yourself; you start to lean and become dependent on others to guide you. You become disempowered and insecure.

Post-Traumatic Stress Disorder

Before we look at how you can recover lost elements of your soul I want to focus on a syndrome, a condition that has taken our attention in recent years and that is post traumatic stress disorder.

post traumatic stress disorder (PTSD) is a condition experienced by servicemen and women, police officers, firemen, first responders and anyone who comes face to face with life's most extreme and traumatic situations involving people or animals. When you are exposed to frequent horrific scenes you will manage the trauma by suppressing your memories. However, the hurt and shock are still there stored away in your cellular memory and eventually, the memories and associated pain will bubble up, creating flashbacks, nightmares, the shakes and panic attacks.

If you suffer from this condition you may have lost a number of elements of your soul, leaving you nervous, anxious, fearful, lacking confidence, weak, insecure and more. Flashback memories caused by intense negative imprints will affect your mind, your spirit and your physicality. The symptoms of this condition can also seriously affect your relationships. Here is the experience of Pete who came to see me some years ago before PTSD was universally acknowledged; he came at the request of his girlfriend in a last-ditch effort to save their relationship.

Once the soul is overloaded and cannot absorb or integrate any more trauma it will ask the body to shut down; we call it a breakdown.

Pete's Story – the horror of his past seriously affected his current relationship

Pete's girlfriend came to me for healing, and after we had finished dealing with her issues and problems she asked me if I would be able to help her boyfriend. He had left the forces after several tours in Northern Ireland. He was having severe and terrifying nightmares, and these were not only awful for him, but impacted her sleep which was affecting her work. Fortunately, Pete was happy to come to see me and he explained his symptoms; he not only suffered nightmares and flashbacks, but he felt unworthy and ashamed.

He shared the cause of his shame. During one of his tours in Northern Ireland his unit was called to an armed confrontation in a residential area. The men were faced with a sniper picking off civilians and soldiers and immediate action was required. Pete was also a sniper and he quickly targeted the shooter and had him in his sights. As he squeezed the trigger, a young girl ran out into his firing line and Pete's bullet killed her. There was an inquest and he was cleared of all blame, but his heart and soul were severely impacted by the experience. He had counselling, but he could no longer face military life. The resulting loss of confidence and self-esteem broke his marriage. Despite knowing that the child died through no fault of his own he felt guilty and that churned into anger, which would burst out from time to time causing him problems with his friends and the law. Years later he met his girlfriend and fell in love. He found it difficult to make love as his sense of worth had left him and his nights were still troubled. He had started to do voluntary work with children and this had helped a little, but he was keen to move on fully and to live a normal life. He wanted this new relationship to be the beginning of an untroubled phase of his life and was desperate to clear the memory of that day.

I used a similar process to the ritual below; I cleared his karma, channelled healing to raise his vibration and reclaimed all that he had lost – it was a long list! He immediately felt a huge load shift as the guilt and attachment to that day left him; a sense of peace and calm had returned after many years. His girlfriend wrote to me later saying that he could now make love and they were sleeping peacefully.

Pete's story is typical of the problems that come from PTSD. Because the experiences are so intense and very often are repeated over and over, they create havoc with the mind and soul. It's always a major blow to the spirit to leave a role you have been in for some time. My husband and his friends all suffered varying levels of depression once they gave up their corporate jobs. Going forward for military or service personnel is particularly hard as their world is so very different, the challenges they face daily often affect their lives, their responsibility for the wellbeing of others is intense and the adjustment to normal life is a huge challenge. Add to this post traumatic stress disorder and you can understand why so many end up suffering from mental health issues and experience spiritual turmoil.

To help smooth the transition from the forces to civilian life, or any major shift in role, it can be beneficial to focus on other skills and knowledge that may previously been a hobby. This is what Lorrie did. Here is his story of transition through following a favourite pastime and turning it into a new career.

Love from any source heals.

Lorrie's Story
Lorrie was a soldier for several years and completed tours in Afghanistan and Iraq. He left the army to join the police force as a first responder with the role of breaking bad news to the relatives of people killed on the motorways and in crime attacks. He says that the emotional impact of forever passing on life-changing news had a deeper effect on his psyche than his wartime experiences, but I believe this was an accumulative situation, and eventually his experiences pushed him over the tipping point and he had to retire with a breakdown.

As with Pete, he had pushed so much of his soul energy away and would spend days laid low, suffering exhaustion, depression and loss of will. He found his salvation, although not a cure, in his hobby of beekeeping. He has turned his hobby into a small business and is now not only selling honey, but other bee-related products. With counselling, the healing from the love and care from his family, and with his own patience and determination he managed to reclaim much of his will and energy and turned his life around. Pete's story is a great example of self-healing!

Love comes as kindness, consideration, care, respect, full acceptance and gentleness.

Journal:
Do you think that you have lost an aspect of yourself because of past trauma or long term emotional, mental or physical abuse? Write your intention to recover, heal and integrate what you have lost.

Ritual: Reclaim a lost aspect of yourself
Your spiritual energy will always belong to you and even though an element of it may be pushed away or seem hidden there is a cord that links it to your soul and is therefore retrievable once you have decided to reclaim it. Call in your protection and your guides and angels.

- Draw this soul Reclaim Symbol.

Soul Reclaim Symbol: Start with the top left hand, top right hand, bottom right, bottom left then the downward stroke then the horizontal from left to right. Draw at least three times.

- Say; 'I reclaim all I have lost in any lifetime; now, right now, right now.' Use your arms to sweep your misplaced soul parts towards you. Do this several times. Then hug yourself.

- Follow on by further healing your soul by using this Soul Healing Symbol three times in front of you. Say, 'The vibration of my soul is raised; now, right now, right now. My soul is healed; now, right now, right now.' Say three times.

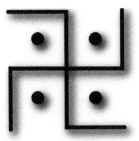

Soul Healing Symbol: Start drawing top left to bottom right then top right to bottom left, then the four dots starting in the top left-hand corner.

- Say, 'I am whole.'

- Use the Preserving Symbol to hold the energy.

Recovering Positive Memories

Of course, there are good memories locked into your soul as well as negative ones. I have been given a symbol that you can use to reactivate those memories to allow you to remember old skills. When I started healing I was told that it was more about remembering than learning how to do it. Within your cellular memory you may have some valuable knowledge that you could use in this lifetime. Here is a ritual and symbol you can use for yourself or for others. This ritual also lifts your energy levels and empowers you.

Ritual: Activate cellular memory for forgotten skills and knowledge.

- Call in your protection and spirit guides.

- Draw this symbol three times over your head.

Cellular Memory Symbol: Start with the top circle then the centre dot, then the bottom right then left.

- Say out loud, 'I reactivate all knowledge and skills that can serve me in this lifetime for the good of all; now, right now, right now. I am empowered; now, right now, right now.'

- Complete with Preserving Symbol to seal in the energies and the intent. Well done.

*Keep in mind that with intention and will, you can take over
the reins of your life rather than let external influences
overwhelm you.*

Your Soul and Mind Connection

Every imprint and scar in your heart and soul has an impact on your
mind. The emotional pain within each imprint sends messages to
your brain to warn of a problem to be sorted, in the same way as
physical pain tells the brain that there is something wrong in your
body so that your logical mind can then go into action to protect
and heal. These messages translate into thoughts. If you read the
messages correctly you will immediately go into action to heal the
source of pain, as you do with a physical problem. Unfortunately, we
often do not see emotions as a sign that there is something out of
balance, something to be dealt with. We have become accustomed
to seeing emotions as a sign of weakness and most often we
suppress and ignore them.

Emotions are signals that something is out of order
– they should not be ignored!

If these emotional messages to the mind are ignored, they can
create havoc as the mind becomes overwhelmed by messages that
it is not dealing with; like an inbox where nothing is done with an
ever-increasing arrival of messages. The mind will then take the
course of least resistance and perceive the messages as 'there is
something wrong with me – I am useless because I can't cope' and
any pre-programmed negative belief about yourself just magnifies.
Instinctively the mind will file the messages in the most used file –
this can be the 'I am useless' file or the 'I am worthless' file, 'I can't

225

manage on my own' file and so on. This state of being overwhelmed and negative thinking can end up as a serious imbalance and a mental health issue. When the messaging system gets overwhelmed and the mind stops coping, then one result can be that reality gives way to the imagination, which will create its own reality, resulting in you living in a la-la land, in denial of the reality of your situation and not taking action to heal it. An alternative result can be a full-blown psychosis filling the mind with imaginary threats and voices. Many post traumatic stress disorder sufferers who have an overload of unresolved imprints and emotions suffer from similar symptoms: hearing voices, haunted by unknown and imaginary assailants, believing that they are in danger and overwhelmed by fearful thoughts.

First step towards healing: acknowledge the problem.

I believe that most mental health issues come from the imprints and associated suppressed emotions that have not been acknowledged, dealt with, transformed into insights and understanding and healed. Once we acknowledge we have a fear and that there is something to heal, then we can then set up a plan of action. Medication can subdue the symptoms but until the sufferer can actually allow the healing, they will continue to be troubled by unwanted thoughts and feelings. Counselling only goes so far because there is a tendency with many counselling procedures to get the sufferer to keep telling their story over and over, recounting the past – this is necessary once but to repeat just relives the experience. Something else needs to be done to heal the soul wound.

I don't presume to have the answer to healing the many aspects of mental illness, but I do know that healing energies of love can do a lot to lift a person out of the spiral of suffering when the mind has taken control of the body, emotions and spirit. Once they can rise above the depths of their negative state, they can then see some future, some light at the end of the tunnel and recover hope. Humans need hope; we all need some reason to get up and face the day; mental illness, unwanted thoughts, negative beliefs all destroy hope. This next ritual is focused on bringing the mind back into balance, healing the negative beliefs that have themselves become imprints – hopefully before they have become part of your DNA and locked into your genes. Remember, however low you have fallen mentally and emotionally, the energies of love are there for you and the symbol will call them in.

When overloaded with negative thoughts, beliefs and attitudes the Mind takes over from your higher self and your heart.

The Mind becomes:

Dictator
Controller
Bully
Saboteur
Critical

Joe's Story

Joe has suffered mental health issues since childhood. His wounding came in with him from a previous lifetime. I saw many lives where he had been disturbed by anxiety and fears, guilt and shame, which in this lifetime he felt as a churning inside. His mind twisted the feelings into blame and for many years he blamed his parents – he lost his mojo completely in his late teens and after some life-changing experiences that confirmed his fears he eventually fell into full psychosis. He spent some time in hospital and was put on a cocktail of drugs that at least subdued his fears and allowed him to function up to a point; not enough to get and keep a job though. Over time he came to realise that there was no one to blame and then he took on the responsibilities of his life and gradually, with love from his family and his own studies on psychology and the workings of the mind, he found his will and took on a university degree course. As his studies went well he recovered his confidence and self-esteem. He went into action and, as soon as he did, his situation changed.

Journal:
Do you have thoughts that you don't want? Do you have anxious thoughts that try to derail you? Do you feel negative emotions about someone that you would prefer to not feel? Do you have a 'monkey mind' that chatters away with low-level messages that distract you from your focus? Write down what affects you and what you would like to heal and, if you know the root cause – the wounding that created it. Set your intention to heal the wounds in your soul that send the messages to your brain and into your mind. What is your action plan to recover your peace?

Your mind can distort what it hears

If you have negative beliefs about yourself and life you may find they distort situations and experiences – even the words that people say to you. They can grab whatever is said and swerve it down the established path of: I'm unlucky, or I'm no good, or I'm ugly, or no one loves me, I'm unlovable and so on. Although you may hear correctly, your mind can interpret comments and twist them so a perfectly normal conversation can be perceived as a criticism, judgement or a personal attack.

Negative Thoughts become Negative Beliefs

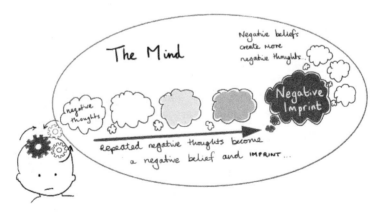

Once your mind starts to create a flow of negative thoughts about yourself and others, you need to set your intentions to heal it and clear the negativity imprints that are taking over. As we saw in Chapter One, every thought has an impact and if negative, pessimistic, critical, unloving thoughts start to take over then they can entrench into beliefs, which are a lot harder to reprogramme or transform.

Journal:

Do your thoughts often run away with you? Do you find it hard to be positive? Do you get depressed frequently? Do you feel your mind dominates your heart? Set your intention of healing your mind and bringing it back into balance with your heart and let your Spirit, your higher self, take back control. Write it and say it.

Break the Cycle of Negativity by Healing your Mind

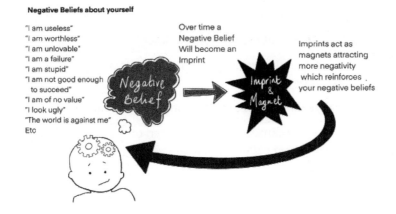

Negative Beliefs about yourself

"I am useless"
"I am worthless"
"I am unlovable"
"I am a failure"
"I am stupid"
"I am not good enough to succeed"
"I am of no value"
"I look ugly"
"The world is against me"
Etc

Over time a Negative Belief Will become an Imprint

Imprints act as magnets attracting more negativity which reinforces your negative beliefs

Negative Belief

Imprint & Magnet

Healing and Balancing the Mind

Once your mind has health issues, it has stepped out of its role of planner, logical thinker and vehicle for the imagination and has become a dominant bully. It has taken over your imagination and using fear to create devastating scenarios. It laces all your thoughts with anxiety and creates visions to keep your spirit and loving state suppressed. When you are balanced, happy and at peace your mind, heart, spirit, emotions and ego are working together and are fully in touch with your higher self. When the connection to the higher self is broken or forgotten then guidance comes from fear, old wounds send messages that get twisted and all sense of balance and harmony is destroyed.

In this healing ritual, you are setting the intention to bring balance back between your mind, your body, your emotions and your soul and to reconnect you to your higher self, so that you can get loving and effective guidance that serves you well rather than fear-based beliefs and thoughts.

Before you start this next ritual of healing ask yourself some questions.

- Before you can heal it's imperative you acknowledge that you have a problem and take responsibility for healing it. It can help if you know the cause of your current situation. Do you understand where your problem has come from?

  – Is it the programming of parents and culture?

  – Is it due to abuse or traumatic experiences in your past?

  – Do you feel that life has let you down?

  – Do you feel it is your fault your mind Is overwhelmed and out of control?

  – Do you blame someone else for your condition?

- Whatever the cause, are you prepared to take over control now to heal and balance the negative beliefs and thoughts that trouble you?

Ritual: Healing and balancing the mind with heart and higher self

- Call in your protection and spirit guides.

- Place your hands together in front of your forehead and as you open them say, 'I open my mind to receive the love and healing I need for my negative beliefs and thoughts and to re-establish a healthy mind and brain.'

- Connect to the energies of healing and love by drawing the Healing Symbol.

- Draw it three times in front of your forehead and place your hands on your head and let the healing energies flow to your head and brain.

- Sweep your head with the intention of releasing and transforming all negative beliefs.

- Draw Release Symbol and say; 'I release and dissolve all negative beliefs I have about myself, others and life. I let them go now, right now, right now.'

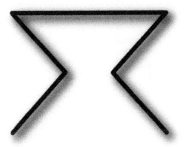

- Say, 'The way is clear for positive vibrations, clear thoughts and a balanced mind; now, right now, right now.'

- Say, 'My ego, my mind, my heart, my soul and my body are connected, are equal and are fully balanced; now, right now, right now.'

- Reconnect to your higher self by clasping your fists together, locking your fingers, bring them up above your head three times saying; 'I reconnect to my higher self, my higher self is my guide; now right now, right now.'

- Draw this symbol to connect to your higher self. Draw three times

Higher self-Connection Symbol: Draw from top left, then top right, finish with the circle in a clockwise direction.

- Draw the Preserving Symbol in front of you now.

All the healing you do for yourself will help to still and quieten your mind.

Here are some further ways you can help to re-establish spiritual balance, quieten your mind and bring yourself back to a harmonious and peaceful state.

The Morning Ritual

You will find this in Chapter One. The purpose of the ritual is to seal and protect your energy and spirit, to open your heart to receive love, to open your mind to allow your consciousness to grow, and to reconnect to your higher self. Do this at any time of the day when you feel you are overwhelmed, stretched, stressed and losing control! I suggest you do this as, at a minimum, part of your morning routine.

A video is available on my YouTube account: Annejoneshealer

Yoga

I love Kundalini yoga; it uses a combination of gentle poses held for minutes and beautiful chants and music. Performed with eyes closed and focusing on the third eye, it will bring you back to your core and centre you both physically and mentally. All yoga practice will help you refocus on your body and your spirit. Whether it is Bikram (yoga practised in a hot room), Ashtanga, (a very physical and strong practice) or the traditional Hathor, it will be so good for you not only to quieten the mind but to keep you flexible. When you are flexible in the body you will be flexible in the mind. Yoga is a wonderful way to keep yourself calm, in balance and spiritually connected.

Meditation

Any form of meditation will help you whether it's the Buddhist practice of emptying the mind or guided journeys where you put all your focus on positive and healing experiences of the imagination. I have recorded several guided meditations that use your imagination to lead you through a healing experience. See the Appendix for a link to my website shop for CDs or download from Amazon or iTunes.

Extreme Physical Exercise

Many people find exercise calms their 'monkey-chatterbox' mind, with its constant mocking and derogatory comments about yourself. Focussing on pushing your body to attain goals and stretching your endurance can give you back self-worth. You may find the pain you go through to achieve your goals distracts you from the pain of emotions. You may find solace in extreme and serious sporting activities. Be careful though – it's not a healing route but a distracting route and you will have to face the underlying problems sometime and heal them as we have so far in this book.

Nature and Gentle Exercise

I find peace from stress by letting my dogs take me for a walk in the countryside. I also find watching the birds on the feeders in our garden bring me back down from hype and worry. Birds and all animals just act out what they are, and connecting with them will open up a new flow of energy that has been constant for millions of years. Just watch a bird or a cow, horse or squirrel and sense what it is like to be them.

Be in the Moment

Eckhart Tolle wrote a great book, *The Power of Now*, describing his wake up, his epiphany, when he realised his emotional turmoil and negative mindset was coming from his habit of living either in the past (going over bad experiences) or living in the future (worrying about what might happen). He discovered that if he focused on 'the now', being in the present moment, he could find peace. Set your focus on what you are doing right now. Shut the door to the past and future. Go outdoors and look at the sky above your head. Focus on a cloud. That is a NOW experience.

Grounding

If you live too much in your mind, you may have lost touch with reality. It's okay to escape for a while to avoid problems, but allowing it to become a way of life is counterproductive; you are here to have a life in this reality, not to skim above it. People who detach from reality live in their make-believe world and it can come as a huge shock when they have to step up to take responsibilities; learn to look after themselves; care for their families or resolve situations... all of which is impossible if you do not have your feet firmly on the ground in this reality. Teenagers can find it hard to step from the self-centred and closeted state of childhood into the harsh reality of responsibility and independence. It's a tough transition, but if you don't transit as a teenager it can be even harder as an adult to become self-sustaining and self-responsible. I had a cousin who was looked after in every way by her father and then her husband. Her daughter left her because my cousin didn't take responsibility for her but passed responsibility for her nurture and support to her in-laws. Up to the age of seventy she had never paid a bill, hadn't cooked, had no idea how to manage a home; she lived in a bubble, like a princess in a castle, completely out of touch with life. She hit reality at seventy when her husband passed away. It was a shocking time for her; being responsible for her own wellbeing and her home and grieving for her husband at the same time.

Journal:

Do you live in your mind? Do you live in such a bubble that you are not in touch with the world? Do you find it difficult to follow society's rules? Do you have expectations that are not met? You may benefit from being more grounded.

Ritual: Grounding

- Close your eyes, take four deep breaths and drop your shoulders.

- Place your feet on the ground.

- Call in your protection, spirit guides and angels.

- Imagine you are a huge tree like an oak or baobab tree.

- Feel roots growing down from the bottom of your feet into the earth beneath you, going deeper and deeper through the Earth's crust.

- Down through underground streams, deeper and deeper towards the centre of the Earth.

- Your roots continue to grow through beds of crystal and rock.

- You go deeper and deeper into the Earth.

- You connect with the centre of the Earth and the heart and soul of Mother Earth. Feel the love flowing up your roots into you now, right now, right now.

- You are filled with the nurturing love of The Spirit of Earth and Nature.

- You are now stable; you are grounded; you are secure; now, right now, right now.

Get Above it All

There are times when life gets really difficult, as I found this year when my husband, Tony, had lymphoma, I couldn't get any solace from being in THE NOW because the Now wasn't a good place to be at all! When I felt the dread and hurt of the situation overwhelming me, I would find great comfort in following my connection from my heart to my higher self then on and on upwards. From this elevated state I looked down on the world and the bigger picture of my life and the people who surrounded us with love. I became filled with gratitude for what I had and what I had already experienced; particularly for the love, which wrapped its arms and wings around me; love from my friends and family and from the angels. I saw that my soul and Tony's would go on regardless to travel through further incarnations, and that this moment was only a blip in the journey of our souls. I saw that when he did pass over we would still be connected through Spirit, and if I stayed on when he went over I would have the most amazing memories and love that we had shared; more than enough to sustain me for the rest of my life.

Ritual: Lifting above pain and stress

- Call in your protection and call in your guides and angels.

- Close your eyes and breathe in four deep breaths.

- Drop your shoulders; sweep them to let go your responsibilities and burdens.

- Visualise a golden staircase in front of you. Climb it slowly and carefully.

- Go higher and higher until you are up in the clouds

- Look down and see your life below you.

- Look around and see the bigger picture; see what messages there are for you.

- What can you be grateful for?

- Can you see the bigger story of your soul's journey?

- When you are ready, slowly come back down, but keep in mind that nothing ever stays the same, 'this too shall pass' and you are stronger than you think!

- Love and hugs to you.

Before I leave the subject of your soul we need to take a look at what happens to your soul when you pass over when you die. Your soul energy will rise up through the cord that attaches your soul and heart energies through your higher chakras, up through the top of your head and your crown chakra and on to reunite with your higher self. You may have seen or felt this happening if you have been with someone as they leave. As you go your soul is met and escorted to the higher realms by angels who shine their light to guide your spirit to the heavenly realms, where you will be met your loved ones. You will then be given any healing and counselling you might need, especially if you have had a particularly difficult time before and during death. Any judgement of the life you have lived will not come from Spirit or God. It will come from you. In all my dealings with Spirit I have never come across any criticism or judgement; only guidance and love. However, you may well be your own fiercest critic; it's from your realisation of the outcomes of choices, lifestyle and spiritual that you made in this life, that leads you on to the agenda you will create for your next life.

If a soul Is deeply troubled with negative emotions such as fear, guilt, anger or extreme distress, then it may not see the angel's light it may be confused and keep its focus back on Earth. There are several reasons why a soul may not wish to move on to the higher planes, to ignore or simply miss the angels sent to guide the way to heaven:

- fear of moving on because of lack of belief that there is such a place as heaven
- fear and reluctance of leaving loved ones behind
- confusion and denial that the body has died following violent and sudden death
- guilt and fear of judgement from God
- anger and revenge for people still living
- extreme attachment to a home or possessions

Any of these feelings or beliefs can keep a soul connected to the earth planes and material world. If a soul continues to stay around for long, they can create and emit disturbing negative energies which give you ghostly, spooky feelings and raise the hairs on the back of your neck! They may haunt their old home or workplace and cause distress for those still living.

These lost and wandering souls are not evil spirits as they are often described. Some can be angry and disturbed and can cause real damage if their energy is violent; one form of these particularly active and troublesome souls is poltergeists who can literally throw furniture around. I released one from a friend's house that threw a wardrobe across a room! Very, very angry indeed! Because they are focused on the Earth they are often more receptive to our thoughts and energies, so with love and encouragement, we can help them to see the divine light that is always shining to show the way home. If you feel you would like to help souls move on then here is a ritual you can use.

Giving love and clearing fears can help a soul move on peacefully before and after death.

Soul Rescue

When you find a place haunted with the disturbing energies of an Earth-bound soul, first check that the soul is lost and wants to move on. In cases of dark souls you should get professional help. To help you make this assessment you can use a pendulum to check if the soul is of the light and wants to go to the light. Place yourself in protection then ask the spirit if it has a human soul. Ask four times and by spiritual law it must answer truthfully by the fourth request. If it says no, stop what you are doing and, in your meditation or prayers ask Archangel Michael to deal with it. If it is a soul, you can use this ritual to help guide it to the light. This is a loving and kindly act for a soul that is hanging around the Earth and allows it to go on and enjoy the benefits of the afterlife.

Ritual: Assisting a lost soul to the light

- Call in your protection and Archangel Michael and his band of angels.

- To Archangel Michael, 'Please, help me to release this soul. Create a column of light leading to the heavens of light.'

- See the column of light and angels hovering around it.

- Connect to the lost soul and say, 'Follow the light. All will be well. Go to the gardens of Heaven where you will be welcomed by friends and family. Go to the light; now, right now, right now.'

- Draw the soul Healing Symbol three times and hold up your hands, knowing that the energy you transmit will raise the energy and consciousness of the soul, making it easier to focus on the light.

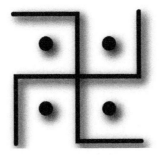

- Use the Release Symbol three times and sweep the soul towards the light. Say, 'With permission of your highest self I cut through your attachments to the earth plane; now, right now, right now.'

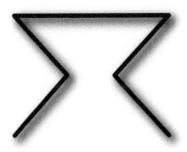

Twenty-two Souls in the Basement

When we lived in Malaysia our basement guest suite regularly showed signs of spirit activity. The bed covers were rumpled as if a child had been jumping on them, the temperature of the room was always low – easily discerned in a country with an average temperature of 32 degrees, and our dogs refused to go down there. A group of local Buddhist monks helped me to release the spirit occupants who turned out to be 22 souls killed by grenades thrown into their cell where they were imprisoned during the Second World War by invading Japanese soldiers. The souls were obviously terrified and had been trapped down there in fear ever since they were killed. As I put my hands down to pull them out of the pit-like void where they were trapped in, one refused to take my hand. After a few moments of cajoling him another hand came up so I pulled the two together. As their spirits flew past me to the light I realised they were brothers, reluctant to become separated! The energy of the massacre was locked in time and haunted us every day at 3.30pm when I would hear the loud bang of the grenade exploding. I am delighted to say the energies of that part of the house improved immensely once the souls had moved on, bless them.

Soul rescue is a special form of healing and not for everyone. If you would like to help when you become aware of lost souls but would prefer not to get involved in the rescue, I suggest you contact one of the names I have put in the back of the book. Never feel you should or ought to do any form of healing for either a living person or an incarnate soul. Trust your own feelings and what feels good for you.

We move on now to see how you can protect yourself if you have been unfortunate enough to be affected by heavy and intense negative energies.

CHAPTER *Seven*

Releasing heavy energies

You will find that once you have cleared your own negative thought forms, attitudes, internal scarring and pain-filled imprints, your loving heart will become your magnet to draw high-frequency energies towards you. Then your life will be filled with loving and uplifting people and situations. Although all dark, heavy, negative energies are on the spectrum of light and therefore not to be feared whilst you are still working on your own healing, it's good practice and sound advice to keep your armour on and every day seal your energy field. There will be times when you may need a more powerful form of healing when you face very dark and malevolent energy.

I now want to focus on, what to many is a taboo subject, the elephant in the room that is rarely spoken of even though most of us know it exists. I want to look at the impact of negative energies that are destructive and aggressive and are deliberately sent to harm you. I have desperate pleas from people all over the world who know that their energies have been compromised, and in some cases their lives ruined, by low-frequency energies that they cannot clear themselves. There are practitioners who will do this work but many charge exorbitant prices to take advantage of people's desperation, and many of my clients come from deprived and difficult circumstances.

I am not going to teach you to clear these energies for other people as this is a specialised field, but I want to show you ways you can protect and manage to avoid the impact of these energies for yourself and to raise your vibrations and that of your living space to disable them. If this is an area that discomforts you or you don't wish to learn about this subject, it's perfectly fine – jump now to the final chapter, which is an overview of all the symbols that I use.

Remember: the light is always, always stronger than darkness and the dark gains its power from fear and fear is dissolved by love. When you get anxious refocus on your heart and remember who you are, a spirit of love.

Why would someone want to harm you deliberately with negative energies?

There are two main sources of dark energies, those initiated from people who have a grudge against you or from dark forces in spirit; entities that want to disable you or your work. Onslaughts with harmful intentions are called psychic attacks and they can vary from slight discomfort to a full-blown assault that can disable you and prevent you from functioning properly. Most people go through their lives without any problems of this nature but there are countries and cultures where the arts of black magic are used frequently, especially against people in certain roles of influence or power. Black magic is the opposite of the light we have been using to help and uplift – it is the art of using energy power to harm and destroy. The energies that are accessed are of the lowest vibration.

What sort of people are likely to be attacked by dark energies?

- **Those involved in the legal system**

  Judges, prosecutors, lawyers, witnesses and the police are frequent targets. It is not unusual in some cultures for intimidation with black magic and curses to be used to affect and deflect the path of truth and justice. I have cleared many professionals in legal roles affected by black magic sent to distort outcomes. Sometimes it is targeted at not only the legal team, but also the paperwork or computers that they use. Electronics are easy prey for a dark arts practitioner because they can be affected by energy surges. A friend of mine has battled his apparently 'open and shut legal case' through the courts for over five years working on getting justice from a member of his family who has swindled him out a very large sum of money and forged his signature on company shares. Each time his case comes up it gets adjourned or put out by the judge. He knows his cousin is paying for black magic to shut down the case, but he cannot prove it! Add to this the normal corruption that is endemic in his country he might still be fighting this case to his deathbed! One of his life lessons must be to learn patience!

- **Politicians**

In many countries the arena of politics is a hotbed of corruption and power play. There are countries where opposition voters are targeted by black magic to prevent them voting either by making them sick or by affecting their minds. The politicians are themselves targeted and they employ their own practitioners to help protect them and in some cases they respond with more black magic, creating a heavy and corrupt environment at the head of society. This percolates down and affects everyone, making life difficult and deterring good people from putting themselves forward for the roles of greatest influence. If you suspect this is the case in your country or district, then use Distance Healing to send love to the leaders and see honesty and cooperation replacing corruption and greed.

- **Lovers**

Throughout history we have acknowledged that love can turn to hate, as quoted from a poem by William Congreve from 1697: 'Heaven has no rage like love to hatred turned, nor Hell a fury like a woman scorned.' Rejection and jealousy have caused many a jilted lover to turn against his or her ex and in some extreme cases led to harmful consequences. Attacks fuelled by jealousy are not uncommon in some cultures. A client in the Far East came to me heartbroken because his fiancée was under constant attack. She got sick for no reason, lost energy and had to leave her job; she was suffering from psychic attack initiated by an ex-lover. By the time I learned of her plight she was under the dominance of the shaman who was being used to send the black magic and she wouldn't come to see me. Eventually she got very sick and she died. With help from myself and other healers her fiancé recovered from the resulting depression and found happiness and marriage with another lovely lady a couple of years later.

- **Businessmen and Women**

Senior men and women in the world of finance and business are probably the most often targeted as the gains can be high when big deals and influential positions are at stake. My husband, in his role of CEO of a company in The Far East, was the target for an attack that caused the local energy grid to suddenly pass thousands of volts through our house rather than the normal 240 voltage; this nearly caused a fire and would have been a catastrophe if it hadn't been for the quick action of our housekeeper's husband who realised what was happening and threw the master switch. Despite his intervention all the fans and many of the electrical appliances were burnt out. We experienced several such attacks, but fortunately we were well protected and came to no harm. However it was an awakening for me to the greed and desperation that leads some to do anything to gain influence, money and power. Some people I know in the world of commerce make the film, *The Wolf of Wall Street* seem like a playful puppy!

- **Celebrities and High Achievers**

When you are in the public eye or stand out in society as a high achiever, you are more likely to attract negativity in the form of envy, criticism and judgement. This is referred to as The Tall Poppy Syndrome – pulling down anyone who achieves more or gets ahead of others. In the Zambian village where we ran our charity Hearts and Hands for Africa, we encouraged children to set up their own small vegetable plots and taught them about good irrigation procedures and new plants. One of the boys worked particularly hard on his plot, watered it every day and kept the weeds down. As a result, his plants grew far better than the rest. One day he turned up to find his garden had been trashed. He was accused of using black magic on his plants to make his garden grow better than the others.

- **Lightworkers**

The description lightworker applies to anyone who brings light to our world, who is loving and caring, compassionate and kind; anyone who has the intention, conscious or not, of raising the vibration of humanity and the world. A lightworker can be a teacher, writer, alternative therapist, business leader, activist, journalist, scientist, politician, mother, nursery teacher, carer, doctor – in fact in any role where you can impact and influence people and the world. We are in a time when there is a concerted effort to move from a fear-based world mind set to a love-based one. Lightworkers lead the way as pioneers to a spiritual age where we are self-responsible and self-loving yet caring and non-judgmental, treating everyone as equals. As you shine your light brightly you may become a target of psychic attack, so it is important to protect your energies daily. I repeat, light is stronger than the dark and love is more powerful than hate!

- **Family Members**

In certain countries the use of black magic, although not talked about openly, is certainly not uncommon. From my experience Indonesia, Malaysia, Africa, South America and the Caribbean are places where you can easily find someone to use negative energies and rituals to do harm to others. Surprisingly, I have also come across – as The Dark Arts, as JK Rawlings describes – in Norway, Great Britain, India, United States and Italy. In family situations it is normally jealousy and envy or inheritance issues that are the triggers. Individuals or an entire branch of a family may be the focus of attack.

This is the plight of one family of highly educated professionals, mother and father are doctors, of Indian heritage, living in Malaysia and their children had been or were studying in higher education. When I met them, they had suffered years of misfortune, illness and financial troubles. The youngest girl was struggling with her master's degree in microbiology and for the second time the cultures used for her experiments had mysteriously died. They suspected a curse put on them by a different branch of the family. Their troubles had started following an incident when they moved close to the parents' family home. They were visited by a sister-in-law who had previously not spoken or visited them. She was from a branch of the family that had always shown antagonism and jealousy. That night she turned up with a big smile and pots of food. They were surprised but accepted her gift with good grace and ate the food. From that moment their good luck, health and wellbeing left them. They had searched for solutions and spent money they could hardly afford on a remedy. As they spoke I could feel the whooshes start that confirmed we could change things that day. I worked with my guides and Archangel Michael to clear the curse and black energies, and as they shifted, all four of them spontaneously burst into tears. They left with their eyes showing how light and happy they felt now the heavy energies had gone.

What are the attacks and who sends them?

Most of the attacks that come from a living person are created by a black magic professional; in Africa and the Caribbean they are referred to as witch doctors, in Southern Africa – sangomas, in Indonesia – bomohs and in South America – shamans. Many start their careers as good and effective healers, but some have been enticed into the lucrative work of dealing in extreme negative energies. Just as we do rituals to bring in light; they do their own rituals to access and channel low vibrational energies with the intention of doing someone harm or manipulating their minds. A common practice in Africa is to infiltrate a person's mind with thoughts and doubts making them believe they are useless or unworthy or even that they are sick, even dying.

In voodoo and witchcraft, religious rituals and symbols are often distorted and perverted. Even in my own village in the New Forest an upside-down cross was attached to the church door and graves desecrated. Black magic is used to destroy crops; to send people insane, (mental illness is a common outcome of a severe attack); to pervert justice by infiltrating the minds of jurors and judges; to make people ill (vomiting and diarrhoea are often the first signs of an attack); to destroy a business or family's finances; to break up a marriage and to create accidents such as car crashes.

Spells

Spells are cast to impose the will and intention of the attacker onto their victim, to manipulate and control their choices and free will. Traditionally they are used to make someone become infatuated and fall in love – or even lust! The effectiveness of a spell depends very much on not only its power but also the strength of mind of the victim. Someone who doesn't believe in the power of black magic, or is not fearful or in awe of it, is far less likely to succumb than a person who is indecisive, lacking confidence and insecure. Most spells tend to wear off after a while as the receiver's own will and thoughts regain their strength.

Curses

Curses are similar to spells in that they are sent to a victim through a ritual of some kind. They are normally more powerful and hold an intention to harm rather than manipulate. A curse can stay with a family for generations. A young mother came to see me to ask for help for her son. She was fearful for him because she believed her family had been cursed. The curse had affected every generation causing the eldest male in her family to lose their head in some way or another. Naturally, as her son approached his teens she was getting extremely worried. Up to this time the curse had manifested in several ways; one young man had died in a car crash where he had been decapitated, another had fallen between a boat and the harbour wall and his head had been crushed, another had lost his mind and another had gone into a coma. We traced the start back to the time when one of her ancestors had been a missionary working in Haiti; a country well known for Voodoo, which is a form of religious magic that can be used for malevolent purposes. The missionary had upset the local headman and witchdoctor by teaching his gospel and converting the local villagers. The voodoo witchdoctor had been called in to cast the curse, not just on him but the family for generations to come. I am glad to say we were able to shift the energy and her son was fine last time I heard.

A curse will most often stay until something is done to release it. When a curse is removed you can feel the energies shifting quite easily as the heavy dark energy lifts. It can feel like a shower of light chasing the heaviness away – it's a wonderful feeling. In some countries there is a thriving business in clearing curses but many who offer help are charlatans and charge ludicrously high fees. I have so often come across the victims who have suffered not only the bad luck of the curse but have been fleeced by their so-called rescuers.

Curses are often set with a pronouncement made out loud such as: 'I curse you so that you will never, ever be happy again', or 'Your wife will be barren', or, 'Your business will fail and you will be destroyed'. Then, some dark entities are invoked to assist. As we call our spirit guides of light and angels to help us when we are channelling light healing energies, the black magic practitioner will call in their own dark masters to enforce the curse. In the Middle East and Indonesia there is another practice that originated in Arabian culture, which is the source of the story of Aladdin and his lamp that held a genie who could grant wishes.

Jinns

Jinns, also spelt djinn, are similar to Nature spirits in that they have their own consciousness so can be good, bad or somewhere in between! They have been around the earth plane as long as humans and virtually in every culture with different names and identities. They appear in many stories and myths, especially in Arabian literature. I was told that in Indonesia and Malaysia they would work alongside farmers and fishermen almost as part of the family. Sadly, farmers began to capture and enslave these Nature spirits and keep them locked down and in receptacles like pots and jars getting them to do their master's wishes – rewarding them – if they managed to help them especially in conflicts and disputes with neighbours. Jinns can be a force for good but like humans, if they have been mistreated they can turn harsh and cruel; they can become an evil force that is more sensed than seen, causing bad luck and disastrous situations. Very occasionally they will move in and inhabit a human, pushing out or overwhelming the soul; a situation that is referred to as 'possession by evil spirits' in the Koran and the Bible. Unfortunately, these tricky spirit life forms are still in existence although mostly dismissed in today's more pragmatic and less superstitious world.

Demons

Demons do not have souls and they have never lived as humans. They are created from repetitive negative thoughts that eventually take on a level of intelligence and consciousness, but they are soulless so can only think and do the way they have been programmed. They are not to be confused with lost souls, which are the souls of humans that have not found their way to the higher planes at the time of death. Like jinns they can be influenced by humans and other spirit entities to harm humans.

JoJo's demon

At the end of a long day giving healing sessions in Kuala Lumpur, Malaysia I was asked if I could fit in another client with an emergency. The client was my promoter and agent and had introduced me to a TV station where I appeared on the Breakfast Show promoting my books and workshops, so I wanted to help her if I could. My instinct was to decline. I was exhausted. I knew the dangers of working when tired but forced myself to raise my game. So, I said yes! My heart sank when she explained why she wanted to see me so urgently. That afternoon she had been psychically attacked by some powerful entities sent by her ex-husband as that day the court case had come up where she had taken him for non-payment of child support. I could feel the dark energies that were attached to her, so I did my usual clearing ritual and felt something very heavy leave her; as it went I saw its red eyes and a wave of nausea flooded through me. She was delighted with the result and skipped out of the room. I spent the entire night in the bathroom and in the morning I couldn't move. I was paralysed! I rang Sal (my mentor) in desperation for we were moving on to Hong Kong that day and I couldn't even move my toes. Bless her; she sent me enough energy to enable me to pack and get out of the hotel. I literally dragged myself around the airport to the plane. Sal told me I had been attacked by the tail end of a very, very nasty demonic entity! I recovered in twenty-four hours, but I certainly learned my lesson about working when tired! I also learned to have great respect for jinns, demons and other nasties and now always protect myself before I open to do any work!

How can psychic attack affect you?

Psychic attack can affect you in a number of ways, but here are some indicators to help you know if negative feelings and thoughts are coming from your own mind and consciousness, or from an external malevolent source.

What you may sense, see and feel:

- shaken and disorientated

- you hear a voice with a critical and judgemental message; telling you that you are wasting your time, you are hopeless, you can't achieve what you set out to do, you are ugly, etc.

- sick with an upset stomach, diarrhoea or bloating

- depressed and losing your energy

- shivery and cold and find it impossible to get warm

- raised hairs on your arms or neck

- tentacles and sense of being entrapped by a malevolent being

- anxiety and panic attacks

- insecure and vulnerable

- Seeing distorted faces that loom up at you

- having many nightmares

- loss of will and determination to overcome or move on

- confused and unsure of a course of action

What to do?

If possible, do not show fear, for fear will not repel the negativity but will feed it. My husband Tony has his own way of dealing with the spooks, as he calls them. He puts on all the lights and turns the television on loud then shouts 'F.... O..', which has worked on every occasion without exception! He shows no fear and by speaking aloud enforces his own will onto the situation. If you crumble and cry, or hide under the blankets, you are giving away your courage and confidence and feeding the demon.

If you hear voices and you are not sure if they are your own thoughts or coming from another source, go and stand under the shower; these energies cannot get to you when you are under running water. Now listen, are they still there? If so, they will be your own thoughts, doubts and fears speaking to you. If you are met with silence you know you are being attacked, so stay under the water and follow one of the following methods of prayer or protection.

If you think you are likely to be attacked or are under attack, then ramp up your protection. Here are several ways that you can call in protection starting with a selection of prayers that have been used effectively for centuries. Speak with authority. If you have seen any of the Lord of The Ring films you will recall the way Gandalf holds up his magic staff and uses a strong, loud voice that brooks no argument. Be like Gandalf and take control!

Even if you are anxious, show no fear and act confidently.

Prayers
When I was in my twenties, I stupidly played with a Ouija board and one of the group was a man I had started to date. He was still smarting from being rejected by his last girlfriend, and in the middle of the session decided to ask his dead mother to call up revenge on her. Immediately, the temperature in the room dropped significantly and I felt a freezing energy wrap around me. I started to shake and lose my voice. Fortunately, my friends were very quick-thinking and grabbed two pens and created a cross and led us all with the Lord's Prayer. After a few moments I recovered. This prayer calls forth a powerful force of light that puts an instant barrier of protection around you. Extracts from the Koran, The Bible and Buddhist Mantras can be equally effective – choose whatever suits you, your beliefs and your culture. I am also sharing a prayer for protection I wrote.

The Lord's Prayer

Our Father who art in Heaven, hallowed be thy name

Thy kingdom come

Thy will be done on Earth as it is in Heaven.

Give us this day our daily bread

Forgive us our trespasses, as we forgive those who trespass against us

Lead us not into temptation, but deliver us from evil

For thine is the kingdom, the power and the glory forever and ever, Amen.

The Twenty-third Psalm

This tract is another powerful extract from the Bible and offers instant connection to God.

The Lord is my shepherd: I shall not want

He maketh me to lie down in green Pastures; he leadeth me beside the still waters

He restoreth my soul: he leadeth me in the paths of righteousness for his name's sake

Yea, though I walk through the valley of the shadow of death, I will fear no evil: for thou art with me, thy rod and staff they comfort me

Thou preparest a table before me in the presence of mine enemies: thou anointed my head with oil; my cup runneth over

Surely goodness and mercy shall follow me all the days of my life: and I will dwell in the house of the Lord forever.

A prayer from the Koran for protection from black magic

I seek refuge in Allah from Satan the outcast. Allah! There is none worthy of worship but He, the Ever-Living, the One who sustains and protects all that exists. Neither slumber nor sleep overtakes Him. To Him belongs whatever is in the heavens and whatever is on the Earth. Who is he that can intercede with Him except with His permission? He knows what happens to them in this world, and what will happen to them in the hereafter. And they will never encompass anything of His knowledge except that which He wills. His throne extends over the Heavens and the Earth, and He feels no fatigue in guarding and preserving them. And He is the Most High, the Most Great.

Jewish Prayer of Protection

Lay us down to sleep in peace, Adonai our God, and raise us up, our King, to life; spread over us the shelter of Your peace. Guide us with Your good counsel and save us for the sake of Your Name. Shield us from foe, plague, sword, famine and anguish. Remove wrongdoing from before us and behind us and shelter us in the shadow of Your wings. For it is You, O God, who protects and rescues us; it is You, O God, who is our gracious and compassionate King. Safeguard our coming and our going, to life and to peace from now to eternity.

Setrap's Mantra – a guardian of the Buddhist Dharma – Spiritual Path

Setrap Chen is a Dharmapala, a spiritual protector from the Tibetan branch of Buddhism, the faith of the Dalai Lama. The mantras to call him for assistance have been in use by monks for over 2500 years. He will clear the inner and outer obstacles you meet on your spiritual path and put a mantle of protection around you.

To call him to your assistance repeat his mantra a minimum of seven times or as many sets of seven as you feel you can do. Do not worry about the exact pronunciation. He will hear you.

OM MA-HA YAK-CHA TSA SO-HA

Optionally, you can make an offering ritual by pouring a cup of black tea and placing it in front of you. Also burn incense and place a lit candle in front of you as you perform your mantras.

Kwan Yin Mantra for Protection

Another powerful Buddhist and Taoist deity is Kwan Yin. She holds the loving power of Divine Mother and Divine Feminine. Her mantra will help clear any negative attachments and thoughts and will help repel negative forces. Repeat this as often as you like. I use it to clear the hall or room I am using before every workshop.

Om Mani Padma Hom

Hindu Mantra for Protection

Maha-Moola mantra is a very powerful potion of divine energies, which takes away any negative energies from within and around your mind and body.

Om

Sat Chit Ananda Parabrahma

Purushothama Paramatma

Sri Bhagavathi Sametha

Sri Bhagavathe Namaha

Sikh Protection Mantra – Gurudwara

Written by the 5th Sikh guru, Guru Arjan Dev Ji 1563-1606, this mantra is recited in Kundalini Yoga classes and also in closing services in Sikh temples. I love this mantra and there are some beautiful versions sung to great music. I particularly enjoy Snatam Kaur's recording. I have put links in the Appendix.

Aad Aad Guray Nameh, Jugaad Guray Nameh, Sat Guray Nameh, Siri Guroo Dayv-ay Nameh

Aad Such Jugaad Such Hai Bhee Such Nanak Hosee Bhee Such

Aad Such Jugaad Such Hai Bhai Such Nanak Hosee Bhai Such

Translation: I bow to the primal Guru. I bow to the truth that has existed throughout the ages. I bow to True wisdom. I bow to the Great Divine Wisdom. true in the beginning, true throughout the ages, true even now, Nanak, truth shall ever be. True in the beginning, true throughout the ages, true even now, Nanak, truth shall ever be.

Prayer for Protection - by Anne

Based on a Buddhist prayer to Setrap

All angels and masters in the heavenly realms

Defenders of truth and guardians of light

Protecting the weak and supporting the faltering

I call you to protect and guard me right now.

I request you to keep me both safe and empowered

To help me along my spiritual path

Repelling negative attacks from those who would harm me

I call you to protect and guard me right now.

I call you to remember and fulfil your promises

Made to those seeking enlightenment on their earthly path

To clear all the obstacles that may block our progress

I call you to protect and guard me right now.

Please dissolve all negativity received from others

Whether consciously delivered or passed unintentionally

That distracts me and disconnects me from my commitments and purpose

I call you to protect and guard me right now.

I call you strong guardians with your band of supporters

To clear and dissolve my fears and anxieties

That create obstacles and doubts in my heart and my mind

I call you to protect and guard me right now.

I ask you to protect not just me but my family

Keep safe my health, my mind and my personal prosperity

That I may share my good fortune with those who may need it

I call you to protect and guard me right now.

Keep detractors at bay and let me be free

To help others and share my love and compassion

As we work together to enlighten our world

I call you to protect and guard me right now.

Ritual for Protection

In Chapter Two I shared a number of protection symbols and rituals but this one is particularly useful when you are faced with a direct psychic or demonic attack.

Ritual: Four Trees – powerful against psychic attack

This is very powerful protection if you feel you are being spiritually attacked. I used this when I was once chased through the streets of Hong Kong by a demonic energy that had attached to one of my clients! I had been working on a woman who from time to time was possessed by a demonic entity, and I was fortunate to meet a healer in Hong Kong, Jenny Lethbridge, who continues to practise in the United Kingdom (see Appendix). She realised that the demon was trying to shut me down and had been stalking me. She shared this protection and I have found it extremely powerful for other situations where I have felt threatened.

- Visualise four large trees, representing stability and security, set around you.

- See gold chains, representing strength and power, wrapped around the trees.

- Call in white light, representing purity and divine presence, to surround you. 'I call in white light to surround and protect me; now, right now, right now.'

How to clear, cleanse and release psychic attack and black magic

Some of the energies and entities I have been describing are powerful and can be dangerous, so I don't advise you to try and disperse or destroy them yourself. You should call on the resources of a professional practitioner or priest who has knowledge and understanding of this area of healing. In the Appendix, I have put the names and contacts of some who work from a distance and whom I can personally recommend.

Call in help from the forces of light, the angels and Gods and deities as I have mentioned above. Do what makes you feel comfortable and don't take on other people's dark energy problems to 'help them out' or because you feel you ought to! I have spent years working with these energies and I have reached a time where I too step back and now pass on my work to the higher forces of light or to other practitioners.

Archangel Michael to clear attacking entities and spiritual attack

The great angel, Archangel Michael and his band of angels, has the role of dealing with the dark forces on Earth and in Spirit. I call him to disperse demonic energy and he uses his sword to break up and scatter the energy form. He will know if the problem you are facing is from a soul or an entity – a demon with no soul. If it is a lost soul he and his angels will escort the soul to the light; if it is a demonic energy he will disperse it. Here is a sample of what you can say to call in Archangel Michael to help you. If you are in an emergency situation call him right there and then, he will come to your aid. You can also call him in to help someone else who needs protection and assistance.

- 'Please Archangel Michael, place your protection around me; now right now, right now.' Repeat twice more.

- 'I call upon Archangel Michael to repel and destroy all negative forces that are affecting me, my family and my business. I call him in now, right now, right now.'

- 'Please take troubled souls to the light and clear all other negative energies.'

- 'I thank you Archangel for your help.'

Ritual: Clearing a Curse

A curse is normally only sent as a one-off event which means that when it's gone it's gone; not like a continuous stream of negativity, which can come from malicious thoughts. To release a curse, we need to summon and channel a light stream of energy stronger and more powerful than the negative intent that initially set it. This ritual will call in the energies of light and also Archangel Michael who will help you. Before you start, allow yourself to relax, play soothing music and let go of all fears, for these will fuel the negative energy and make it harder to release. Have a bowl of salt water by your side.

- Start by setting the Four Trees Protection that we looked at earlier and any other protection of your choice.

- Call in Archangel Michael, Jesus Christ or a protective deity of your choice; 'Place me in your protection and assist me in bringing in light to remove negative influences.

- Draw the Healing Symbol three times in front of you to bring in channelled healing energies.

- Sweep your hands through your aura and say, 'With the power of divine light and with Archangel Michael by my side, I fill this curse and associated energies with light and disperse and clear it; now, right now, right now.' Say three times as you sweep and flick the energy into the bowl.

- Thank Archangel Michael for his assistance.

- Preserve the energies with the Preserving Symbol.

After you have been through any close association with negative energies whether it is a jealous sister-in-law, an overbearing boss or an argument with your partner, let alone a psychic attack, it's a good idea to give yourself a good cleanse. Here are some ways that you can purify your energy field.

- A swim in the sea. The salt is a natural cleanser and the sea will leave you uplifted and refreshed.

- Take a shower and rub sea or Himalayan salt all over your body, include the soles of your feet.

- In your shower rub yourself with fresh limes or use a good concentrate of lime shower gel.

- Smudge yourself (cover with smoke) with burning

Frankincense or sage. If you don't have the fresh natural product use either a good quality incense stick or burn essential oils in a burner in your room.

- Wear or have near you, crystals and gemstones that have cleansing and protecting properties such as obsidian, malachite, red agate, black tourmaline, amethyst, selenite and moonstone.

- Spray or anoint yourself (dab oil on pulses on your wrists and temples) with any of these essential oils that clear negativity: juniper, sage, peppermint, palo santo, frankincense and lavender.

- The Violet Flame was given to us by the ascended master Saint Germaine. It will transform any negativity you may have picked up or created and will also protect you. Either visualise it burning around you or say, 'I am surrounded by the Violet Flame and all negativity is transformed.'

Possession
Possession occurs when a spirit, either a lost soul or a dark energy in the form of a demon or jinn style energy, moves into a person's body. The soul is pushed out and a full-blown possession occurs; the new energy will change the personality, character, mood and choices and the victim will act out of character. Sometimes the possession is permanent but often it will come and go.

How does possession occur?
Firstly, let me reassure you that possession is very rare. There are certain circumstances where a person is vulnerable and there has to be a 'way in' for the invading spirit. A hole in the boundary that surrounds the energy field can be an entry point for a lost soul who wants to continue their life experience after their own body has died.

What creates a hole in the aura?
A hole occurs when your thoughts are constantly focusing on something outside of yourself, the most common cause of this being addiction. When you have an addiction or craving over a period of time for alcohol, drugs, power or sex and you no longer can control your thoughts and emotions, then your auric boundary becomes perforated and negative

energies can enter. In other words your defences are down, just as when your immune system is low, you are vulnerable to invasion by viruses. The souls of addicts who have died can hang around the earth plane waiting for an opportunity to satisfy their cravings, and they will enter a living addict's body and energy field to satisfy their cravings. This makes giving up an addiction so much harder; the addict is not just battling his/her own cravings but those of visiting spirit addicts as well.

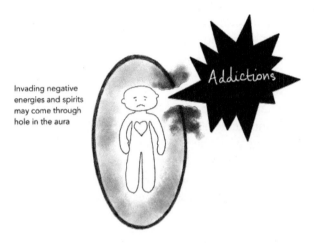

Invading negative energies and spirits may come through hole in the aura

What makes a person vulnerable to possession or psychic invasion?

- Addictions of any kind where the craving is constant, and they are out of control of their thoughts and desires.

- Being unconscious.

- Allowing another person to dominate to the point where they lose their will.

- When in the depths of despair, they open up and surrender without any protection.

- They sink into negative thoughts and behaviour and their vibration drops into the spectrum of darkness.

- When they are 'out of their mind' with grief, guilt or hatred.

- They have an extremely weak sense of self and are filled with fear.

- Completely ungrounded and disconnected from reality.
- They open up to channel unknown spirit entities without a focus or protection.
- Victim of a sudden accident.
- Using a Ouija board or other methods of channelling without protection.

Please join me as I send love, strength and healing to all those people who suffer the debilitating, destructive and humiliating conditions of addiction. Bless them. No one has a life ambition to end up in a gutter with only a needle for a friend.

Salesha's Possession

A month before Salesha's wedding she behaved out of control; she threw tantrums and acted like a child. She stamped her feet and refused to go ahead with the wedding. Her family, whom I knew well, were extremely distressed and they asked me to help them. I was reluctant to exorcise her in person, so I worked at a distance asking Archangel Michael to assist me. I was giving a workshop at the time on healing negative energies based on my book, so I thought it would be useful for the attendees to get involved. I asked them to hold the energy for Salesha, to focus on her soul and set the intention of keeping it safe. I called Michael and he helped me to release the spirit of a young child that she had attracted. She was most definitely possessed as her voice and her facial expressions changed but I wondered if at some level, reluctance to the marriage may have allowed the spirit to come in, as possessing spirits are often encouraged in by a mindset of the host. This can be a fear or a reluctance to move into a new state or stage of their journey. Once we had released the invading spirit, I suggested her mother talk to her and reassure her that it was her choice whether or not she went ahead with the marriage. Once the spirit had gone Salesha showed no reluctance to getting married and is now the mother of teenagers.

Brian's Story

I met Brian on a Nile cruise organised by the spiritual teacher Drunvelo Melchizedek's organisation. One evening his uncle gave a talk and told us that Drunvelo was a walk-in – with a prior contract his soul had stepped into another person's body in his late twenties. I was fascinated by the idea that a soul could swap bodies. Apparently, it occurs very infrequently but in order to miss out the years while the body develops, an old and experienced soul, maybe a Master, who needs to come to Earth with a specific and important purpose, can swap into another body. They would swap places with the resident soul who wants to leave at that age because they have completed their own life purpose. This is a positive situation all round as the departing soul will have achieved all they want and is happy to pass over his body to another soul.

Brian was one of the audience, and after the talk he and I went for a coffee to continue the discussion of walk-ins, possession and other extreme circumstances where a soul may leave the body or swap with another soul. He then went on to share his concerns about his wife.

His wife, Jessie, had undergone a massive operation some two years previously. It had taken nine hours, far longer than expected. Physically she was left with a chronic health problem and needed constant care which Brian was happy to give. But he was concerned about her character and personality, which had changed drastically since her operation. He asked me to check out what had happened. We went to my cabin and there I meditated and connected to Jessie's soul. Jessie was no longer in her body. She was still attached by the cord that connects a soul to the body, but her body had been taken over while she was unconscious in the hospital by another invasive soul looking for attention and further life experience. Jessie could not get back into her body and the invading soul refused to leave. I passed this on to Brian who tearfully told me that this was his fear. He said that the new spirit was mean and cruel and was making his life hell. However, he didn't want to abandon Jessie. I told him that Jessie was still attached but was in a state of limbo, neither on Earth nor in Heaven. Brian asked me to see if she wanted to go to the light or return to her body. He proposed it would be better for her to leave as her body was sick, old and damaged and he didn't want her to suffer. I reconnected with Jessie and she was very happy to move on. She sent her love and gratitude to Brian for the life they had shared and when I called in the angels she went to the light quickly. The cabin filled with an amazing feeling of peace and although Brian cried as he said farewell, he relaxed and said a huge weight had lifted from him. He was so happy she was at peace at last. Later we went to a channelled musical event where a woman channelled the most beautiful song. Brian cried and told me it was a personal farewell, from his wife! The singer said she didn't know the source but was overwhelmed by the love and the sense of peace she experienced while singing Jessie's farewell of love and gratitude. Brian wrote to me later, telling me he had put his 'wife' into a care home and walked away knowing that his Jessie was happy and well cared for in the higher realms.

Protect yourself in hospital

A lesson from Jessie's experience: surround yourself with light and call in your protection whenever you go through a procedure in a hospital where you will be unconscious, even for a short time. If you know anyone who is going in for an operation, call Archangel Michael to protect them.

- If you are a strong-minded and determined person who predominantly thinks positively, any possession or severe psychic attack will be only temporary.

- If you feel you are vulnerable or have been affected, get help from a competent therapist. See Appendix for suggestions.

Ways to avoid dark energies, spirits and psychic attack

As you can see there are some pretty nasty energies out there! So it's important to take care just as you would take care when visiting a new city; be conscious of your spiritual safety.

- Do not ever meditate, channel healing or open yourself spiritually without setting up your protection first.

- Do not talk to spirits without knowing who or what you are speaking to. If you want to be a medium, get training from a reputable teacher first.

- Never play with a Ouija board.

- Have absolutely no contact with people who play around with the occult.

- If you are a healer or therapist, never take on any clients when you are very tired.

- Avoid visiting places that have a name for being haunted.

- Be discerning about whom you choose as a spiritual teacher or healer.

- Protect yourself when going into hospital for an operation.

- If you have an addiction, get help; in the meantime use protection.

- Keep your energies uplifted and positive. If you feel low or depressed, play good music and use essential oils to lift your spirits.

You are the strong one; you have free will and a direct connection to the divine through your own higher self; keep that connection open.

Clearing your Space

Negative energy activity can affect your home and workspace. Here is one of my own lessons on the way negative energies can affect us.

The Crystal Bowl

After I had the experience of receiving the gift to clear karma in my friend Karen's kitchen as I described in Chapter Five, we decided to use my new gift on a group that gathered weekly at her house for meditation and planetary healing. The word got out that I was going to clear karma and we had a packed house. I duly went around to each one and cleared their karma, some I felt an instant shift, others not so much but it was well received, and we celebrated with a feast of cake and curry puffs. Afterwards everyone was standing around socialising and eating; one of the girls went to Karen's crystal singing bowl that was sitting on the side and took the wooden stick that we used to set off the vibration and spun it round the bowl. This would normally make the bowl 'sing' but almost immediately there was a loud crack and the bowl exploded into pieces. Everyone in the room froze and I walked over to look at the broken bowl. As I got close, I felt a wind blow and a strong force knocked into me, hitting me on the chest; it then moved into the room and bounced off another woman hitting her arm, and then sent another woman flying. Finally, it flew out of the window. We were struck dumb! No one could speak for a few moments, then we rushed to pick up the woman who had landed on the floor and calm her down for she was hysterical at this point – it's not every day that an unseen force sends you flying! I soon realised that all the karmic energies we had cleared had lodged in the crystal of the bowl; crystal attracts negative energies in a similar way to salt. If I had put salt in the room, it would have taken the toxic energy and we would have saved the bowl and saved ourselves from being knocked about. The lesson I learned that day was to always keep the room clear by putting salt close to where I do healing. The next day a psychic in the group came with a message from Sai Baba, a spiritual guru in India, to tell me to call him in to collect and transform any energies I shift. Now, I always call for help to do this when I give a group healing session.

Here are a few of the situations that can infect the space you use for living and working.

- Conflict and arguments.
- A person who is depressed, needy or has negative thoughts and attitudes has spent time with you.
- The toxic energies you release when healing, especially if you haven't been able to use some salt to attract and disperse these.
- A lost soul has taken up lodging.
- Illness or long-term disability.
- Your own fears, anxieties or depression.
- You have been the victim of a psychic attack.
- People you don't know have visited and you feel they have lowered the vibration.
- You are the target of jealous, envious or mean thoughts from neighbours or family members.
- There has been a traumatic event on the land or in the building in the past.

Fortunately, there are many ways that you can clear and uplift the energies of your living and working space.

Smudging
You can use the smoke from herbs to clear yourself or space.

- **White Sage** is a herb that contains powerful cleansing properties and is perfect for this use. You can buy prepared bundles of dried sage specifically for this purpose. Light the end of the bundle but knock out any flames; when it is smouldering take it around the building and waft the smoke into every corner. You can blow on the embers to increase the volume of smoke and use a large bird feather to direct the smoke. This is the traditional method used by North American Indians who have used smudging as a way to purify and heal for centuries. You can also use smudging to clear yourself, clothes, furniture and jewellery.

- **Frankincense** is a resin and also has very powerful cleansing properties. The smoke reacts with negative energies and transforms them. A space clearer I knew would visit the accounts department of a company he was helping and burn frankincense to detect any negative energies emanating from the files of suppliers. The colour of the smoke became darker, yellow and thicker when any negativity was detected. In the case of suppliers, it was an indication that they were cheating the company in some way! Frankincense comes from Oman and is quite expensive to buy but it is worth getting the best you can.

- **Palo Santo** is a holy tree found in South America and has extremely powerful properties for renewal and for clearing dark energies. When a branch falls, it is left for six months while fungus grows; shamans will then use it for smudging or turn it into an oil for healing.

Essential Oils

Plant oils have many healing and transforming properties. Use good quality, preferably organic oils for clearing energies; use in a burner, with reed diffusers or as a spray. The most effective oils for clearing space are peppermint, sage, frankincense, juniper berry, sandalwood and cedarwood. Clear and Cleanse is a spray I have developed, which you can purchase from my website.

Incense

Incense has been traditionally used in churches and temples to purify the atmosphere and ward off negative entities. Sandalwood

Incense sticks are my favourite and they have a pleasant fragrance.

Salt

Sea salt is an excellent absorber of negative energy and I have cleared rooms simply by sprinkling the salt around the perimeter, then smudging. I also put a bowl of water containing sea salt in my healing room to clear the energies released in sessions.

Symbol to clear thoughtforms of fear

This symbol can be used to clear thoughtforms created by fear or anxiety. You can clear a room by visualising this spinning, enveloping and transforming negative clouds.

Fear Release Symbol: Transforms negative energies. Draw from the top left, then top right, then the circle.

Ritual: Clearing Negative Thoughtforms

Here is a simple meditation you can use to clear away negative thoughtforms, blocks and attachments.

- Call in your protection and guides.

- Close your eyes and ground yourself by seeing yourself as a great tree with roots growing into the ground and fully connecting to Planet Earth.

- See a white vortex of swirling energy like a tornado coming down into the top of your head and enveloping you.

- It moves down you slowly spinning and clearing your energy.

- It clears all thoughtforms, all attachments and takes them down into the centre of the Earth to be transformed into light

I have a recorded version on my CD, *Healing Visualisations* in Shopify and it is also available on my YouTube account: Annejoneshealer, *Clearing Negative Thought Forms.*

As you clear your clutter you clear your mind. As your mind clears, your vibrations rise.

De-clutter and clean
Where clutter collects in your home or workplace, so does stagnant energy. This brings down the energy and attracts negativity. Check your home cupboards and corners for rubbish and clear it away.

- Discard piles of old magazines and papers.
- Throw on the compost heap dying and dead house plants.
- Take clothes that have not been worn for two years to the charity shop.
- Recycle old ornaments and décor that's pushed away in the loft, the garage and cupboards.
- Take children's toys and games to be recycled to the charity shop or pass to friends and schoolmates.
- Check what's hidden under the bed; do you really want or need it?
- Check there are no piles of rubbish in the corner of the garden or behind the shed.
- Clear out your sheds and recycle what you can.
- Kitchen cupboards; clear out those products significantly past their sell-by date; tidy and clean too.
- Cleaning and painting can be very therapeutic for you too. One client pulled herself out of depression by redecorating her house. She said she felt renewed as she spruced up her surroundings.

Music and Flowers
Playing your favourite music and bringing fresh flowers into your home can shift the energy after a time of conflict or grief.

Ritual: House Blessing

This is a lovely ritual that you can do for your home at any time you feel it needs an uplift, but is especially powerful when you first move in. I have this blessing done in houses after I have helped souls to the light or cleared away dark energies. Perform the ritual of clearing and blessing in every room.

Set up a tray with:

- a flower

- a bowl of sacred or blessed water; channel healing energies into spring water using the Healing Symbol or a reiki symbol

- a burning incense stick of frankincense or sandalwood

- a small bowl of uncooked rice; this represents food for you and your family

- a small bowl of salt; this represents cleansing and clearing the atmosphere and is also a sign of prosperity

- a lit candle representing the light

Take this tray into each room.

- Set it down in the middle of the room.

- Take the flower and dip it into the water and sprinkle the water into the corners of the room.

- Draw the Peace and Harmony Symbol in the air three times and say, 'I call in peace, love, harmony, prosperity and joy into this house; right now, right now, right now.' Choose the words that suit you.

Peace and Harmony Symbol: start drawing from the bottom and finish with the flame

- Draw the Healing Symbol three times and channel healing energies into the room.

- When you have blessed each room leave the tray in the centre of the house for a week.

Keeping yourself uplifted and strong

Negative energies have the least effect on you when you are feeling positive and uplifted, they will then skim off you like water off a duck's back. There is only one person who can make sure you are physically fit and strong, eating good food, sleeping well and allowing yourself downtime and holidays: you!

Journal:

Write down your own plan for maximum wellbeing. If you like spas, book one; if you enjoy exercise classes, enrol now; if you enjoy running, walking or cycling schedule time in your diary now. Plan your food in advance so that you don't slip into lazy fast-food habits. You know what to do; love yourself enough to do it now, right now, right now!

That more or less completes my sharing of the techniques and understanding I have developed during the last twenty years. I am sure there will be far more for me to learn in the years ahead because healing is not an exact science and I am learning something new all the time. What I do is driven by the needs of those that seek my help. I am now moving away from face-to-face sessions towards group work and online healing and teaching using the latest technology. This makes me laugh because although I am quite at ease facing a demon, the thought of live webinars, trusting new apps, the ever-changing layouts as software updates and fighting broadband speeds continues to send a chill down my spine!

I hope I get the chance to meet you either at a seminar or online but in the meantime, I wish you well with your healing progress. The last chapter is an overview of all the symbols I use. Let them work for you and enjoy their energies.

Love and hugs to you

Anne xx

Love is the key!

CHAPTER *Eight*

Ancient Symbols for Healing and Transformation

Through this book I have introduced the symbols where their energies can enhance the effects of the rituals and procedures of healing. Here is a full list of the symbols; many of them can be used in a variety of situations and ways. They initiate and invoke the power of universal healing energies and activate rays of energy that are channelled to Earth for healing and transformation. These rays of energy are controlled and mastered by a select group of evolved beings in Spirit. These advanced souls, ascended masters, have all gone through the cycle of life on Earth, sometimes many, and have become enlightened, which means they no longer need further incarnations on Earth and will not move amongst us in human form. However, they all have the soul purpose of helping humanity and guiding us through our challenges and evolvement here.

Masters who are involved with the guidance of the symbols include Kwan Yin, Dwal Khul, Lord Lanto, Serapis Bay, Lady Nada and El Morya. You will find further information on the Ascended Masters in 'Lords of the Seven Rays' by Mark and Elizabeth Clare Prophet and 'The Ascended Masters' by Dr Joshua Stone.

Although each symbol resonates with a different vibration and a different intention, they are all on the highest spectrum of light and come to us with love and compassion.

The symbols were used for healing as far back as Atlantis, a highly evolved ancient civilisation which eventually blew itself up with the misuse of crystal power – does that sound familiar? Just before Atlantis was destroyed, several high priests left with their advanced esoteric knowledge and took this with the symbols to the four corners of the Earth – The Himalayas, South America, North America and Egypt where they were used for healing and the raising of consciousness by the Ancient Egyptians, the North American Indians, the Incas and Mayans and other ancient cultures.

As people started to become less spiritually connected and lost focus on their intent, so the symbols were taken away and hidden. From a past life recall I was involved in placing them away for protection as I mentioned earlier, so I have a personal connection to them and that is why they have come back to me in this lifetime. Fortunately, they are now being released for use by everyone anywhere who has the intention of using them for good. They have been revitalised and recalibrated – the words of the Master Keeper of the Symbols – and are stronger than ever.

Through my teaching of these symbols, I have met people who recognise them in one form or another from many cultures around the world, where they have been passed from generation to generation. They are now fully activated and are being brought out into full public profile for use by mankind to help at this time, to assist us in our healing and personal empowerment. They also raise our energetic vibrations and help us to attain enlightenment. We are all connected through our universal energy stream, so as we use them we raise the level of love and light in the world and affect everyone and every living thing. So use them freely and generously and you will be helping mankind and the entire planet to come back to the state of love.

Integrity

The Masters have declared that we can use these symbols and pass them to others. The symbols are no longer secret but are only effective when used with love and with positive intentions. They cannot be misaligned and perverted by those with negative intent.

When you draw the symbols you invoke powerful healing energies, so you need do no more than add your love and caring as you work with them. They have their own energy and so you will not deplete your own energy store. They hold their own integrity, but I would ask you to always work with unconditional love and confidentiality. If you use these on someone else, please honour their personal confidences and have the intentions of the highest good for all in your heart at all times.

Frequently Asked Questions

- Q. What if I make a mistake when drawing the symbol?

  A. Don't worry – any mistakes you may make when drawing them will be corrected by the Masters. Draw them at least three times and then your intention to use them and their message is very clear.

- Q. I am a Reiki Master; will they clash with the reiki symbols?

  A. They will not cause any problem as they enhance positive energies. I am a Reiki Master and I have found they make the healing more powerful.

- Q. Can I use several symbols in one healing session?

  A. Yes, each holds a different intention and energy.

Healing

Healing Symbol: Be a channel for love.

Draw three times from right to left, then the dot.

This symbol can be used in all situations where healing energies are needed. It invokes the healing energies of the divine feminine, which resonates with love and compassion. Draw or visualise it three times to turn on the energy flow, just like a tap. The highest frequency of energy will channel into you through your crown chakra and out through your hands.

Draw this symbol three times to unlock your personal power to heal yourself and others by connecting to the universal energies of unconditional love. Use your hands to direct the energies to any living being or situation; the energy stream will raise the vibration of the recipient and transform negativity. Use for emotional, mental and physical problems.

You may feel a slight tingling in your hands as you channel the energy. However if you feel nothing don't worry because the energies will still be flowing. See Chapter Three for healing rituals and advice and situations where this symbol can be used to great effect. Avoid direct healing to the heart, if someone has a heart problem direct healing to their heart chakra.

Uses
- To invoke the energies of love for healing for yourself or friends, family, clients or groups.
- Use in the workplace by visualising the symbol and knowing it will be raising the energies of everyone around you.
- Integrate it into any therapy or counselling. Visualise the symbol to raise the energies of your session.
- Place under flowers or plants to help them stay fresh
- Place under food.
- Use over food that you eat outside of the home when you don't know the person who cooked it or their mood and energy.
- Use on or under drinking water.
- Draw this symbol and send the energies to the soul of a dead animal (roadkill) as an act of respect and acknowledgement.
- Draw over a map where there is conflict.
- Draw over any name or situation in a newspaper or magazine that needs love.
- Draw in your home or workplace to invoke loving energies when there is disharmony and the energies have dropped.

- Use with the Distance Healing Symbol to send love and healing to friends, families or clients if you are a therapist.

- Use on your pets and farm animals. Use for zoos and anywhere animals need extra care.

Release
Symbol Power· Clearing blockages, releasing congestion.

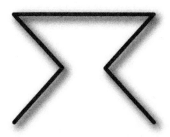

Draw left to right at least four times then sweep away the attachments or blocks. Breathe in deeply then blow out the blocked energy.

Use this symbol to cut the cords of attachment to old issues that still churn away inside you. Write down any feelings you still hold about past trauma, unresolved disputes, guilt and perceived injury from others. Draw the symbol over the paper then burn it and watch the old emotions transforming into light. Use to clear any blockage or congestion whether mental, emotional or physical. Let go and move forward.

Uses
- Clear your own thoughtforms, hovering in and around, your aura; heavy energy created by fear, worry and tension.

- Cut through cords and attachments to your heart centre connecting you to past and lost love.

- Cut through your own attachments to negative behaviour and thoughts, including addictions, obsessions, strong and out-of-control desires and yearnings for anything that don't nurture you.

- Releasing imprints of past pain and trauma that are now lodged deep in your subconscious and your cellular memory. Use with the Healing Symbol. See Chapter Three.

- Clear congested noses and sinuses. Use the symbol four times then sweep vigorously for a few moments. Have a handkerchief to hand!

- Relax muscles and joints and release tension.

- Clear a congested and constipated digestive system. Draw the symbol four times then sweep down through the body at least ten times.

- Helps with period pains and cramp.

Pain Release
Symbol Power: Releasing emotional and physical pain.

Draw three or more times starting at the point of pain and throwing the end as though letting the pain go from your hand. Draw from left to right.

Releasing the pain you carry, your own and other people's. Draw the symbol over the pain area then flick the symbol releasing the pain with the intention that it transforms into light. Repeat many times. Look for the root cause of your own pain and set the intention of healing the underlying cause, whether it's holding on to the past, feeling inferior, holding guilt or not nurturing your body. Avoid carrying the pain and suffering of others but send them love instead.

Uses
- Clearing out physical pain, such as headache, toothache, joint pain etc.

- Releasing emotional pain.

Peace and Harmony

Symbol Power: The inner flame.

Start drawing from the bottom and finish with the flame.

This symbol represents the universal flame of love that exists in all our hearts. When you recognise this light within you, it radiates from you and flows to everyone in your life and transforms discordant energies. To reignite this flame within your own heart and those in your home draw the symbol and say, 'I radiate the energies of peace and harmony, let all conflict be resolved, let all live together in acceptance and love.'

Uses

- Bring peace to your own heart when feeling hurt or troubled.

- Bring peace and harmony to a situation, person or home.

- Use with the Distance Healing Symbol to send peace to places of conflict in the world.

- Use it with photographs of people who are distressed.

- Bring harmony where there is friction between the occupants of a home or workplace.

- Include in a house blessing.

- Peace and harmony, calm, connecting to your own inner spark of divine love.

Distance Healing

Symbol Power: Connect from a distance.

Firstly, draw the Distance Healing Symbol once from the middle then round to the right in a clockwise direction, then the line, then the dot. Secondly, draw the Healing Symbol three times.

When you draw this symbol you create an energetic and spiritual connection with someone or a situation that needs healing and love. If you have a photograph of the person you are helping, first draw this symbol over the photo, then draw the Healing Symbol three times. Finally, hold the photo between your hands and let the healing energies flow into them through their photograph.

Alternatively, visualise the name of the person in lights and focus on them as you draw the symbol in the air in front of you. Hold the image or intention that the recipient is happy and well. Use as an antidote to worry. Anxious thoughts are negative energies but love uplifts and transforms.

You only need to take a few moments; this is a very powerful form of healing and your connection is instant. Remember the recipient is free to use the energy for whatever purpose they wish. You can emphasise your intention by saying out loud, 'I am sending love and healing to ...; now, right now, right now.'

Uses

- Sending healing to someone who is not with you.
- Sending healing and love to places in the world suffering disaster.
- Sending healing to the victims of accidents.

HOW TO *Heal*

- Sending love to war and conflicts by drawing with healing symbol over newspaper articles or towards the television or phone where you see people in trouble.

- Send healing and comfort to animals in distress.

Manifesting

Symbol Power: Creating with the power of the universe.

Draw three times, from bottom, left to right and end with the dot.

This is a powerful symbol so take care when you use it as it will attract whatever is in your mind when you draw it. It activates and works with the spiritual law of attraction that manifests and creates your will and intention. I call it the Wish Symbol. However, make sure you know what you truly want! When using this for someone else – draw the symbol and say or hold in your mind these words, '(*name*) will manifest whatever she/he holds in her/his mind at this moment if it is for their highest good.'

Here is a simple ritual for using the symbol; find a fuller description in Chapter One.

- Be clear and positive about what you want. Mixed thoughts give out mixed messages and dilute your power of attraction.

- Draw the symbol to invoke help from spirit and to send the message that you want to attract, matching energies to those held in your mind.

281

- Connect to your heart centre, open it and be thankful for all your blessings.

- Write, draw or visualise yourself with your goal realised.

- Release your expectation of when, how or where this will occur.

Uses

- Creating and manifesting desires and wishes.

- Setting goals and aspirations.

- Activating your ability to create with your mind, your heart and your will.

- Sends out the intention and vision in your mind and heart so that the universe can match this and bring it into reality.

The Chamber of Light and Colour

Symbol Power: The healing energy of the Chamber of Light and Colour.

Draw three times, first the top to bottom line, then left to right then the dots, starting in the top right-hand quarter.

When souls who have been suffering illness reach the heavenly realms, they are first taken to heal in the Chamber of Colour where each brilliant hue performs a holistic healing role. I saw a friend of mine who recently passed in this chamber and she was covered in colour, light and flowers for several days before she was strong enough to move on.

To replicate the healing experience on Earth find a quiet and peaceful place to lie down. Draw the symbol with first the downward stroke, then the cross stroke and then the four dots starting in the top left-hand quarter. Connect to the amazing healing properties of these vibrant colours as the colours of spiritual healing are directly beamed to Earth just for you.

If you wish to heal with colour, this symbol will help you to visualise the bright strong psychedelic colours of the spirit world. Each colour has its own vibration and healing powers, so choose the one that best suits your needs.

The following are some examples.

- Red is warming, stimulating and activating. It clears away negative energies, breaks up arthritic deposits and is good for blood disorders and circulation.

- Orange can be used for cleansing and clearing toxins and increasing immunity. Good for colds and lung problems.

- Yellow is purifying and good for meditation as it brings love and peace. Good for broken bones and skin problems

- Green is very soothing and excellent for calming down anger. Heals the nervous system.

- Blue is a strong healing colour. Good for epilepsy, depression, removing pain and reducing inflammation and fever. Good for sleep. Use with the sleep/peace symbol.

- Purple/violet. A very powerful colour to open up the third eye chakra for psychic and spiritual powers.

- Gold is the most powerful protective colour against negative energies and emotions.

Fulfilling your life purpose

Although I was originally given this symbol accessing the healing colours of spirit as used in the Chamber of Light and Colour in Heaven, I was subsequently given another use of this symbol which is to invoke a ray of healing energy that acts as an empowering wave and energy force that will help you to step forward and do the work you have contracted to do on Earth.

It will release barriers and open doors. You will find opportunities opening up and you will meet the right people at the right time. It raises the vibrations of all it touches, and once it is within you it will stay and be passed to all you meet. It is the energy of action. In colour vibration, the energy stream has gold on the outside, then silver, then aquamarine, then violet, with the centre of golden yellow.

Ritual: Activate your life purpose

- Breathe deeply four times.

- Hold your intention to connect to and complete your life purpose.

- Draw the symbol. Draw the vertical line then the horizontal then the first dot in the left-hand corner then the others clockwise over the head.

- Use your hands to sweep the energies down the entire length of the body.

- Say, 'I connect to and fully accept my life purpose as the plan I agreed to follow in this lifetime. I see all obstacles dissolved and my way clear; now, right now, right now.'

Uses

- Allows you to replicate the colour healing of the Chamber of Colour from the Heavenly Realms.

- Activates and reconnects you to your life purpose.

- Clears barriers and brings synchronicity and motivation to help you move forward.

Sleep/Peace
Calming turbulent energies.

Visualise this as the gentle flow of a blue wave. Draw down the body several times.

When you are feeling agitated and cannot find peace, draw this symbol several times and visualise it flowing through you as a blue light. Take three deep breaths, use your hands as combs to smooth through your troubled aura and say, 'I bring in the energies of peace and calm, all is well, all is still and all is at rest.' Use it to encourage sleep for restless legs or for hyperactive children.

This is one of a quartet of symbols used for bringing peace to the world with the Silver Ray. See the end of this chapter.

Uses
- Encourages sleep.
- Calming after a traumatic experience.
- Use with the Excess Energy Symbol for a small child who is restless in bed and overexcited.
- With distance healing to bring peace to troubled situations in the world.

Empowerment
Symbol Power: Empowering you to fulfil your potential.

Draw three times, the top then the bottom line underneath.

The power of this symbol will allow you to embrace the wholeness and fullness of who you are and allow you to expand into your potential. Use to overcome low self-esteem and negative ego. Let go all thoughts of inadequacy and accept that you are a powerful spiritual being and have much, much more to give and be.

It also has practical uses. One of my clients approached me for help to become a cook! She lived overseas and had been brought up with a housekeeper who did the family cooking. She had recently given birth and wished to cook her child's food herself. So would I make her into a cook please! I convinced her that we are all cooks inside, and it was more about empowering her desire to learn and to infuse her food with love than any magical formula to become a good cook. I drew the symbol over her head while she visualised herself cooking wonderful food for her child. Two years later she gave me a Healthy Cookery Book that she had written!

Uses

- Empowering.
- Restoring self-esteem and ego.
- Helping you to reach your full potential.
- Strengthening your self-belief, resolve and determination.

Preserving

Symbol Power: Preserving energies.

Draw three times, first the half cups then the vertical line.

I had a past-life recall of using this symbol in China to protect children from plagues and epidemics of viruses. I was shown that we can use it to preserve energy. At the end of your working day sit down and relax. Draw this symbol to reinforce your intention to contain yourself, take time out, to conserve your physical and emotional energies.

Use after a healing session to hold the new energy state and help prevent slipping back into old habits and negative beliefs.

Draw on paper and place beneath indoor plants, flowers and food.

Uses

- Preserving your own energy.

- Holding energy after a healing session.

- Preserving plants, flowers and food.

Trauma and Stress Release

Symbol Power: Releasing stress and trauma.

Start in the middle of the symbol and spiral outwards anti-clockwise, then point the middle finger into the centre.

This symbol clears away the pain and shock of injury and prevents stress. To be most effective it should be used as soon as the event has occurred whether the trauma is from a sports injury or an accident. My mother was always fairly accepting of my healing work and the symbols, but she became completely convinced when she fell down a short flight of steps and hit her head. The resulting pain in her head was sharp and intense, so I picked her up and sat her down and immediately drew this symbol to draw out the shock. She looked amazed as the pain stopped instantly and she became a huge fan of all the symbols from that day!

The symbol's energy swirls in an anti-clockwise fashion and goes straight to the core of the impact, drawing out the imbalance and shock of the trauma. It also helps prevent bruising developing if you use it straight away.

It can be used to release imprints from chakras and bring them into balance. Draw over the chakra and remember to circle in an anti-clockwise direction as this draws energy out; clockwise sends energy in. When worn as an amulet it prevents stress from settling;

it dissolves shocking energies; calms down turbulent energy and helps keep you free of extreme anxiety.

Uses
- Clears the impact of shock from emotional or physical trauma.
- Releases stress and anxiety.

Digestive Tract Healing
Symbol Power: Healing the digestive tract.

Draw up the body using two hands several times then sweep downwards with both hands clearing out any toxins and flick the negative energies into a bowl of salt or one in your imagination. Follow up by using the Healing Symbol over the solar plexus chakra and the sacral chakra to fill the entire digestive system with healing.

This symbol was originally given to me to heal the entire digestive tract. Later I was shown it can be used for DNA healing (see below). It helps to bring your digestion into balance if it is either too acid to too alkaline. It helps with hiatus hernia, irritable bowel – in fact, any digestive tract ailment.

Uses
- Balancing and healing the digestive tract.
- Helps with acidity, indigestion and irritable bowel syndrome.

DNA and Genetic Imprints

Draw up the body and above the head three times using both hands, then sweep down through the length of the body and down to the ground.

This symbol was originally given to solve and improve the flow of digestive problems (see above) but its other powers were shown to me later. It will help with healing the imprints of inherited genetic weaknesses – see Chapter Five for a full description of how to heal DNA and how you can be impacted by the genes you inherit.

Ritual: DNA Clearing

This is a simple use of this symbol. See Chapter Five for a fuller version.

- Place yourself into protection.

- Breathe in deeply four times and hold your intention of clearing all the negative beliefs, attitudes and imprints passed from the experiences of your mother and father and their ancestors – your entire natural family tree.

- Using both hands draw the symbol from your head up into the air and say, 'If permission is granted by my higher self, I am healing the souls of my mother and father and their parents back to source.' Repeat this three times.

- With your hands above your head, draw the Healing Symbol three times, then sweep down to the feet, saying, 'I am healing through this generation and the next and the next.'

- If you suspect there have been negative energies directed at your family in the past such as jealousy or even a curse, then as you draw the symbol up, you can also say, 'I clear all attachments and negativity placed on any member of my family and clan back to source.'

- If you do this for someone else before you start say, 'If permission is granted for this healing from all ancestors and your higher self.'

Uses
- Clearing genetic imprints.

- Healing weaknesses passed through the generations.

- Healing the souls of your ancestors.

- Releasing negative influences passed from generation to generation.

Excessive Energy Release
Symbol Power: Releases excessive energy.

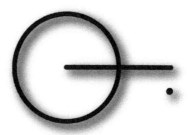

Draw three times in an anti-clockwise direction, starting with the circle then the line then the dot.

This symbol releases excess energy and is particularly useful for calming hyperactive or hysterical thinking or behaviour. Use this when you are feeling wired, overwhelmed, disoriented or losing focus. One of my students used it with great success on her neighbour's dogs when they became noisy and excited when people passed along their lane. She would lean out of her upstairs window and draw the symbol instead of shouting abuse at them as she had in the past!

Use with the Peace and Sleep Symbol for over-active children at bedtime.

Ritual: Water Energising

- Take a glass of water.

- Draw the Healing Symbol over it three times and hold your hand over the water for a few moments.

- Use a pendulum (anything weighty on a thread such as a gemstone drop) to check the energy in the water. You will find the pendulum will either swing or circle the water.

- Draw the Energy Release Symbol once over the water.

- Test again with the pendulum – you will find the pendulum falls straight again, indicating a neutral energy situation.

- Use the Healing Symbol to re-energise the water.

Uses

- Calming hysteria and hyperactivity. When overwhelmed or feeling over-charged.

- Calming over-excited children at bedtime.

Fracture

Symbol Power: Healing rifts and separation.

Draw the line over the break. Then draw the two sets of little lines on either side of the break.

You can use this symbol to help heal broken bones by drawing over the break. Use the symbol to heal rifts and differences in your own relationships and those of your family and friends. Draw the symbol and visualise the person with whom you wish to connect. Visualise old cords of discord and disagreement dissolving and see cords of love and acceptance flowing between you. To help other people's relationships, draw over their photos. This brings the healing energy in, then let go and let them work it out for themselves.

You can use this symbol on a map between countries that have disagreements or conflicts.

Uses

- Help to speed up the healing of bone fractures.
- Will help to bring people back together where there is a rift in the relationship.
- Setting the intention of healing breaks non-communication between people or countries.

Abundance

Symbol Power: Attracting prosperity and abundance.

Draw the curly part on the left first, then down and round to the right then the horizontal line second. The symbol represents a pouch of money! Draw three times.

Draw the symbol and be open to receive and allow the benefits of life to flow to you. If you have self-worth issues, overcome these by daily confirming out loud, your intention to attract and receive prosperity. Say three times 'I deserve and am open to love, financial rewards and security, friendship and exciting opportunities.' Remember that abundance comes in many forms, and gratitude for the benefits you already have will make you more receptive.

See Chapter One, lesson for living abundantly and the Attracting Abundance Ritual.

Uses

Attracting abundance and prosperity.

Clearing the blocks created by low self-esteem and low self-worth.

Meditation

Symbol power: Going within and connecting to your spirit.

Close your eyes and either envisage the symbol or draw it in the air in front of you four times starting at the top and swirling down – there are not a specific number of loops, allow it to flow naturally.

Use this symbol to assist you to go down deep within yourself for meditation and to connect to your subconscious feelings and thoughts.

Initiate a Meditation

You can use this to start any meditation for healing, self-development and understanding or for manifesting; anytime you wish to get into your own private and deepest thoughts and feelings or wish to connect to your higher self and Spirit.

- Use the Protection Symbol before you start and take four deep breaths. Call in any other protection that suits you.

- Call your spiritual guides and angels to be with you.

- Say, 'I call the Four Great Archangels to hold the space around me, in the four corners of my room: Archangel Gabriel (the divine messenger), Archangel Michael (the Protector), Archangel Raphael (the Healer) and Archangel Uriel (the Light bringer).'

- Breathe in deeply into your solar plexus.

- Hold whatever intention and purpose you have for your meditation.

- Draw the symbol four times from top to bottom.

Uses

- Meditation.

- Going deep within one's conscious and subconscious mind.

- To create a sense of oneness with your true self.

- Assisting you to connect to your higher self for your own personal guidance and wisdom.

- For contemplation to find your own answers and connect to your own truth.

Connect to Spirit

Symbol Power: Connecting to Spirit for guidance and help.

First draw the top vortex then the upturned pyramid.

Use this symbol in meditation to connect to your personal spiritual guides or to channel the wisdom of Ascended Masters. You may wish to have paper and pen to hand when you make your connection to note any messages. Call in your protection then open to their guidance; they will speak to you through your thoughts, insights and dreams. If you are in danger or dire circumstances angels may appear disguised as humans to help you.

I used this to connect to and channel the guidance of Enoch who is a spiritual master mentioned in the Bible. He helped me to understand the workings of the soul and higher self. I found it interesting that when I drew the symbol for this book I took the triangle from Microsoft's flow chart icons and its caption is merge! It's probably not been used for spiritual merging before!

Sit quietly, call in your protection then draw the symbol three times and invoke the Master or soul in Spirit you wish to connect with, then ask for the help or information you need.

See Chapter Three for a full ritual.

Uses

- Connecting to angels, your personal spirit guides and your loved ones who have passed on.

- Channelling guidance and wisdom from Spiritual Masters.

Opening your Heart
Symbol Power: Healing and opening your heart.

Draw the circle then the lines, draw three times.

Use this symbol to emphasise your intention of opening the doors of your heart. You can enjoy the effects of giving and receiving love when your heart is open and all blocks are cleared.

Put one hand onto your heart centre in the middle of your chest. Draw the symbol with the other. Close your eyes and visualise a set of doors representing the doors to your heart. Say to yourself, 'The doors to my heart are opening to receive love.' Love comes from family, friends and partners, strangers who step forward to help you and from Spirit in the form of our personal guides and angels, God and spiritual masters. When your heart is open, you allow love from all sources to flow towards you.

See Chapter Four for rituals and further guidance on healing and opening your heart.

Uses

* Setting your intention to open your heart to improve relationships, to attract love into your life.

Shapeshift

Symbol Power: Changing yourself to meet your aspirations.

Draw from left to right three times as you visualise what you want to be.

Shamans, healers of indigenous cultures, embrace the belief that everything is a form of energy and therefore it can be changed and manipulated at will. These priests of pagan practice, without reservation connect to nature and, with their own ability to manifest, can change their physical form. This practice allows them to shapeshift to any animal that suits their purposes and enables them to perform their healing and magic through various guises. For example, they can become an eagle and soar overhead seeing far further than they can through the eyes of a man.

A modern-day version of this art is to allow yourself to shapeshift, to change as you move through a transition and allow yourself to consciously shift into a new role, or transition into a new way of living. This symbol opens the opportunity for you to change and recreate yourself.

Examples of change and transition: from student to teacher from single to married, into motherhood, into retirement etc. Use this symbol daily with your intention as an affirmation.

Focus on what you would like to be, then draw the symbol and visualise yourself morphing into the new you. See yourself in your new role. See yourself developing new skills and expertise. See yourself happy and fulfilled. Are you ready to step into your full potential? If so allow the power of the shamans and the energy of the shapeshifter to renew you, revitalise and re-energise you.

Uses

- Use for rebirth and renewal when you are ready for change.

- Transitioning to a new role.

- Acceptance of new circumstances.

Solar Logos

Symbol Power: Personal empowerment and inner strength.

Start drawing with the circle then the centre downward stroke, next the left to right stroke, then the diagonal from the left and finally the right diagonal downwards.

The energy of this symbol comes from the spiritual energies of the sun, the solar logos; the most powerful energy in our universe. This powerful force will help you dissolve any anxiety and fear held in your own solar energy centre, your solar plexus. Use to strengthen your personal power, your will and your self-esteem.

Focus on your solar plexus, the seat of your solar energy and your personal power of will. Draw the symbol and visualise a beam of golden light flowing from the sun directly to you. Let it fill you and allow yourself to expand beyond your body, your home, your town, your country and the world. Keep expanding your consciousness beyond all earthly limitations and become at one with the universe.

In Chapter Two there is a ritual to activate and empower your solar plexus energy centre, releasing and dissolving suppressed fears and anxieties.

Uses

- Personal empowerment and strength.
- Strengthen your self-esteem.
- Develop courage to face your challenges.
- Dissolve fears and anxieties that are suppressed in your solar plexus.
- Heal the solar plexus chakra and all associated energies.
- Boost your will and determination.

Higher Self Connection

Symbol Power: Reconnect to your higher consciousness.

Draw from top left, then top right, finish with circle in a clockwise direction.

This symbol will raise your vibrations and allow you to rise up through levels of consciousness. Use it to connect your heart and soul and align yourself with your higher self, your higher consciousness. This higher, more evolved aspect of yourself is your true self and is unaffected by the wounds and imprints of painful life experiences that affect your soul energy. It holds the blueprint of your unique-self and the wisdom you have accumulated through all your lifetimes. When you hold this connection you become more in tune with your intuition, your accumulated innate wisdom and your true-life purpose.

Use this symbol to take you through to all that Is, to the universe, to the divine.

Ritual: Rising to Higher Consciousness

- Hold your intention to connect to your soul and rise above the darkness and troubles you are experiencing.

- Call in your protection of choice.

- Draw this symbol three times.

- Visualise a staircase ahead of you leading upwards through the clouds to the heavens.

- You are surrounded by angels and your spiritual guides.

- Imagine yourself climbing this staircase; you become lighter and lighter.

- Look down and see your home and life below as a speck in the universe.

- See the bigger picture of what is happening in your life.

- Allow yourself to be above the suffering and pain on Earth and feel the light and love of Spirit that is you, with you and surrounds you.

- All is one and one is all.

For further rituals with this symbol go to Chapter Six.

Uses

- Connect with your higher self, your oversoul, your I AM presence.

- Align to your intuition.

- Rise above the suffering of your life and connect to the Spirit that makes us all one.

- Connect to your higher self to become less emotional, more intuitive and open to your own guidance.

Fear Release
Symbol Power: Transforms negative energies.

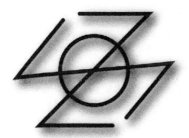

Draw from the top left hand and finish with the circle. It moves around like Pacman gobbling up negativity!

This symbol is used for releasing fear. It will help dissolve imprints on the energy field caused by trauma from this and other lives. The fear can manifest as a phobia or aversion; It can also become a physical problem e.g. digestive illness, panic attack, skin complaint etc.

Draw the symbol three times, focus on the fear you wish to release and see it dissolving and leaving your body, e.g. see black balloons leaving you taking all toxic energy, rising to the sun and turning into light, transforming the energy from dark to light, from negative to positive. This symbol can also be used to shift negative mindsets, fears and doubts.

Clear space with this symbol. Visualise it spinning through your home and workplace in anti-clockwise direction sucking in and clearing the negativity; lightening and uplifting the atmosphere.

Uses
- Clearing fears, phobias and negativity.
- Clearing space of residual negative energies.

Clarity

Symbol Power: See clearly - clearing illusions and negative perceptions

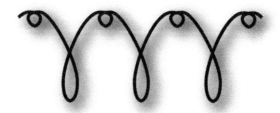

Draw from left to right three times.

Whenever you are confused or unsure then this symbol will help to bring you clarity. It brings focus when your mind goes off at tangents or you are easily distracted. It's good for a failing memory; I am still working on mine! As an experiment to test its power I used it to recall my primary school days, and I was amazed how I could see every detail of my classrooms, even to the style of handle on the doors! Use when healing or visiting past lives to give you a clear recall of memories that have been suppressed into your subconscious and soul.

When you are in a conflict or there are many arguments presented for a situation to be resolved, use the symbol to cut through preconceived ideas, expectations and illusions.

Sit in quiet contemplation and think of something you wish to achieve, a goal you have set or a problem you wish to solve. Draw the symbol before you. Ask for clarity to see through the illusion and the distorted energy that surrounds the situation. Relax and the answer will come to you as an insight, a dream, a suggestion from a friend or something you hear or read that creates a light bulb moment of clarity.

Uses

- Focus on difficult subjects or situations.

- Clarity of mind to see through the fog.

- Memory recall.

- Past life regression.

- Clears muddled thinking.

- Cut through illusion and see people, yourself and situations more clearly.

- See yourself and those around you clearly for who they truly are and let go of illusory expectations – see the truth and let it be.

Fertility

Symbol Power: Creating the opportunity for birth and growth.

Start drawing from the top and finish with the dot, three times.

The Fertility Symbol will help encourage and enhance any new growth, whether this is for seeds you plant in your garden or projects you have conceived with the germ of an idea. It will help you evolve your ideas and aspirations into full-blown actuality.

It can assist in the conception of a baby; it works to clear the blocks that may be in your own energy or that of your partner that subconsciously resist the fertilisation of an egg. Through the healing and your intentions that the symbol emits, any barriers can be cleared and the solution can come through to you, whether this is a new type of fertility drug, a therapist who can clear the physical and mental blocks or raising the energy and wellbeing of sperm so that fertilisation can occur.

Use this symbol to open all opportunities for you to create something new and special. Focus on the desire in your heart and as you draw the symbol say out loud what it is you wish to create. Once you have sown the seeds let the powerful energies of universal love nurture your creation and see it flourish and grow. Use the symbol until it is fully-fledged and has its own energy.

Uses
- Fertilising and encouraging the conception, growth and development of seeds, concepts, projects, ideas, love and babies.

Protection
Symbol Power: Sealing and protecting your energy and possessions.

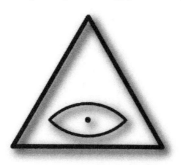

Start drawing with two hands at the middle of the base line of the pyramid, then draw the sides and meet at the apex. Then draw the eye and then the dot. If you are protecting someone else you can draw this over their picture or envisage them in the pyramid.

This powerful Protection Symbol invokes universal energies that will seal, strengthen and protect your spiritual energy and your aura. It helps you to withstand the negative energies that can drain your life force; energies that you pick up from needy or sick people or are targeted at you by jealous or manipulative people.

You can use it for yourself or other people, a place or an object. It is based on the Eye of Horus, an Egyptian power symbol and creates an energy shield around you that helps protect from unseen dangers. Use it when you are feeling vulnerable or when you are with negative people or dangerous situations. When worn as a talisman it can strengthen your energy field and make you less likely to be bullied or dominated by others. You can attach it to your keys, your phone, your car or your pets. You can draw it on the bottom of your shoes, put under your bed or, as one of my clients has done, tattoo it on your back!

There is more information on protection techniques and rituals in Chapters Two and Seven.

Uses:

- Protection for yourself from all sources of negative energies, other people's thoughts and emotions or deliberate psychic attacks.

- Helps prevent heavy vibrations and challenging atmospheres from draining your own energy, e.g. hospitals, care homes, city centres, gatherings where people are in conflict etc.

- Protection for your possessions; keys, pets, car etc.

For more help with Protection and Clearing Negative Energy see my books *Healing Negative Energies* and *Protect Yourself.*

Balance
Symbol Power: Balancing all aspects of your being.

Start drawing the left sphere, then the lines, then the right sphere, three times.

Use this symbol to bring yourself or a situation into balance. It has the properties of the ying/yang symbol. Use to commit to a lifestyle balance allowing time for play as well as work; time for exercise as well as relaxation; time for quiet contemplation as well as social activity. You can use it to help bring balance back to your physical state: acid/alkaline digestion, blood, hormones, actual balance and stability. Use to balance your mind to keep it focused and active but not overwhelmed by chitter-chatter or negative thoughts.

Draw the symbol and hold the intention of reclaiming balance in your life. An orderly and balanced life needs to be planned, so work out now what aspects of your life need more attention or more focus. Decide what needs to be given more emphasis. Keep your feminine and masculine aspects and your spiritual and earthly activities in equal time and consideration. When you are balanced you are secure and strong.

Uses
- Commitment to a balanced lifestyle.
- Balancing the need to care for others and for yourself.
- Balance your physical body; active but not hyper, strong but not overworked, controlling your food but not depriving yourself etc.
- Balance your mind between active and somnolent, focussed and careless, etc.

Empower and Activate Cellular Memory
Symbol Power: Reactivate lost knowledge.

Draw the three circles in any order then put the dots inside.

This symbol encourages the recall of past life experiences that have become embedded in your cellular memory. Use it to improve your abilities in this lifetime and also unlock latent skills and talents you have not developed so far, but are part of you. Activate creative skills such as art, music, or acting and psychic abilities that you have hidden in your subconscious.

The symbol can be used in a ritual for the Activation of Cellular Memory, to allow these skills, abilities and wisdom to be resurrected into your consciousness in this lifetime, this is explained fully in Chapter Six.

Uses

- Recalling lost skills.
- Activating cellular memories and old knowledge.
- Empowering skills and attributes.

Healing Damaged and Infected Cells

Symbol Power: Healing and transforming damaged cells.

Draw the left, then the right as an infinity sign, then the top and bottom. Draw four times. Can use with the Healing and Distance Healing Symbols for people who are not present.

Use this symbol to send love and healing directly to any cells that are malformed, damaged or attacked by viruses. I use it to send healing to cancer. See the person you wish to help or yourself, in a beautiful, sparkling ball of light. Say, 'I send healing energies of love for your highest good.' Say, 'I send love for healing all cells: now, right now, right now.'

Uses:

- For misaligned or damaged cells.
- Help with healing cancer, viruses, immune system disease.

Soul Healing

Symbol Power: Healing and raising the vibration of the soul

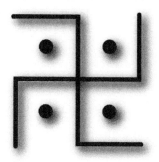

Start drawing top left to bottom right, then top right to bottom left, then the four dots starting in top left-hand corner.

Use this symbol for healing soul imprints and fractures and raising the overall vibration of your spirit.

Use to heal the soul after it has become fragmented or overloaded with emotions or when involved with traumatic events involving human tragedy; for example, as experienced by accident and emergency medics, police, armed forces, relief workers and social services.

The soul holds the imprints, wounds and scars of all the most shocking and upsetting things you have experienced such as abandonment, abuse or betrayal. Each lifetime you come with the intention to clear and resolve these deepest wounds and will therefore create opportunities to experience them again. Illness, upset emotions and mental distress all point to underlying soul wounds. With a positive approach and dedication, look deeply within to identify the underlying problem; the trauma you have experienced as part of your journey of self-development and spiritual evolvement. The issues, problems and challenges of your life will be markers that show you that there is healing to be done. Your quest to find the underlying cause will lead you to imprints that are held at cellular level in your soul and heart. These imprints hold emotions that were experienced at the time of the past trauma. This symbol holds the intention to heal the damage caused by challenges you faced that were intended to teach you a life lesson. With healing you can unlock these emotions, dissolve the scars and learn the lessons.

To use for yourself draw the symbol several times and see it zooming into you. Hold the intention that all imprints and scars will be healed and you will understand why those traumas occurred. Remember anything that was not completed in the past will have occurred again in this lifetime, so you have it in your conscious memory as well as in your subconscious. You may feel your entire being become lighter as the toxic energies of old traumas release. Refer to Chapter 6 for full description of usage of this symbol and techniques for healing soul imprints and fragmentation.

Take time to sit in a quiet space and contemplate your life and relationships. If you have been the victim of other people's hurtful actions, you need to heal the resulting soul scars. These act as magnets attracting negative energies and causing you to shut down to aspects of life. It's time to heal with love and forgiveness. Draw this symbol and invoke the energies of universal love you need to heal these deep wounds.

To help heal the soul of someone else, send from a distance with the Distance Healing Symbol. See the symbol entering them and sense their whole being filled with light.

Ritual: Sending souls to the Light
This symbol can also be used to help release the souls of the departed who are stuck in this earth plane. You can use this ritual if you want to help a 'ghost' or troubled soul that is stuck down here, unable to move up onto the higher vibrations of the heavenly planes. The symbol invokes the light energies that are needed to lift the soul and release the guilt or fear that keeps it down on Earth.

- Protect yourself.

- Either do this in the place where the soul is hanging around or draw a simple map with the address where it can be found.

- Draw the symbol four times and then cup your hands and sense the soul is in your hands.

- Say, 'You are filled with love and light and all pain from your earthly life is healed; now, right now, right now.'

- Say, 'I call your spirit guides and angels to guide you to the light.'

- 'With love, I send you to the light; now, right now, right now.'

There is more information about helping souls to the light in Chapter Seven.

Uses
- Healing the soul of imprints, damage and fragmentation.
- Raising the vibration of a person's essence.
- Helping lost and confused souls to the light.

Group Healing
Symbol Power: To initiate healing for groups.

Start anywhere, then draw in a continuous flow back and forth three times.

This is the symbol I use when beginning a group healing live. Draw this three times then bring your hands down as though you are drawing down the energies into the group in front of you.

Call in protection for yourself and the group; say out loud the purpose and intention of the healing, call in spiritual assistance and continue to use any symbols you need including the Healing Symbol. This symbol effectively sends you a broadband width of energy to meet the needs of everyone in the group.

Uses
- Healing a group of people or animals.

Karma Release
Symbol Power: Transforming and releasing karma and redundant vows.

Draw three times, the infinity loops then line one, then two, then cup underneath and finally the dot.

I use this symbol whenever I need some heavy-duty energies! In this case, we are using it to release you from your karmic cycle and dissolve old redundant vows. Contacts, vows and promises that you have made in any lifetime can stay with you and seriously affect your life and particularly your relationships. Old contracts can create karma if they are broken, so release all vows that are not active and no longer have your commitment.

The spiritual law of karma of cause and effect is covered fully in Chapter Five.

As you draw the symbol say out loud, 'If it's appropriate for my highest good I release and dissolve my karma turning my guilt and shame into wisdom. I dissolve all redundant vows that no longer serve me. I dissolve the vows, now, right now, right now.' Say this two more times.

Uses
- To clear the burdens of guilt and shame.
- To clear your karmic debt if you have learnt your lesson and/or atoned.
- To release old and binding vows, which are no longer to your benefit.
- To dissolve karma and transform the lesson into wisdom.

The Ascension Symbols

This set of symbols came to help my clients raise their energy to the vibration of the fifth dimension, where love and inner peace are the norm. The symbols help us to reclaim personal powers that we have lost over many lifetimes on Earth where judgement and fear have shut us down to our spiritual selves. They can help you to work consciously on moving onwards and upwards without limitations. Confidence and self-belief are so often elusive in our challenging world, but by connecting to the intentions of the symbols you can overcome your own fears and inhibitions and follow your dreams, take on new directions and expand your consciousness, allowing you to believe that 'yes you can'!

Reclaim your lost aspects

Symbol Power: To help you claim back all aspects of your power, skills and soul fragments that you may have lost in this and previous lifetimes.

Draw three times. Firstly the down line, then the across line, then the infinity sign from the left, then the right. Then bring all lost aspects back by sweeping your arms towards you saying 'I claim all that I have lost that is mine; now right now, right now'

When we experience trauma, persistent bullying or abuse we may push away the memory to save ourselves from pain and that can work well as a managing process, but we often lose some of our power and aspects of our character at the same time. Aspects lost in this way include: your voice to share your feelings and thoughts, your self-esteem and confidence, your self-worth, your trust in yourself or others. You need these aspects of your character to have fulfilling and complete relationships and to live your life fully without limitations.

This symbol is useful for calling back aspects of yourself lost in a past life. If you died in a traumatic way with strong emotions at the time you passed over, there is a chance that you may have lost strong attributes and character aspects that may still be missing in this lifetime. For example, a client was a trusting loving child but was dreadfully abused and abandoned by her father; she died alone and disillusioned. She lost her trust and her confidence with men from that lifetime. We used this symbol to reclaim her faith, trust and confidence.

Uses

- Reclaiming soul fragments.

- Make yourself spiritually and emotionally whole again and claim:

  – confidence

  – voice

  – trust

  – inner peace

  – self-worth, esteem, value

  – courage, will, security, balance

  – lost and forgotten skills

- Lose your inhibitions and self-doubt.

Clearing Obstacles

Symbol power: Clears limitations and obstacles that are in the way of your spiritual journey of evolvement.

Draw three times. Firstly the large circle, then the small, then the spokes

Use when you are stepping forward with a new project, job or change in direction in your life. It helps you release your fears of the unknown when embarking on new ventures of all kinds and has a similar energetic effect as calling in the assistance of the Indian God Ganesh. The symbol represents a wheel that rolls forward without effort or stress.

Uses

- Releasing fears and the limitations they create.
- Opens your mind to all possibilities for your success.
- Clears the way for new ventures and new directions.
- Propels you forward on your spiritual journey.
- Releases barriers of mind and spirit.

Expanding Consciousness

Symbol Power: To raise yourself above low and dense vibrations and to open your mind to greater understanding of your spiritual self and your place in this universe.

Draw three times. Firstly, draw the dot at the top then the vertical line, then another dot. Draw the large circle, the smaller, then lastly the smallest circle.

Use this symbol when with all your heart and soul you wish to grow and expand your consciousness. To open your mind to new understanding, to let go of old restrictive beliefs and patterns and to evolve. This is particularly powerful when you are consciously raising your vibrations as you seek to reach the fifth dimension, which is our next level of consciousness. This is the spiritual goal of us all, but we often become disconnected from our spiritual senses; this symbol will reconnect you to your spiritual needs and the desire to become lighter and to release old self-inhibiting thoughts and fears.

Uses

- To raise your spiritual energy frequency and vibration.
- Working towards ascension and the fifth dimension.
- To open your mind and consciousness to new and lighter ways of thinking and being.
- To set your intentions for your journey of self-discovery.

Release Burdens

Symbol Power: Releases the heavy and debilitating energies of the real and perceived burdens and responsibilities you carry.

Draw three times. The downward line then the line across, then the left circle and finally the right circle. Sweep your hands over your shoulders and upper back and flick heavy energies into a bowl of salt water (imagine it if you don't have one to hand)

Use the symbol to release burdens you are carrying; they can be people who are depending on you, people you are carrying, responsibilities that are overwhelming you or a sense of heaviness on your shoulders from the difficulties and challenges in your life.

Draw the symbol then sweep your shoulders three times and imagine flicking the heavy energy into a bowl of salt water. If you tend to try to sort out other people's lives, then use this frequently. Hold the intention of letting go of any controlling thoughts or intentions on your part. If you are a carer or responsible for other people's welfare, then use this every day.

If you are a worrier and experience anxiety, then use this symbol to clear the burden or worry. If you suffer from a stiff neck or upper back, you will benefit from using this to release tension.

Uses
- Clearing the burdens of responsibility.
- Releasing the energy attachments of people who depend on you.
- Letting go of the need to control and fix other people's situations.

- Releasing the tension in your neck and back from your burdens.

- Lightening the load when you feel overwhelmed by your life.

Freedom – Set Yourself Free
Symbol Power: Releases you from the prison of thoughts, attitudes, beliefs and programming.

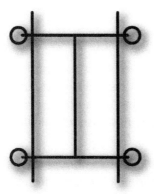

Draw three times. Draw the two outside vertical lines first, then the cross lines, the middle line, then the four circles starting with the top left hand.

Use the symbol to release ties, attachments, mindsets and fears that hold you back and create limitations. See yourself flying high and free as you draw this symbol. You are releasing yourself from third dimension rules, regulations and inhibitions. You are allowing yourself to be as great as you can be! This is your get out of jail card! Permission to fly and take a chance, to give yourself the opportunity to follow your dreams and be and pursue whatever your heart and passion call you to do.

Uses
- Release any chains that hold you back.

- Move forward at the rate that your heart dictates.

- Release yourself from self-limiting thoughts and feelings.

- Release the programming that makes you think you cannot fly.

- Use when you feel blocked.

- Use when you feel it is time to step forward for new directions and ventures.

Planetary Healing Symbols and the Silver Ray

Background

I was first introduced to the symbols for planetary healing during a regression to a past life in Egypt. I was a High Priest and placed a gold casket containing the entire set of symbols in a chamber under the Sphinx. I connected with a spirit of green light that announced itself as the Guardian whose role it was to keep secure the ancient wisdom held in the chamber. The Guardian told me that I and other Ancient Egyptians had stored away valuable information about healing and alternative therapies and practices; this wisdom and knowledge would be revealed to mankind when the time was right.

I asked to see what was in the casket and I was shown the symbols displayed in light. There were some that I recognised which I have shared in this book, some that I couldn't see clearly and also a set of four new ones that shone brightly. The set of four is for the purpose of healing mankind, specifically for balance and equality and for bringing peace to Earth.

Several nights later I was woken up by my spirit guides and requested to sit and be ready to receive. I was surrounded and filled by the most intense silver light; the Silver Ray that was coming to Earth to bring peace and healing for mankind, Planet Earth and all that live upon her. I was surrounded by the Mer Ka Bah light body, which is a star tetrahedron and I was told that there would now be a constant light body around me. This would protect me and enable me to raise my energy and lift me above the earth plane at a time in the future without going through the process of dying. I felt the amazing and comforting presence of an angel wrapping its wings around me. Since that time several psychics have seen the angel behind me and the Mer Ka Bah light body surrounding me.

The Mer Ka Ba light body. This is two 3-dimensional pyramids interlocked

When you draw these symbols, you too will invoke the power of the Silver Ray and receive the Mer Ka Ba light body that will surround you and assist in your journey of healing and evolving, and ultimate enlightenment. It is believed that we will move to a higher dimension, to a place of love and harmony; this shift to a higher vibration is called ascension. It is believed this will happen sometime in the next 20 years. For further information on the predicted ascension, you can read the books and writings of Drunvalo Melchizedek, Bob Frizzel and Greg Bradon.

The Symbols of the Silver Ray bring Love and Peace for the Planet

The Sun – representing power and strength and the male energy.

The Moon – representing Unconditional Love and the Female Energy.

The Bird – representing freedom and freedom from fear.

The Wave – representing peace.

Ritual: Invoking the Silver Ray and Planetary Healing

- This is a ritual that you can do alone or in a group. If there are several of you, create a circle and place a representation of the Planet Earth in the centre. Also, in the circle place the names of anyone you feel needs healing and the vibrations of love.

- To Invoke the Silver Ray and planetary healing say the following as you draw the symbols, and repeat three times.

'When the male energy of strength (pause to draw the sun) and the female energy of love (pause to draw the moon) are in balance and humans are free from fear (pause to draw the bird); Then we will have peace on earth' (draw the wave).

- Spend a few moments visualising a world at peace and a world where love is the norm.

- Raise your right hand and feel the healing energies flow from your hand and direct them to Planet Earth.

- Close your eyes and feel the energies of the Silver Ray and the Mer Ka Ba envelop you. Sense the angel wrapping her wings around you.

- Take a few minutes of meditation while you enjoy this amazing vibration of love. Then you can follow the meditation below to send healing to our planet.

Hearts and Hands Planetary Meditation – you can do this meditation after the symbols. There is a recording of this meditation on my YouTube account: Annejoneshealer.

Use your hands to direct the energies of the ray towards the world representation and the names in the circle.

'We call upon our guides to be with us now for this planetary healing. We call the angels, archangels, masters and the spiritual hierarchy to be with us now as we use the Silver Ray to bring love and peace to our world.

'We send beams of love and light from our hearts and our hands to the seas and water of the world. We see them blue, crystal clear and free from toxins and pollution. We see healthy fish, dolphins and whales swimming in these clear waters and we see this all in a world filled with love and a world without fear.

'We send beams of love and light from our hearts and our hands to the air of our world. We see blue skies, we see the air clear and free from pollution, we see the ozone layer complete and healed. We see the birds flying through air that is clear and free from toxins and we see this in a world filled with love and a world without fear.

'We send beams of love and light from our hearts and our hands to the vegetable kingdom of our world. We see forests of trees thriving, we see the flowers that bring so much beauty and we see our vegetables growing in soil that is free from toxins and pollution. We see all vegetation thriving in a world filled with love and a world without fear.

'We send beams of love and light from our hearts and our hands to the mineral kingdom. We see the crystals of the world bringing us beauty and healing, we see the great rocks of the world as our foundation and we see all this in a world filled with love and a world without fear.

'We send beams of love and light from our hearts and our hands to the animal kingdom. We see the animals of the wild running free, unhurt and unfettered by mankind. We see all farm and domestic animals respected and nurtured. We see all animals free from hunger and harm. We see the animal kingdom thriving in a world filled with love and a world without fear.

'We send beams of love and light to the children of the world. We see them loved and loving, we see them cherished, and we see them sheltered and free from hunger and harm. We see them with confidence, self-esteem and respect. We see all our children thriving in a world filled with love and a world without fear.

'We send beams of love and light to the women of the world. We see them tender and caring, loved and respected, free to speak and filled with self-esteem and self-worth. We see them free from hunger and pain surrounded by love and we see them in a world filled with love and a world without fear.

'We send beams of love and light to the men of the world. We see them strong and respected, loved and loving. We see them at peace with themselves and each other. We see them free from hunger, free from repression, free from hate. We see them treated with equality with opportunities to thrive. We see them in a world filled with love and a world without fear.

'We see our beautiful planet shining in light – we see all sentient beings filled with love, filled with compassion and free from fear.

'We call this love back into our hearts and fill ourselves with this love. Sweep your arms round to scoop up the love and bring it into your heart.

'We send this love as beams of light to all those who are in need of help, strength, love and care at this time.'

Thank you for allowing me to share the knowledge of these powerful symbols. They have helped me and many people all over the world step into our personal power. With your own natural ability to heal and the help of the symbols and the universal energies they invoke, you can help yourself, your family and friends and anyone you meet who may be struggling with the challenges they face.

I have painted a set of Symbol Oracle Cards, which you can use to bring the power of the symbols into your life on a daily. See Appendix.

Appendix I

Your Questions Answered

Here are answers to some of your most frequently asked questions.

Q How do I know if the feelings I am experiencing are from my own fears and self-created thoughtforms and demons or if I am under psychic attack or black magic?

A. If you are affected by negativity from outside of you, whether it is from someone's jealous thoughts or full-blown black magic, you will not feel it when you are standing under a shower or waterfall. The flowing water will shield you, so you can test out your situation quite easily this way.

Q In my meditation I get spirits talking to me and offering to help me. Should I listen?

A. Ask them if they stand in divine light, or The Christ Light. If they answer anything other than a direct yes, then do not continue to listen to them. Ask this question four times. By spiritual law they have to answer honestly.

Q I think I am cursed. What can I do about this?

A. I have included a ritual for clearing curses in Chapter Seven. If you would rather get help, you can ask for help from someone who specialises in clearing such negativity. See below for recommendations of therapists who clear curses and negativity from houses and the workplace.

Q I think my house is affected by negative energies; how can I check this out?

A. A space-clearing practitioner can dowse at a distance to check the energy status of a building. In my book *Healing Negative Energies* I give instructions how you can do this for yourself. I suggest you use the techniques in Chapter Seven, and if you continue to feel the energy is depleted or disturbed get professional help. See below.

Q Can I send any bad vibes that I receive back to the sender?

A. The best place to send these energies is to the light. There, they can be transformed and will not harm anyone else in the future. Use your intention to do this. Say, 'I send all energies that are not positive to the light; now, right now.'

Appendix II

Clearing negative energies, possessions and attachments from people and buildings

- **Debbie Rye of www.alternativetherapies.co.uk**
  Debbie works from a distance so can help you anywhere in the world. Clearing houses, buildings, helping souls to the light, clearing possessions and curses. Email: dar@alternativeways.co.uk.

- **Emma Loveheart**
  Emma works on healing energy in homes, and specialises in clearing psychic activity of a dark nature including curses. She works remotely from the UK and is contactable via her website www.homehealer.co.uk. 'My mission is to heal as many homes as possible to bring light and healing into people's lives, including yours.'

- **Soo Kong Beow Temple, Penang, Malaysia**
  Consultations, including expelling evil spirits, exorcising houses, clearing black magic and curses etc. Lot 297, MK 10, Sungai Ara, 11900 Penang, Malaysia. Tel: +6 04 642 1234 Contact: Mr CH Ooi (English speaker) Tel: +66001986681. chikhoe@yahoo.com
  Soo Kong Beow Temple,Jinjang. Kuala Lumpur, Malaysia No. 36A Jalan Kepong, Jinjang Selatan, 52000, Kepong, Kuala Lumpur, Malaysia.

Past Life Regression – Janet Thompson
Janet works from home in East Grinstead, Sussex. www.janetthompson.org. For bookings and Past Life Regression CD please contact Janet directly: mailme@janetthompson.org

Conscious Café
Changing the Consciousness of the World one conversation at a time.

Find a group near you http://www.consciouscafe.org

Distance Healing and Channelled Readings for People and Animals –

Debbie Atkinson www.naturesmessage.co.uk.

In my online shop on www.annejones.org you will find:

Silver symbol jewellery – the symbols created into beautiful pendants, protection, healing and heart healing.

Ancient Symbol Oracle Cards – connecting to the power of the symbols for energising, healing and guidance.

Heal and Be Healed – *Discover The Secrets of Ancient Symbol,* A6 booklet. E-book version available from Amazon.

Protect Yourself – *Protect Your Energy,* A6 booklet available on my website www.annejones.org and from Amazon as an e-book.

Clear and Cleanse Aura Spray – Essential Oil Ingredients: spanish sage, juniper berry, cedarwood, peppermint. To clear negative energies from your energy field or work or home space.

Heart Balm. This organic body lotion contains geranium, ylang ylang and rose organic essential oils. Use for helping to heal heartache and attracting love into your life.

Snatam Kaur – Add Guray Nameh. Mantra for protection. YouTube.

Acknowledgements

Thank you to Trina and Trevor for taking my manuscript and producing a book! Thank you to Jacq Forrest for producing the illustrations. Thank you to all my clients and the friends who have been willing and had faith to receive the magic of the symbols and the amazing energies they bring; I have learnt from every single one of you. Huge love and thanks to Brenda and Tony who have battled on supporting me on all fronts even through their dark days – thank God and the medical teams for your recovery. And I thank the spiritual masters who have given me the symbols and shown me to their incredible power.

Index

Command 106, 107, 108, 109, 110, 164

Compassion 34, 35, 37, 48, 49, 57, 94, 103, 104, 113, 133, 142, 145, 148, 151, 162, 180, 181, 256, 273, 275, 322

Conflict 216, 266, 269, 276, 279, 302, 305

Connect to Spirit 4, 105, 295

Corporate 62, 163, 221

Counsellors 63

Crystal bowl 265

Crystals 68, 87, 260, 322

Cursed 247, 325

Curses 111, 242, 247, 248, 325, 327,

D

Dating 174

Death 25, 32, 33, 61, 141, 184, 197, 236, 237, 238, 249, 252

De-clutter and clean 269

Demonic energy 256, 257,

Demons 4, 22, 181, 182, 248, 249, 325

Depression 32, 61, 73, 74, 75, 112, 118, 165, 176, 181, 204, 212, 221, 222, 243, 266, 269, 283

Distant Healing 130, 131

Divine source 8

Divine timing 18, 40, 42

DNA 71, 227, 288, 289,

Dominating parent 63

Dowse 325

E

Earthly realm 6, 7, 21

Ears 13

Ego 51, 56, 99, 112, 113, 147, 152, 154, 175, 176, 177, 229, 231, 285, 286

Empathy 26, 34, 37, 61, 148, 151, 180, 217

Empower 84, 88, 201, 298, 306

Energy field 24, 58, 59, 64, 68, 70, 71, 82, 86, 87, 115, 118, 127, 135, 191, 241, 260, 261, 301, 305, 328

Essential oils 51, 68, 75, 92, 104, 113, 260, 265, 267, 328

Excessive energy 290

F

Fear release 268, 301

Feet 15, 51, 65, 78, 85, 86, 88, 89, 93, 94, 169, 183, 204, 234, 235, 259, 262, 289

Fertility 194, 303

Finance 20, 152, 154, 156, 244

Financial security 15, 47, 139, 156, 192

Finding love 180

Flow of abundance 193

Forgive 35, 36, 37, 38, 145, 148, 149, 156, 162, 163, 204, 206, 252

Forgive yourself 37, 38, 145, 148

Forgiving 35, 36, 37, 155

Four Trees 256, 258,

Fracture 124, 292

Frankincense 68, 75, 92, 105, 113, 198, 260, 267, 270

Freedom 317, 320

G

Golden Pyramids 65, 67, 169
Grief 28, 29, 32, 61, 80, 143,
    155, 158, 159, 261, 269
Grounding 234, 235
Guardian angel 30, 101

H

Happiness 14, 56, 137, 139,
    140, 146, 147, 162, 167,
    175, 177, 182, 192, 211, 243
Harmony 36, 75, 120, 136, 230,
    270, 271, 279, 319
Headaches 26, 84, 85, 121, 181,
    212, 278
Healing your soul 196, 211, 223
Heart attack 142
Heart opening 45, 139, 140,
    142, 155, 156, 195
Heartbreak 158, 159
Heart spheres 150, 151, 175
Heavenly realm 6, 7, 21, 29
Heavy energy 84, 85, 126, 134,
    150, 161, 163, 277, 316
Higher consciousness 8, 9, 25,
    299, 300
Hooks 40, 63, 82, 83, 84
Hospital 62, 64, 82, 132, 182,
    227, 263, 264, 265
How to forgive 35

I

Immune 60, 68, 261, 308
Imprints from your past 192
Incense 104, 113, 183, 253, 260,
    267, 268, 270
Infinity 307, 311, 312
Insomnia 27

J

Jasper 68
Jealousy 61, 166, 243, 245, 246,
    290
Joints 84, 116, 212, 278
Judgement 8, 9, 14, 47, 69, 95
    97, 122, 123, 155, 218, 228,
    236, 237, 244, 312

K

Karma release 311
Karmic ties 191

L

Lesson of forgiveness 34, 36
Letting go 38, 40, 78, 91, 160,
    162, 164, 165, 166, 167,
    168, 316
Life lessons 5, 13, 14, 56, 57, 82,
    91, 189, 212, 243
Love is the key 137, 272
Loving partnerships 157, 175

M

Malachite 68, 260
Managing loss 28
Manifest 19, 44, 90, 106, 281,
    297, 301
Manifesting 43, 140, 281, 282,
    294,
Mantra 63, 107, 139, 192, 194,
    196, 253, 254, 294, 328
Mass consciousness 55, 61, 134,
    135, 136

Meditation 29, 51, 87, 94, 95,
100, 109, 110, 135, 136,
140, 169, 171, 198, 233,
238, 265, 268, 283, 294,
295, 321, 325
Mental wellbeing 58
Meridian lines 85, 86, 115
Moods 59, 61, 62, 69, 75, 76
Muscles 94, 278

N

Needy 63, 82, 266, 304
Negative beliefs 5, 107, 108,
180, 182, 226, 228, 230,
231, 286, 289
Negative feelings 34, 87118,
147, 159, 167, 181, 190, 249
Nurse 19, 63

O

Obsidian 68, 260
Obstacles 18, 19, 20, 21, 41, 42,
253, 255, 284, 314
Open heart 24, 137, 151
Opening your heart 45, 46, 91,
139, 141, 148, 149, 296
Oracle cards 323, 328
Overcome fear 26

P

Pain release 278
Panic attacks 27, 219, 250
Past lives 145, 154, 179, 185,
189, 191, 193, 194, 215, 302
Past life regression 4, 198, 201,
202, 203, 205, 303, 327
Past trauma 222, 277, 309

Peppermint 51, 75, 113, 260,
267, 328
Pine 68
Post-traumatic stress disorder
219
Power of love 31, 97
Prayers 142, 238, 251
Preserve 63, 129, 259, 286
Protecting yourself 23
Protective shield 24, 25, 66
Psychic attack 243, 245, 249,
256, 257, 259, 264, 266, 325
Pyramid 31, 66, 67, 105, 114,
295, 304

R

Rejection 97, 130, 136, 151,
153, 243
Relationships 23, 24, 27, 40, 45,
49, 80, 97, 138, 139, 151,
152, 161, 164, 165, 166,
171, 172, 174, 175, 188,
190, 218, 219, 292 297, 309,
311, 312
Releasing heavy energies 241
Rosemary 68

S

Sage 68, 92, 113, 198, 260, 267,
328
Salt 79, 84, 85, 86, 115, 126,
258, 259, 266, 268, 70, 288,
316,
Sandalwood 68, 92, 113, 267,
270
Sea salt 68, 79, 113, 205, 214,
268
Self-acceptance 51

Visualisation 84, 106, 107, 108,
    109, 110, 148, 171
Vitality 23, 62, 82, 212

W
Wheel of wisdom 5, 11
White light 65, 68, 89, 91, 94,
    95, 256
White sage 267

Y
Your soul purpose 7, 9, 16, 19